Agricultural Options

Trading, Risk Management, and Hedging

Agricultural Options

Trading, Risk Management, and Hedging

Christopher A. Bobin

John Wiley & Sons

New York · Chichester · Brisbane · Toronto · Singapore

This publication is designed to provide accurate and authoritative information in regard to the subject matter covered. It is sold with the understanding that the publisher is not engaged in rendering legal, accounting, or other professional service. If legal advice or other expert assistance is required, the services of a competent professional person should be sought. *From a Declaration of Principles jointly adopted by a Committee of the American Bar Association and a Committee of Publishers.*

Library of Congress Cataloging in Publication Data

Bobin, Christopher A., 1961–
Agricultural options: trading, risk management, and hedging / Christopher A. Bobin.
p. cm.
Includes bibliographical references.
ISBN 0-471-52429-8
1. Commodity futures. 2. Produce trade. 3. Options (Finance) 4. Hedging (Finance) 5. Risk. I. Title.
HG6046.B63 1990
332.63'28—dc20 89-70468

Printed in the United States of America

10 9 8 7 6 5 4 3 2 1

For my parents, Stephen and Virginia,
my brother, Stephen, and my sisters,
Gail and Joanne.

Preface

The aim of this options book is to bring together, in a readable form, a wide and diverse body of technical information on options in general and agricultural options in particular. This information is always presented in terms of its usefulness in trading and hedging situations and in managing option risk. Accordingly, traders, merchandisers, and managers will have one source of knowledge about options that is easily accessible.

Much emphasis is given to understanding the determinants of option prices and the risks associated with those determinants. This is because, whereas futures risk is one dimensional, option risk is multidimensional. That is, an options trader must deal with futures price risk, market volatility, and premium time decay; a futures trader deals only with futures price risk.

Consequently, the usual cookbook approach to option strategies—where options are often presented as surrogates for futures—is de-emphasized because these strategies cannot be fully understood or appreciated until the major aspects of option pricing and risk are digested and absorbed.

The first chapter of this book begins with basic definitions; it will be helpful for people who are unfamiliar with options or for those who need a basic review. The second chapter elaborates on the determinants of option prices and familiarizes the reader with the three sources of option risk: futures price, volatility, and time. The rudimentary tools for option risk analysis are presented here.

Inherent to agricultural markets is seasonal price volatility; therefore, a third chapter discusses the nature of this seasonality, its limits, and the implications for options trading. Special emphasis is placed on the behavior of market volatility during the 1988 drought. Once the second and third chapters are covered, the reader is ready to approach the fourth chapter on the problems of strategy formulation, analysis, and position monitoring.

Chapter 5 covers the basics of options hedging for those involved in domestic and international grain marketing and merchandising. Finally, Chapter 6 contains four case studies of actual trades. Each trade is analyzed in order to uncover the factors that contributed to its success or failure.

It is recommended that traders focus most of their energy on understanding the first four chapters, as the pain of absorbing this information will be minimal compared to the pain of a trading misfortune.

The conceptual material in this book is based on the Black formula for pricing options on futures. I have chosen to present the Black formula, its derivative equations, and some lengthy mechanical examples in an appendix rather than in the main body of the book. This is done in order to first emphasize the concepts behind the formula and its derivative equations rather than the formula itself.

Our objective is twofold: (1) gain a good conceptual understanding of how an option is priced, and (2) manipulate and derive meaningful information from the numbers that result from the formulas. Our goal is not to learn how to plug numbers into formulas or how to read a statistical table. I believe this also facilitates the flow of the reading material without diluting the rigor of the concepts. Therefore, the reader is unlikely to hit any snags, and the most that is required is a knowledge of arithmetic.

But there is a more fundamental reason for de-emphasizing the presentation of the actual Black formula: Most option books present the formula and encourage readers to calculate the "fair" option price given the various option price determinants (futures price, time to expiration, volatility, and interest rate). The problem here is that there is a great undercurrent of debate as to whether the Black formula actually gives the fair price of an option, because significant differences have been noted in actual premiums and those generated by the Black model. Most of the controversy centers on the appropriate volatility to use in the Black model.[1]

Therefore, I have chosen to take an alternative approach: Analyze the effect that *changes* in each price determinant have on actual option premiums, because these are readily observable and identifiable phenomena in trading. In other words, the core of this book deals with how option values change given relative changes in the underlying determinants, and not with the calculation of absolute levels of options values in order to determine which market premiums are under- or overvalued vis-à-vis the formula.

It is my conviction that the former approach provides the base for sound trading and strategy formulation, while the latter approach is a recipe for disaster. This is because we would all like a magic formula to resolve difficult trading decisions, and the reader must understand from the beginning that this is not what the Black formula can do for us.

[1]An outline of this debate is beyond the scope of this book, and the reader is encouraged to consult some of the articles cited in the bibliography.

If everyone knew what the correct values of the option price determinants were, and thus the fair value of any option, I doubt there would be much interest in options markets. Indeed, the functions of the options market is to continually search for the correct price determinant levels—and thus the correct option values—as new information is incorporated into the market. Traders who buy and sell by correctly anticipating changes in option price determinants (especially volatility) profit; those who do not lose money.

It will be shown that correct volatility determination is paramount because it is the only unknown that the options market must determine itself; all other variables are given to the options market exogenously. Academics will dispute this; they argue that volatility is given by the actual statistical variation in the underlying futures price. This is only a half truth, and much debate will be resolved once it is recognized that an options market performs the function of volatility discovery, much as the futures market performs the role of price discovery.

This is how professional traders approach options markets, and it is somewhat different from the dogmatic approach of determining the fair value of an option a priori simply because that is what a model dictates. That is why in the first chapter I chose to present options pricing in terms of a market supply and demand model. The model is theoretically correct as long as supply and demand is determined by the inputs given in the Black model. One can then see, within the construct of an understandable market mechanism, how option prices change with fluctuations in the underlying option price determinants. But more importantly, it drives home the point that option prices are determined by market participants and not by mathematicians or statisticians.

Acknowledgments

A special thanks goes to Martin Graf for encouraging me to put in writing the knowledge and experience gained from options trading; much of those early writings form the basis of this book. I am extremely grateful to a few key people who took the time to read and criticize parts of the original draft: Jin Choi, Bob Dix, Martin Graf, and Bob Utterback. Jin Choi's input was invaluable for sorting out some of the technical difficulties of the option supply and demand model; Bob Dix and Martin Graf helped keep the book pragmatic and towards trading, while Bob Utterback's comments on hedging were invaluable.

Many other people were helpful either directly or indirectly: Harry Ambrose, Mario Balletto, Tom Coyle, Jean Louis Drei, Paul Fribourg, Noriko Fuku, Dale Jackson, Paul McAuliffe, Tom Medd, Paul Moravek, Paul Mulhollem, Bernard Nicole, Dick Smetana, Denis Smith, and Paul Smolen. Finally, I would like to thank Karl Weber, my editor at John Wiley, for recognizing the value of the material.

Christopher A. Bobin

New York, New York
May 1990

Contents

Agricultural Options

Trading, Risk Management, and Hedging

Chapter 1

Options and Options Trading

This book was written with two goals in mind: First, to use a trading approach to explain the concepts and applications of options on agricultural futures, and second, to provide the tools for evaluating and managing the risks associated with trading these instruments.

A trading approach begins with the development of a base of knowledge about option pricing. This entails a thorough explanation of how option prices behave with respect to the underlying futures price, the expected volatility of these prices, the progression of time, and the interrelationships among these variables. It elaborates on how factors particular to agricultural markets, such as price seasonality, also influence agricultural option premiums.

The result is a set of conceptual tools that a trader can draw upon to construct option strategies that are consistent with his or her market convictions. Risk management tools then translate conceptual instruments into dollars and cents; they show what is at stake in terms of profit and loss.

Preliminaries

Options Trading

Good traders approach options with a market outlook, a certain degree of conviction, a profit objective, and a risk preference. They have goals but lack an options strategy to achieve them. To advise them to buy undervalued options and sell overvalued options is meaningless because that is a trading goal, not a trading procedure.

Alternatively, to provide a strategy cookbook only causes confusion since option cookbooks present numerous exotic strategies with similar profit and risk outcomes; many are complicated formulations.

Unless a solid base of conceptual material is digested first, the connection between canned recommendations and the traders' objectives is tenuous; no logical choice is obvious.

This causes beginning option traders to oversimplify their approach by buying and selling uncovered options[1] or to complicate their approach by using an exotic canned formulation. They quickly learn that buying uncovered options is usually a waste of money, selling uncovered options often leads to open-ended disaster, and complicated strategies usually yield little profit. *Artful simplicity is the most common ingredient to successful options trading.*

Wise traders withdraw from trading options until they have digested the necessary conceptual base and gained the confidence to formulate strategies. At the very least, they can then understand the cookbook approaches and acquire the ability to discern and reject among them. Again, to provide the base for developing this skill is the goal of this book; it is not a drawback if certain exotic strategies are not covered or if all theoretical pricing formulas are not elaborated.

The Black Model for Pricing Options on Futures

The conceptual tools presented here are derived from the Black model for pricing options on futures. Experience suggests that the model mirrors reality to a reasonable extent; accordingly, it provides a way to demonstrate conceptual relationships.

But the Black formula must always be kept in perspective. When used in a vacuum, the formula tends to confuse rather than to enlighten. It conjures up the image that an option premium is only a mathematical formulation that is traded by mathematicians. Or worse, it leads to the belief that one can calculate the "theoretically correct" value of an option and make a profit by trading it accordingly. This is just one more recipe for disaster.

Indeed, a secondary goal of this book is to bring the reader back to the options market, where value is determined by the actions of option buyers and sellers. There is a demand for options and a supply of options, and where the two meet is where the market-clearing price is determined. The Black formula is only a method for estimating this point or, more importantly, for showing how this point fluctuates with changes in the underlying futures, market volatility, and the progression of time.

[1] Uncovered options are often referred to as "naked" options. This entails the simple purchase or sale of a put or call without ownership of the underlying futures or without an offsetting purchase of a different put or call in a spread or combination.

Let there be no doubt that an option's value reflects all the anxiety, conflicting opinions, and anticipation that occurs in the underlying cash and futures market. That is why an options market—indeed, any market—can exist, and that is why determining undervalued and overvalued options is ultimately a subjective decision. Traders can only be guided by a rigorous set of conceptual tools that enable them to optimize the profit outcome based on their market expectations or to minimize the loss according to their risk preference.

Basic Definitions

Options markets consist of option buyers and option sellers. An **option seller** grants the buyer the right but not the obligation, to buy *or* sell an underlying asset at a predefined price at or before a fixed date called the expiration date.[2]

The **option buyer** pays the seller a fee or premium to acquire the right. **Call** options grant the owner the right to *buy* the asset at a predefined price; **put** options grant the owner the right to *sell* the asset at a predefined price.

The underlying asset in agricultural options is a futures contract; thus the term **options on futures.** The predefined price is referred to as the **strike price.** Exchange-traded option contracts specify uniform strikes, strike intervals, and expiration dates.

To carry out the right to buy or sell the underlying asset is called **exercising the option.** The option buyer exercises the option only if it is profitable to do so. If a call option enables the owner to buy futures at a lower price than the price they are trading for in the market, the owner has the incentive to exercise. Conversely, if a put option enables the owner to sell futures at a higher price than the price they are trading for in the market, the owner has the incentive to exercise. Consequently, *an option buyer's profit is limited only by the amount that futures can rise above a call's strike price or fall below a put's strike price.*

But the option buyer is never obligated to exercise a losing proposition, that is, to buy at the call strike price and sell at a lower price, or to sell at the put strike price and buy at a higher price. The option buyer's maximum loss is therefore the premium.

The seller (sometimes referred to as the **writer**) is obligated to

[2] There are two types of options: American options and European options. American-style options can be exercised anytime before expiration. European-style options can be exercised only during a specific time period. Options on agricultural futures are American-style options.

TABLE 1–1 Maximum and Minimum Profit for an Option Buyer and Seller

Position	Maximum Profit	Maximum Loss
Option buyer	Unlimited	Premium
Option seller	Premium	Unlimited

fulfill the buyer's right even if it subjects the seller to open-ended losses. The seller has no rights: If he or she sold a call and the buyer exercises, the seller is assigned a short futures position at the call strike price. Conversely, if the seller sold a put and the buyer exercises, the seller is assigned a long futures position at the put strike price.

The option premium provides the incentive for the seller to take on the obligation. The seller's expectation is that the buyer is purchasing a losing proposition and thus will not exercise his or her right. The premium is therefore the seller's maximum reward. (See Tables 1–1 and 1–2 for summary.)

Interpreting Option Tables and Quotes

Option features are best illustrated by some examples. Table 1–3 shows soybean options quotes as they appeared in the *Wall Street Journal* on July 28, 1989. The first line shows the commodity, the exchange where the option is traded (CBT is the Chicago Board of Trade), the amount of commodity represented by one contract, and the money units in which the premiums are quoted.

Under the headings of put and call settlements are the contract months that correspond to the underlying futures. The first column contains the strike prices. Note that they have uniform increments as defined in the option contract.

Expiration dates are not given; however, options cease trading and expire in the month prior to the last trading day of the underly-

TABLE 1–2 Results of Exercising Calls and Puts

	Call Buyer Exercises	Put Buyer Exercises
Result for Buyer	Receives a long futures position at strike price	Receives a short futures position at strike price
Result for Seller	Assigned a short futures position at strike price	Assigned a long futures position at strike price

TABLE 1–3 Option Quotes

Soybeans (CBT) 5,000 bushels; cents per bushel						
Strike	**Calls—Settle**			**Puts—Settle**		
Price	Sept. - c	Nov. - c	Jan. - c	Sept. - p	Nov. - p	Jan. - p
575	. . . .	38½	. . . .	2½	14	. . . .
600	25	26½	38	8½	26½	31
625	12	17½	26	20½	41½	45
650	6	12	21	39	61	62
675	3	8½	16	61	82	80½
700	1½	5¾	12	84½	104	101½

ing futures. Hence, options on January futures expire in December, options on March futures expire in February, and so on. Trading ceases on Friday and the options expire on Saturday at 10:00 A.M. The decision to exercise can be made up to that point.[3]

The option premiums follow vertically in Table 1–3. For instance, the value of a November 650 soybean call is 12 cents per bushel and the contract is worth $600 ($.12 · 5000). A January 675 soybean put is priced at 80.5 cents per bushel and the contract is worth $4,025 ($.805 · 5000). Soybean option premiums trade in fractions down to one-eight of a cent. A summary of contract specifications for agricultural options is given in Table 1–4.

Call Option Example

Consider the September 600 call in Table 1–3. The seller of the call grants the buyer the right, but not the obligation, to purchase a September soybean futures contract at a price of 600 cents per bushel at or before expiration. In return, the writer receives a premium of 25 cents per bushel. For simplicity, the following analysis will be limited to outcomes at expiration.

If futures are above 600 cents per bushel by expiration, the call buyer has the incentive to exercise because he or she can buy futures at 600 cents and sell at the current (higher) futures price. However, to earn a *net* profit, futures must be above 625 cents. Otherwise, with futures at 625 the call buyer breaks even since he or she can exercise, receive a long futures position at 600, sell futures at 625, and earn a 25 cent profit that nets out the original 25 cent cost.

But if futures are below 600 cents per bushel by expiration, the buyer will not exercise the call option. Why would the buyer buy futures at 600 and sell at a lower price for a loss? Because the call

[3] Contact the Education and Marketing Services Department at the Chicago Board of Trade for an exact schedule of expiration dates: 1–800-THE-CBOT.

TABLE 1–4 Options on Futures

Commodity	Exchange	Contract Size	Tick Size	Price Limits	Strike Increments
Soybeans	CBT	5,000 bu.	1/8 cent/bu.	30 cents/bu.	25 cents
Soybeans	MID-AM	1,000 bu.	1/8 cent/bu.	30 cents/bu.	25 cents
Soymeal	CBT	100 short tons	5 cents/ton	10 dollars/ton	5 dollars
Soyoil	CBT	60,000 lb.	1/200 cent/lb.	1 cent/lb.	1 cent
Corn	CBT	5,000 bu.	1/8 cent/bu.	10 cent/bu.	10 cents
Wheat	CBT	5,000 bu.	1/8 cent/bu.	20 cents/bu.	10 cents
Wheat	MID-AM	1,000 bu.	1/8 cent/bu.	20 cents/bu.	10 cents
Wheat	KCBT	5,000 bu.	1/8 cent/bu.	25 cents/bu.	10 cents
Wheat	MPLS	5,000 bu.	1/8 cent/bu.	25 cents/bu.	10 cents
Live cattle	CME	40,000 lb.	2 1/2 cents/100 lb.	none	2 cents
Feeder cattle	CME	44,000 lb.	2 1/2 cents/100 lb.	none	2 cents
Live hogs	CME	30,000 lb.	2 1/2 cents/100 lb.	none	2 cents
Pork bellies	CME	40,000 lb.	2 1/2 cents/100 lb.	none	2 cents

CBT = Chicago Board of Trade
MID-AM = Mid-America Commodity Exchange
KCBT = Kansas City Board of Trade
MPLS = Minneapolis Board of Trade
CME = Chicago Mercantile Exchange

represents a right that nobody wants, it expires worthless, and the call buyer loses the initial investment of 25 cents per bushel or $1,250 per contract. However, this is the maximum loss even if the underlying futures fall to 550 cents per bushel. The seller then keeps the initial 25 cent premium or $1,250 per contract; this is the seller's maximum reward.

Figure 1–1 shows the call option's value at expiration as well as the profit and loss of the call buyer and seller over a range of futures prices. The notation used for the call value at expiration is:

$$\text{Max}\ [0,\ (F-S)]$$

where

$$F = \text{Futures price}$$
$$S = \text{Call strike price}$$

This is read "the greater of zero or the difference between the futures price and the strike price." To illustrate, if soybean futures are at 675 cents per bushel by the expiration of the 600 call, the call's value is the greater of zero or 75 cents (675 − 600). Obviously, 75 is greater than zero so the call is worth 75 cents.

In addition, note the profit and loss symmetry between the call buyer and seller: The buyer's net profit or loss at expiration is the

FIGURE 1–1

600 Soybean Call Option
Expiration Value and Buyer & Seller Net Profit
Call Bought/Sold for 25 Cents

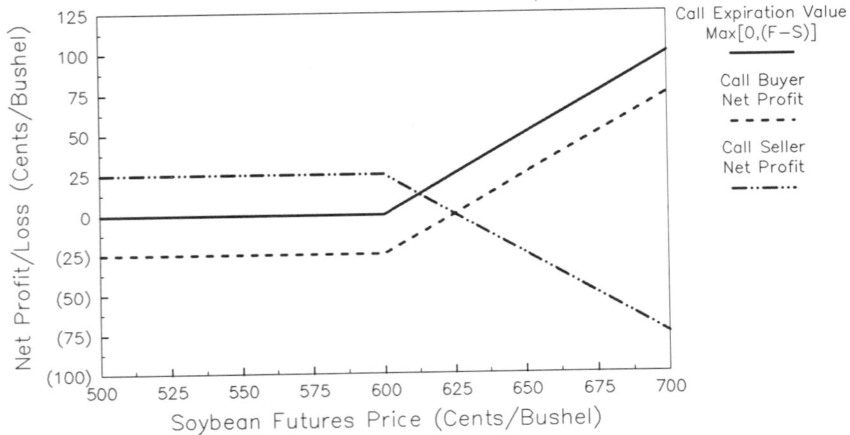

option's value at expiration less the initial premium; the seller's net profit or loss is the initial premium less the option's value at expiration:

$$\text{Call Buyer's Net Profit/Loss} = \text{Max}[0, (F - S)] - P$$

$$\text{Call Seller's Net Profit/Loss} = P - \text{Max}[0, (F - S)]$$

$$\text{Call Buyer and Seller's Breakeven Point} = [S + P]$$

where

$$P = \text{Initial Call Premium Bought or Sold}$$

It is evident from these formulas and from Figure 1–1 that the call option buyer has a bullish market outlook while the seller takes a neutral-to-bearish stance.

To use the formulas, we can analyze the impact on the buyer and seller of the November 625 soybean call option in Table 1–3 at three hypothetical futures prices at expiration: 575, 640, and 680 cents per bushel. From Table 1–3, the 625 call is worth 17.5 cents per bushel. To simplify the analysis, assume futures were trading at 625 (at the call's strike price) when the call was bought and sold.

	CALL BUYER	CALL SELLER
Premium Bought/Sold:	17.5	17.5
Breakeven:	642.5	642.5
Net Profit at Expiration:		
At 575:	Max[0, (575 − 625)] = 0 (0 − 17.5) = −17.5	Max[0, (575 − 625)] = 0 (17.5 − 0) = +17.5
At 640:	Max[0, (640 − 625)] = 15 (15 − 17.5) = −2.5	Max[0, (640 − 625)] = 15 (17.5 − 15) = +2.5
At 680:	Max[0, (680 − 625)] = 55 (55 − 17.5) = +37.5	Max[0, (680 − 625)] = 55 (17.5 − 55) = −37.5

(*Note*: All premiums are in cents per bushel)

This example also underscores the difference between the market outlook of the call buyer and the call seller. The buyer profits if the futures price rises *dramatically*, but the seller can profit if the futures are either slightly above the call's strike price (at 640) or below the strike price (at 575) by expiration. Again, the call buyer is bullish on futures and the call seller is neutral to bearish. *In general, the call's breakeven serves as a benchmark*. The call buyer is bullish above the breakeven (642.5 cents per bushel in the previous example), while the call seller is bearish below it.

Put Option Example

Consider a March 260 corn put worth 10 cents per bushel. The seller of the put option grants the buyer the right, but not the obligation, to sell March corn futures at 260 cents per bushel. In return, the writer receives a premium of 10 cents per bushel. Again, the analysis is limited to outcomes at expiration.

If futures are below 260 cents per bushel at expiration, the put buyer has the incentive to exercise because the buyer can sell futures at 260 and buy them back at the current (lower) futures price for a profit. Nonetheless, futures must be below 250 before the buyer earns a net profit. Otherwise, at 250 the buyer breaks even, because he or she can exercise, receive a short futures position at 260, buy futures at 250, and earn a 10 cent profit that nets out the premium cost.

But if the futures price at expiration is above 260 cents per bushel, the put buyer will not exercise, since to sell futures at 260 and buy at a higher price results in a loss. Because the put represents a right that nobody wants, it expires worthless. The buyer abandons it and incurs a 10 cent per bushel loss, even if futures are at 300 cents per bushel. In turn, the put writer earns a 10 cent per bushel profit.

Figure 1–2 shows the put option's value at expiration as well as

FIGURE 1–2

260 Corn Put Option
Expiration Value and Buyer & Seller Net Profit
Put Bought/Sold for 10 Cents

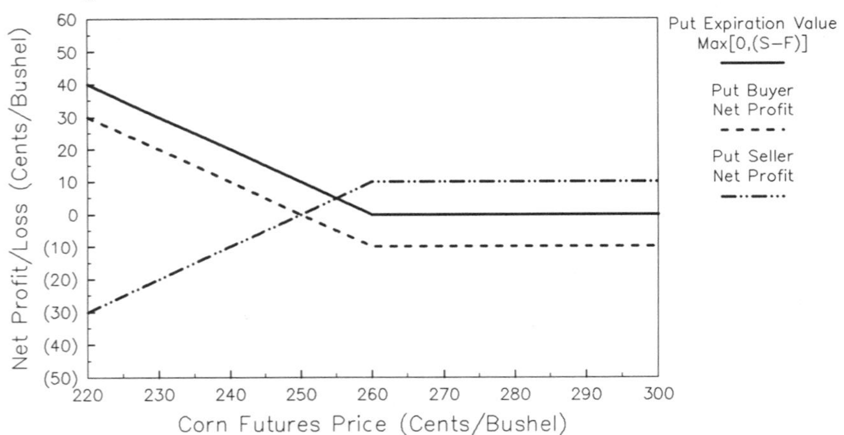

the profit and loss of the put buyer and seller over a range of futures prices. The notation for the put value at expiration follows:

$$\text{Max}[0,\ (S-F)]$$

where

$$S = \text{Put Strike Price}$$
$$F = \text{Futures Price}$$

In the put case, one takes the greater of zero or the difference between the strike and the futures price. For example, if corn futures are trading at 220 cents per bushel by expiration, the put's value is the greater of zero or 40 cents (260 − 220). Since 40 is greater than zero, the put is worth 40 cents.

As in the call example, there is a symmetry in the profit and loss between the put buyer and seller:

$$\text{Put Buyer's Net Profit/Loss} = \text{Max}[0,\ (S-F)] - P$$
$$\text{Put Seller's Net Profit/Loss} = P - \text{Max}[0,\ (S-F)]$$
$$\text{Put Buyer and Seller's Breakeven Point} = [S-P]$$

where

$$P = \text{Initial Put Premium Bought or Sold}$$

These formulas and Figure 1–2 demonstrate that the put buyer is bearish on futures and the put seller is neutral to bullish.

To put these formulas to work, we can take the example of a July 230 corn put worth 8 cents per bushel and analyze the impact on the put buyer and seller at expiration at three hypothetical futures levels: 260, 225, and 205 cents per bushel. For simplicity, assume futures were trading at 230 cents per bushel (at the put's strike price) when the put was bought and sold.

	PUT BUYER	PUT SELLER
Premium Bought/Sold:	8	8
Breakeven:	222	222
Net Profit at Expiration:		
At 260:	Max[0, (230 − 260)] = 0 (0 − 8) = −8	Max[0, (230 − 260)] = 0 (8 − 0) = +8
At 225:	Max[0, (230 − 225)] = 5 (5 − 8) = −3	Max[0, (230 − 225)] = 5 (8 − 5) = +3

At 205:	Max[0, (230 − 205)] = 25	Max[0, (230 − 205)] = 25
	(25 − 8) = +17	(8 − 25) = −17

(*Note*: All premiums in cents per bushel)

This example clarifies the difference between the market conviction of the put buyer and the put seller. The put buyer is speculating that the market will fall dramatically, while the seller is still profitable if futures fall slightly (at 225) or rise (at 260). *Again, the put's breakeven serves as a benchmark.* The put buyer is bearish below the breakeven level (222 cents per bushel in the example), while the seller is bullish above it.

Trading the Option

An option can be traded before expiration to take profits, to reduce losses, to avoid exercising and receiving a futures position, to avoid being assigned a futures position, or for some combination of these reasons. No option buyer or seller is stuck with a position until expiration. Traders always have the alternative of selling or buying back the option in the market before expiration.

Intrinsic and Extrinsic Value

Intrinsic value is equal to the gross profit earned by exercising the option. Conversely, the **extrinsic value** of any option is the option premium less intrinsic value.

Call Option Examples

With soybean futures at 650 cents per bushel, a 600 soybean call option with 150 days to expiration and a premium of 134 cents is worth 50 cents intrinsically because a trader can exercise, receive a long futures position at 600, and then sell futures at 650 for a 50 cent gross profit. The remainder of the premium (84 cents) is extrinsic value:

Futures:	650	Call Premium:	134
Call Strike:	600	Less Intrinsic:	−50
Intrinsic Value:	50	Extrinsic Value:	84

However, with futures at 550 cents per bushel and 150 days to expiration, the same 600 soybean call has a premium of 77 cents. The call has no intrinsic value, as the strike price is above the futures price, and no rational person will exercise at a loss. *Therefore, since intrinsic value cannot be negative, the entire 77 cent premium is extrinsic value.*

This begs the question of why an option has value even though it has no intrinsic value. Extrinsic value is often called **time value** because over time any option has the chance of getting or adding intrinsic value due to price movements in the underlying futures; accordingly, a trader must pay some amount for it. Nevertheless, it will be shown that an option's value falls as time progresses. This is tantamount to a decline in extrinsic (time) value and is referred to as **time decay.**

Put Option Examples

If corn futures are at 240 cents per bushel, a 260 corn put with 150 days to expiration and a premium of 53 cents is worth 20 cents intrinsically because the trader can exercise, receive a short futures position at 260, and offset by buying futures at 240 for a 20 cent gross profit. The remainder of the premium (33 cents) is extrinsic value:

Put Strike:	260	Put Premium:	53
Futures:	240	Less Intrinsic:	−20
Intrinsic Value:	20	Extrinsic Value:	33

However, with futures at 280 and 150 days to expiration, the same 260 put is worth 38 cents; that is, the entire premium consists of extrinsic value, because the strike price is below the futures price and to exercise would result in a loss.

Finally, it is important to understand that the trader will not necessarily exercise in the previous examples. A gross profit is earned, but not a net profit, because the extrinsic (time) value is forfeited upon exercising.

Table 1–5 summarizes the notation of intrinsic and extrinsic value.

TABLE 1–5 Intrinsic and Extrinsic Value

Option Premium = (Intrinsic Value) + (Extrinsic Value)
For Calls: Intrinsic Value = Max [0, (F − S)] Extrinsic Value = (Option Premium) − (Intrinsic Value)
For Puts: Intrinsic Value = Max [0, (S − F)] Extrinsic Value = (Option Premium) − (Intrinsic Value)

In-the-Money versus Out-of-the-Money Options

When a call (put) option's strike price is below (above) the futures price, it has intrinsic value and is thus **in-the-money**; otherwise, it has only extrinsic value and is termed **out-of-the-money**. When an option's strike price is equal to the futures price the option is said to be **at-the-money**. Option strikes that are closest to the future's price but still out-of-the-money are termed **near-the-money**.

Traders use additional terms to indicate the extent to which an option is in- or out-of-the-money, such as **"deep" in-the-money** and **"deep" out-of-the-money**. Although there is no rule to determine when an option is deep in- or out-of-the-money (as opposed to being just in- or out-of-the-money), a good rule of thumb is ± 15 percent of the underlying futures price. To illustrate, if corn futures are trading at 280 cents per bushel, ± 15 percent of 280 is ± approximately 40 cents, which equates to strikes of 240 and 310.

Table 1–6 summarizes in-, at-, and out-of-the-money options.

Minimum and Maximum Values of Option Prices

Minimum Option Prices

An option's price at expiration is equal to its intrinsic value if it expires in-the-money, or zero if it expires at- or out-of-the-money. But an option's price at expiration is also the minimum price of an option before expiration. First, no rational seller will pay a buyer for an obligation; thus, an option's price cannot be less than zero before expiration. Second, any American option that has intrinsic value can be worth no less than that value. Otherwise, a risk-free profit can be

TABLE 1–6 In-, At-, and Out-of-the-Money Options

For Call Options:	
In-the-money when Futures Price	> Strike
At-the-money when Futures Price	= Strike
Out-of-the-money when Futures Price	< Strike
For Put Options:	
In-the-money when Futures Price	< Strike
At-the-money when Futures Price	= Strike
Out-of-the-money when Futures Price	> Strike

earned by buying the option, exercising, and then making an offsetting trade in the underlying futures.

To illustrate the second point, assume soybean futures are trading at 675 cents per bushel. By definition, a 650 call option has an intrinsic value of 25 cents, but suppose a trader could buy it for 10 cents. In that case, the trader could buy the call, exercise, receive a long futures position at 650, and then sell futures at 675 for a net profit of 15 cents:

Buy 650 Call:	−10	
Exercise:	+25	
Net Profit:	+15	cents per bushel

Such profits—if they were available—would not exist for long; all rational market participants would buy the 650 call and sell futures in order to execute the trade and earn the risk-free profit. Trying to do this would push the option premium up and the futures price down until the premium would be worth at least its intrinsic value and thus no risk-free profit opportunity could exist.

Maximum Option Prices

If the minimum price of an option is its intrinsic value, what is the maximum price of an option? For call options, the maximum price is equal to the underlying futures price. If it were greater than the futures price, a risk-free profit could be earned by selling the option and buying the futures. All traders would undertake this trade until the call price was in line with the futures price. For a put option, the maximum price is its strike price. No trader will buy a put for more than its strike price, because futures prices cannot go below zero.

Figures 1–3 and 1–4 use the 600 soybean call and the 260 corn put examples to show the minimum and maximum price boundaries over a range of futures prices. These are essentially the arbitrage boundaries of the call and put option. Note that the minimum price line is also the expiration price line. Maximum prices can occur only prior to expiration. Table 1–7 summarizes these concepts.

The Option Pricing Problem

Prior to expiration, an option can take on any value between its minimum and maximum allowable price, that is, the gray area in Figures 1–3 and 1–4. As explained in the section Intrinsic and Extrinsic Value, an option premium is the sum of intrinsic value plus extrinsic or time value. As such, the shaded area in Figures 1–3 and

FIGURE 1–3

Call Option: Maximum and Minimum Values
600 Soybean Call

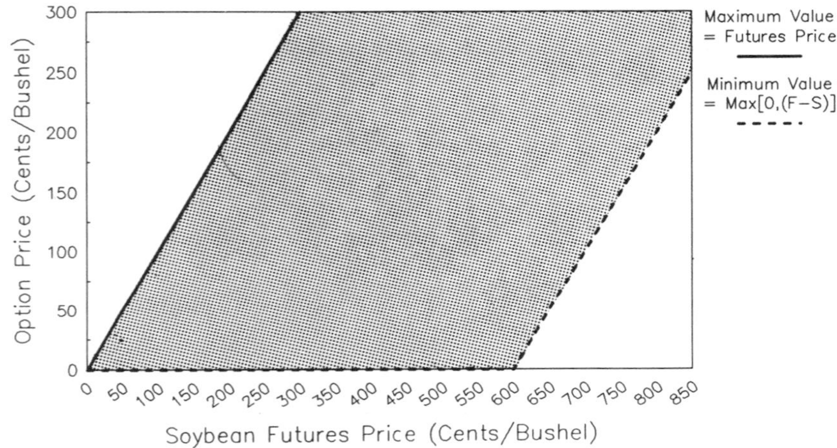

FIGURE 1–4

Put Option: Maximum and Minimum Values
260 Corn Put

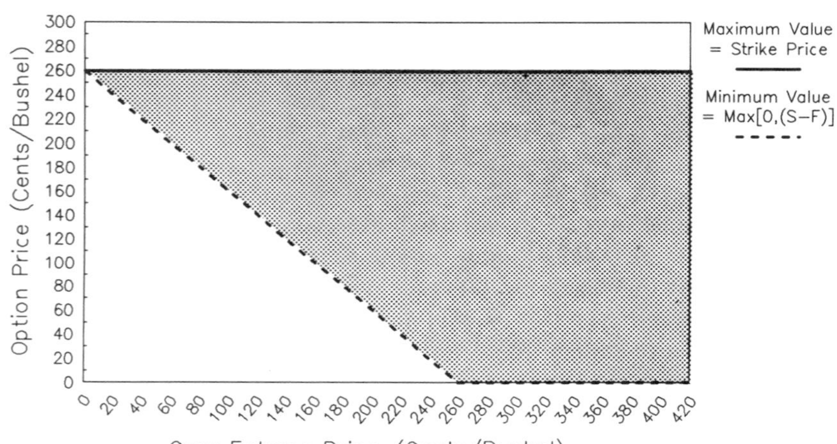

TABLE 1–7 Maximum and Minimum Prices for Calls and Puts

	Call	Put
Max Price	F	S
Min Price	Max [0, (F − S)]	Max [0, (S − F)]

Note: F = Futures Price; S = Strike Price

1–4 represents extrinsic value. Nonetheless, how much extrinsic value should be added to intrinsic value at any futures level? This is the option pricing problem.

Part of the solution can be obtained from the minimum price lines in Figures 1–3 and 1–4: *The futures price is an important determinant of an option's value*. Intuitively, as the futures price rises, call options become more valuable; as the futures price falls, put options become more valuable. This relation holds even though an option has no intrinsic value, because it is sufficient that an option be nearer-to-the-money for it to be worth more (as long as there is time left to expiration).

Witness the 600 soybean option in Figure 1–3. Assuming an equivalent number of days to expiration, a trader will demand a higher price for the call when it is near-the-money than when it is out-of-the-money because there is a much higher probability that the option will gain intrinsic value. The same logic holds for the put option in Figure 1–4. The put is more valuable when corn futures are at 270 than when futures are at 300 or 350, because there is a higher probability that the put will go into-the-money.

But the futures price is only a partial solution to the option pricing problem. Figures 1–3 and 1–4 also show that at any particular futures level, the option can take on several prices. For instance, when futures are at 550 cents per bushel, the 600 soybean call in Figure 1–3 can be worth 50 cents, 100 cents, 150 cents, all the way up to the futures price of 550 cents per bushel. This is shown in Figures 1–5 and 1–6, where two hypothetical levels (A and B) of call and put prices are possible at every futures price. Clearly, there must be other factors at work that determine an option's price.

Specifically, the Black model considers two other variables when an option is priced: (1) the expected volatility of the futures price, and (2) time to expiration. Expected market volatility gauges the potential speed and extent of movement in the futures price. Time to expiration is simply the number of days to expiration. Therefore, we can account for the difference between the two levels of prices in Figures 1–5 and 1–6 by our assumptions regarding expected volatility

FIGURE 1–5

Two Possible Levels of 600 Soybean Call Option Prices at Different Futures Prices

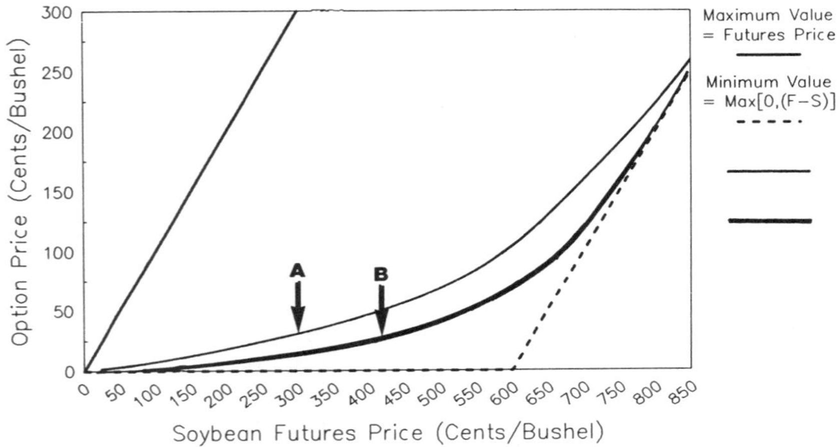

FIGURE 1–6

Two Possible Levels of 260 Corn Put Option Prices at Different Futures Prices

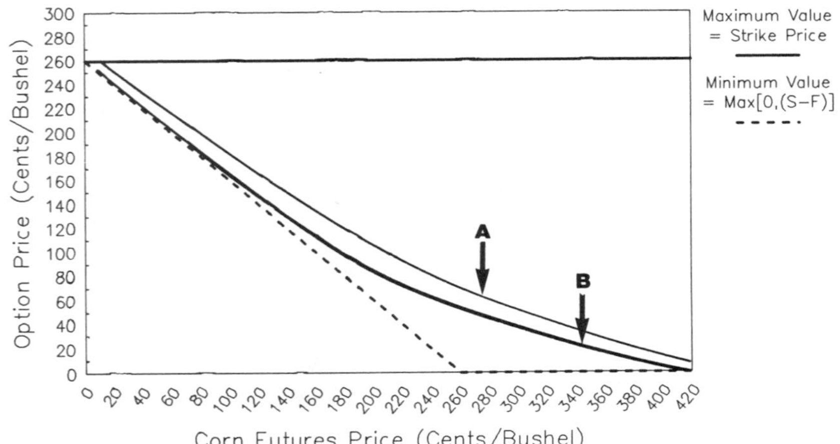

and time to expiration. The impact of these variables on option prices is analyzed next by using a simple supply and demand model for options.

Supply and Demand Model for Call and Put Options

Before the supply and demand model for options is introduced, it is important to reiterate one point. One of our original objectives was to understand what motivates option buyers and sellers, for it is their collective action that determines an option's market price within the arbitrage restrictions discussed earlier.

The Black formula attempts to model the actions of option buyers and sellers through mathematics and statistics. There is, however, more intuitive power behind a market (supply and demand) approach. Ultimately, this makes it easier to understand the Black formula and to put it to use without being intimidated by it. It will also underscore some of the difficulties in basing trading decisions on the Black model.[4]

The following assumptions are made in constructing the supply and demand schedule of a call or put option with a given strike price: (1) the futures price is held constant, (2) both buyers and sellers have an outlook on expected market volatility,[5] and (3) there are a fixed number of days to expiration. In addition, the analysis is limited to options with no intrinsic value, that is, out-of-the-money options. This presents no problem, as the point of the supply and demand model is to determine extrinsic value, that is, value beyond intrinsic value. *Our concern as option traders is to understand value determination at the extrinsic level, since intrinsic value is a simple function of arbitrage relationships.*

Supply and Demand of a Call Option

Figure 1–7 shows the supply and demand model for a call option. As in Figure 1–3, the graph on the right defines the arbitrage limits for the call option. At a given futures price F_1, the supply and demand lines must lie below F_1. At the lower end of the graph, the supply and demand lines must lie above zero; however, before expiration they are above the minimum tick price (M) or perhaps the cabinet price.[6]

---

[4] The supply and demand model is not an alternative to the Black model. Rather, it is a market model predicated on Black's variables and assumptions.

[5] Black originally stipulated that actual market volatility (not expected market volatility) would determine the fair value of an option. However, even purists will concede (and it will be shown in Chapters 2 and 3) that the volatility implied in an option premium will often differ from actual market volatility. Thus, a volatility expectations effect is operating in the options market.

FIGURE 1–7

The Supply and Demand for a Call Option

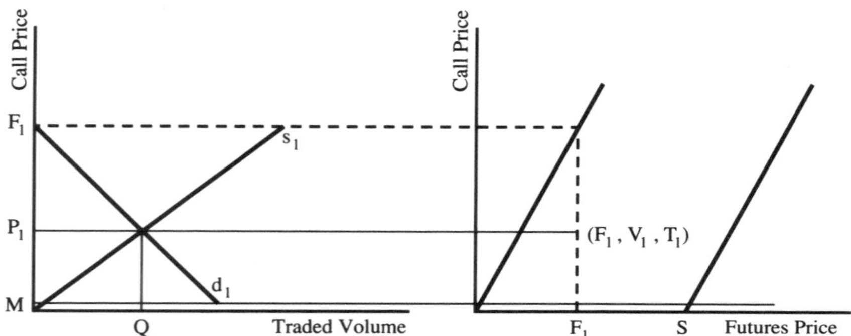

The downward sloping demand curve and upward sloping supply curve come from the rational economic assumptions that option demand is small at high prices and option supply is large; conversely, option demand is large at low prices and option supply is small. Where the supply and demand line meet is where the price of the call option (P_1) is determined as well as the traded volume (Q). We are more interested in the determination of price level than in the traded volume, however; accordingly, Q will be dropped from Figures 1–8, 1–9, and 1–10.

At P_1, market participants have priced the option according to the futures level (F_1), an expected volatility level (V_1), and the number of days to expiration (T_1). If a call option with the same strike but with different pricing assumptions enters the market, it will not clear the market as long as F_1, V_1, and T_1 hold. For instance, if V_1 holds for all buyers and sellers, and an option is offered that is priced at a higher volatility level, no other trader will buy it. The option's price will be lowered until it is priced at the V_1 level.

Changing the Variables

We now relax the assumptions regarding futures price, expected volatility, and time to expiration in order to see how the call supply and demand changes and thus how the call price changes. For the call option analysis, three situations are explored: (1) the futures price is *increased* while holding expected volatility and time unchanged, (2) expected volatility is *increased* while holding futures and time unchanged, and (3) time to expiration is *decreased* while holding futures and volatility unchanged.

If the futures price increases, demand for the call increases and

---

[6] Some option contracts specify a cabinet price such that a deep out-of-the-money option can be liquidated at a price of one dollar, as opposed to the minimum tick of one-eighth of a cent or $6.25 per contract.

FIGURE 1–8

The Effect of an Increase in Futures Price on the Price of a Call Option

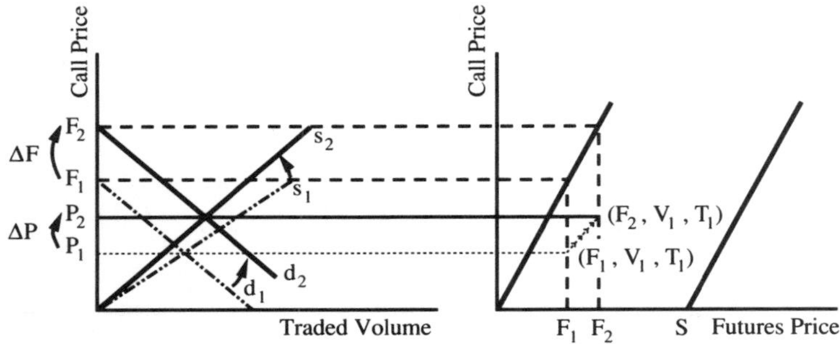

supply of the call decreases. At every price call, buyers are optimistic and demand more because there is a higher likelihood that the call will go into-the-money. Conversely, call sellers are cautious and sell less, since they are reluctant to assume open-ended risk in the wake of a rising futures market. The combined action of buyers and sellers makes the call more valuable, and its price rises to P_2 in Figure 1–8. Notice the option's price is not a function of the buyer's or seller's *expectation* of the future price level of the underlying. Buyers may be optimistic and sellers cautious but always relative to the *current* futures price and its distance from option strike price. Trading will occur only when optimism or cautiousness is reflected in the the new premium. At that point, all who want to buy will buy and all who want to sell will sell.

An increase in the expected volatility of the futures price has a similar impact. If futures prices are expected to fluctuate greatly, the call has a higher probability of going into-the-money. Therefore,

FIGURE 1–9

The Effect of an Increase in Expected Volatility on the Price of a Call Option

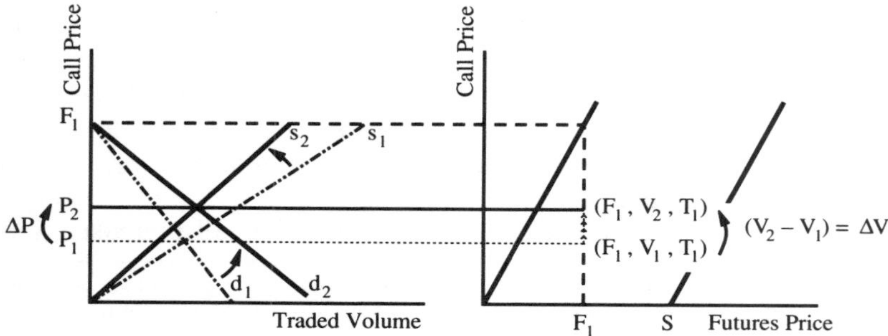

when call buyers anticipate a more volatile market, they increase their demand at every price. Conversely, sellers become cautious and sell less at every price because they perceive a higher risk of losing money. The combined result is a higher call premium even though futures and time to expiration are unchanged. This is shown in Figure 1–9, where volatility increases from V_1 to V_2 and the call's price rises from P_1 to P_2.

If the number of days to expiration is reduced, demand for the call decreases and supply of the call increases because there is less time for the call to acquire intrinsic value or gain additional intrinsic value. Call buyers become pessimistic and withdraw from the market, especially if the call is out-of-the-money, that is, ultimately worthless. But call sellers are encouraged and become optimistic; they enter the market in an attempt to earn the extrinsic value (time decay) as it erodes when buyers withdraw. As demonstrated in Figure 1–10, the combined action of buyers and sellers lowers the price of the call option from P_1 to P_2 as time moves from T_1 to T_2.

Supply and Demand of a Put Option

Figure 1–11 shows the supply and demand model for a put option. As in Figure 1–4, the graph on the right defines the put's arbitrage limits. At the upper end, the supply and demand lines must lie below the strike price (S) of the put. At the lower end, the lines must be above the minimum tick price or the cabinet price before expiration. Where supply and demand meet is where put price (P_1) and the traded volume (Q) are determined. Again, our concern is with price, not volume; Q will therefore be dropped from the construction of Figures 1–12, 1–13, and 1–14.

The assumptions for a downward sloping demand curve and an upward sloping supply curve are the same as in the call example. At

FIGURE 1–10

The Effect of a Decrease in Time to Expiration on the Price of a Call Option

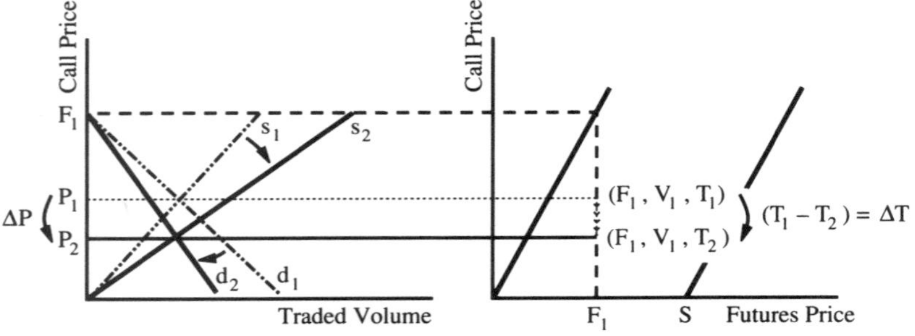

FIGURE 1–11

The Supply and Demand for a Put Option

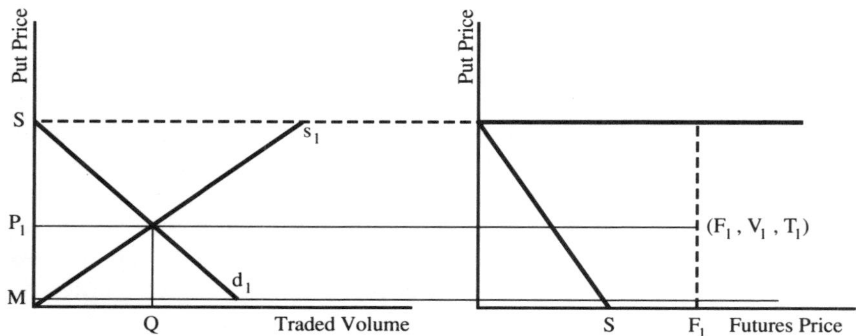

higher prices, buyers demand less of the put option, but sellers are willing to offer more. Conversely, at lower prices, buyers demand more of the put option, but sellers offer less.

At P_1, market participants have priced the option according to the futures level (F_1), an expected volatility level (V_1), and the number of days to expiration (T_1). As long as these levels hold collectively for all participants, any put option with the same strike price that is priced differently will not clear the market, and its price must adjust accordingly for it to be bought or sold.

Changing the Variables

As in the call example, we now relax the assumptions regarding futures price, expected volatility, and time to expiration in order to understand how the put supply and demand changes and thus how the put price changes. For the put option analysis, three situations are studied: (1) the futures price is *decreased* while holding expected volatility and time unchanged, (2) expected volatility is *increased* while holding futures and time unchanged, and (3) time to expiration is *decreased* while holding futures and expected volatility unchanged.

If the futures price decreases, demand for the put increases and supply of the put decreases. At every price put buyers are optimistic and demand more, because there is a higher probability that the put will go into-the-money (gain intrinsic value). Conversely, call sellers are cautious and sell less because they are reluctant to assume open-ended risk in a collapsing futures market. As demonstrated in Figure 1–12, the combined action of buyers and sellers makes the put more valuable, and its price increases from P_1 to P_2 as futures move from F_1 to F_2.

An increase in the expected volatility of the futures price has the same effect. Buyers increase their demand at every price, since the

FIGURE 1–12

The Effect of a Decrease in Futures Price on the Price of a Put Option

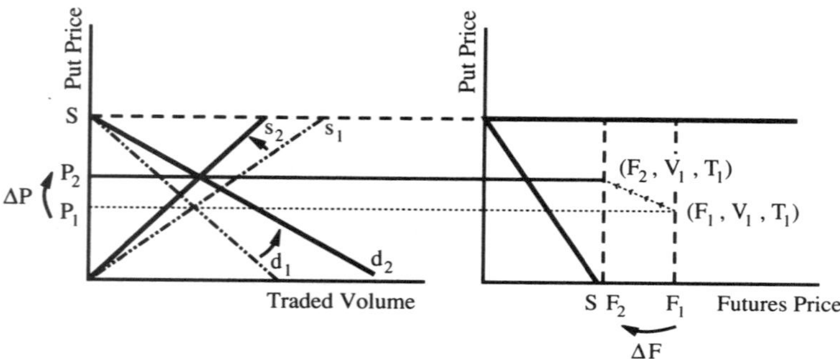

likelihood that the put will go into-the-money is greater in an environment of high volatility. Conversely, sellers offer less at every price, as they are unwilling to assume greater risk at current prices. In Figure 1–13, the combined actions of buyers and sellers raise the price of the put from P_1 to P_2 as expected volatility rises from V_1 to V_2.

Note that the volatility effect for put option prices is the same for call option prices. *It is important to understand that volatility is not unidirectional*. Rather, it measures the extent of any potential (anticipated) increase or decrease in the futures price during a specified period of time. Therefore, if volatility expectations increase, all options—calls *and* puts—must increase in value. Volatility is the rising tide that lifts all boats.

Finally, if the number of days to expiration is decreased, there is less time for the put option to acquire or add additional intrinsic value. This discourages put buyers, since the put is ultimately worth-

FIGURE 1–13

The Effect of an Increase in Expected Volatility on the Price of a Put Option

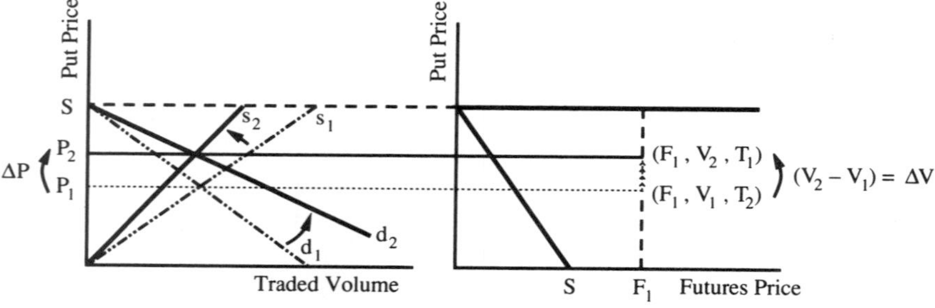

FIGURE 1–14

The Effect of a Decrease in Time to Expiration on the Price of a Put Option

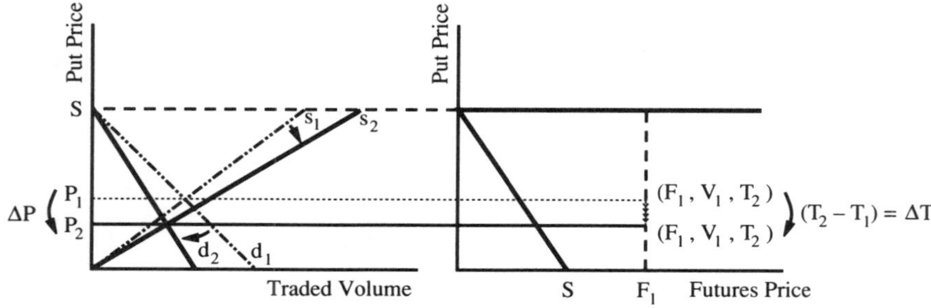

less if it is out-of-the-money; thus, buyers reduce their demand at every price level. Put sellers are encouraged, however, as they seek to earn the time decay as buyers withdraw. As Figure 1–14 shows, the combined action of buyers and sellers lowers the price of the put from P_1 to P_2 as time progresses from T_1 to T_2.

Expected Volatility

In the jargon of options trading, expected volatility is referred to as implied volatility, that is, the volatility implied by an option's market premium given a certain futures price and time to expiration. Implied volatility is represented by the symbols V_1 and V_2 in the call and put supply and demand model. Specific descriptions of how to measure this variable are given in Chapter 2.

In the meantime, the expectations aspect of volatility is emphasized for a good reason: Implied volatility is really a receptacle for every other prevailing anxiety in the market that cannot be explained via the futures price or time progression. Market anxiety—and thus implied volatility—can increase for several reasons: weather problems, anticipated government reports, political events, and nuclear accidents. Hence, although we have always talked of volatility in terms of expected moves in futures price, there are diverse factors lurking behind those expectations.

To that extent, volatility is the real unknown in options trading. It is the ghost in the machine, since every other variable can be accounted for. Speculation on the direction of the futures price in options trading is no different from such speculation in pure futures trading and nobody will argue over the number of days to expiration, because it is a known quantity defined by the expiration date. But there is no precise or accepted method for predicting future implied volatility; thus, volatility risk is unique to options trading. To realize this is to understand the difficulties in using the Black formula to make trading decisions. The formula is always imperfect if future implied volatility is an unpredictable black box.

This is powerful knowledge. First, we must be cognizant of this thing called implied volatility before we try to trade options; otherwise, it is bound to frustrate any strategy based solely on futures price direction or time decay. Secondly, once we are aware of implied volatility, we can learn how to trade it; alternatively, we can dilute it if we do not want to trade it. Third, it is not suggested here that the Black formula is useless because it is imperfect. On the contrary, it has already been stated that the formula is a powerful trading guide and risk-management tool. However, it is only rational that a trader must keep the formula's limitations in mind before using it.

Introduction to Risk Management and Trading Tools: Delta, Vega, and Theta

The diagrams of the supply and demand model for calls and puts (Figures 1–8 to 1–10, and Figures 1–12 to 1–14) provide some very useful concepts for trading and risk management. A brief introduction is given here.

First, Figures 1–8 and 1–12 define two quantitative changes: ΔF and ΔP. When we combine this in a ratio ($\Delta P/\Delta F$) we have calculated the option's **delta**. For any given change in futures (ΔF), the change in the option's premium (ΔP) can be estimated via delta. For instance, if a call's delta is .50, then a 10 cent increase in futures results in a 5 cent increase in the call premium:

$$
\begin{aligned}
\Delta P/\Delta F &= .50 \\
\Delta P &= (.50)(\Delta F) \\
\Delta F &= 10 \\
\Delta P &= (.50)(10) = 5
\end{aligned}
$$

We can derive any option's delta from the Black formula; such calculations and more examples are given in Chapter 2 and in its accompanying Appendix.

Second, any change in volatility can be quantified as follows:

$$\Delta V = (V_2 - V_1).$$

By combining ΔV with ΔP in Figures 1–9 and 1–13, a ratio can be formed ($\Delta P/\Delta V$) to help measure the impact of any given volatility fluctuation on an option's premium. This ratio is called **vega** and it can be derived from the Black formula. Since the tools needed to give an example of vega's usefulness are not developed until Chapter 2, an illustration is not given here. However, it suffices to say that if one can anticipate the change in an option's premium given a fixed increase *or decrease* in volatility, one has a powerful trading and risk management tool.

Finally, any change in time can be quantified as follows:

$$\Delta T = (T_1 - T_2).$$

The combination of ΔT and ΔP from Figures 1–10 and 1–14 provides us with the ratio ΔP/ΔT, which allows us to analyze the impact of some defined change in time on the option's premium. This derivation from the Black formula (ΔP/ΔT) is called **theta**. We will see in Chapter 2 how a trader can calculate his or her risk or income from time decay for any fixed period of time, that is, one day, one week, one month, and so on.

Summary: The Multiplicity of the Options Pricing Problem

The previous analysis demonstrates that there are several factors that determine an option's price. The futures price is just one factor. To that extent, an option is only in part a vehicle for speculating on the underlying futures. *Indeed, the impact of other variables can offset any beneficial move in futures prices.*

The first order of business for any serious trader is to fully understand the multiplicity of the options pricing problem. Table 1–8 summarizes the different impacts stemming from changes in the fu-

TABLE 1–8 Futures, Volatility, and Time Effects on Call and Put Premiums

Change in Variable	Call Option Premium	Put Option Premium
Futures price increase	Increase	Decrease
Futures price decrease	Decrease	Increase
More expected volatility	Increase	Increase
Less expected volatility	Decrease	Decrease
More time to expiration	Increase	Increase
Less time to expiration	Decrease	Decrease

tures price, expected (implied) volatility, and time to expiration.[7] Note that the effect of rising or falling futures prices is the only delimiting factor between put and call option price movements. All other factors affect puts and calls equally.

But again, these impacts can be complementary or offsetting. To illustrate, envision a situation in which futures rally but the call option's price *decreases* because volatility expectations fall. The trader who bought the call will obviously be disappointed since he or she was correct on the futures forecast but did not anticipate the decrease in expected volatility.

The point is that traders must approach options as options. They must have an outlook on the direction of expected volatility just as they have an outlook on the direction of the futures price. Their outlook must be consistent with their strategy: If they are bullish on futures and believe volatility expectations will fall, they should not buy a call; they should consider modifying their strategy or implementing an alternative. And to the extent that they are wrong in their outlook, they must be able to anticipate the potential loss.

Questions

1. A broker calls you with a recommendation to buy a November 625 soybean call option on the premise that the futures are bullish and the call option is still cheap. November soybean futures are trading at 590 cents per bushel, and the 625 November call is worth 12 cents per bushel. There are 25 days left to expiration.

   a. If you purchase the call, what is your total cost per contract excluding transaction costs?

   ANSWER: The size of the soybean option contract is 5,000 bushels (refer to Table 1–4). Hence, the cash outflow per contract is $(.12) \cdot (5000) = \$600$. The \$600 cash outflow is also your maximum potential loss if the call is held to expiration and expires out-of-the-money.

   b. What is the intrinsic and extrinsic value of the call?

   ANSWER: The intrinsic value is the greater of zero (0) or the difference between the futures and the strike price (590 − 625

[7] Option prices are also influenced by interest rates. However, interest rate effects operate over the long term and are not important for the analysis at hand. A more detailed explanation is given in Chapter 2.

= − 35); thus, the intrinsic value is zero. The extrinsic value is the call premium less the intrinsic or (12 · 0) = 12.

c. To what price must futures rise in order for you to break even at expiration?

ANSWER: In order to recoup the intial 12 cents per bushel cost, the call must have 12 cents of intrinsic value at expiration. This equates to a November futures price of (625 + 12) = 637 cents per bushel, or a 47 cent rally from the current futures level.

d. Besides a collapse in futures, what else could go wrong with this trade?

ANSWER: The other risks associated with buying a call are falling volatility and time decay. Try to put a subjective probability on acheiving the break-even level within the next 25 days. If you view this as a low probability trade, avoid it.

Of course, the value of the call will increase before expiration if futures rally without reaching the break-even level, but then reassess the market at that point and consider a contingency plan to keep any profits if you consider further increases in futures prices as unlikely.

e. If you are willing to risk the entire cost of the call premium, what would be an alternative futures trade?

ANSWER: If you agree with the broker's bullish market outlook and are well-capitalized, don't buy an out-of-the-money call option. Buy futures and place a stop-loss order 12 cents below the market.

If the futures rally to 625 in the next 25 days, you will make 35 cents or $1,750; if you bought the call option, you are down by $600.

2. You sell 100 contracts of the November 600 soybean call for 16.50 cents per bushel and buy them back after seven trading days. Calculate your cumulative profit/loss given the following settlement prices:

	Time	Settlement (cents/bu.)
Enter	Day 1	17.00
	Day 2	12.00
	Day 3	10.25
	Day 4	11.00

	Time	Settlement (cents/bu.)
	Day 5	9.25
	Day 6	13.25
Exit:	Day 7	10.00

ANSWER:	Time	Profit/Loss	Cumulative
	Day 1	−$2,500	−$2,500
	Day 2	+$25,000	+$22,500
	Day 3	+$8,750	+$31,250
	Day 4	−$3,750	+$27,500
	Day 5	+$8,750	+$36,250
	Day 6	−$20,000	+$16,250
	Day 7	+$16,250	+$32,500

Chapter **2**

Determinants of Option Pricing and Risk

The trader who understands the intricacies of option prices and risk is more likely to trade options successfully than the trader who buys and sells options as surrogates for futures. To reiterate: Option values reflect not only flat-price direction, but also market volatility, time value, and less importantly, interest rates. Thus, even though a trader's flat-price forecast is correct, the trader could fail to profit, as one or more of these additional factors can work against the trade.

This chapter elaborates on and quantifies the determinants of option prices that were introduced in Chapter 1. The material that follows is analogous to the instructions for a tool kit rather than the tool kit itself, though every effort has been made to link theoretical concepts with trading applications. Chapter 4, on options strategies, will further refine the conceptual material into a trading approach.

Option Premium and Futures Price: The Concept of Delta and Gamma

Chapter 1 demonstrated that option premiums will change as the underlying futures change. The precise relationship between changes in an option's premium and changes in the underlying futures is given by the option's **delta**:

$$\text{delta} = \frac{\text{change in option premium}}{\text{change in futures price}} = \frac{\Delta P}{\Delta F}$$

The formula for calculating delta from the Black equation is given in Appendix A.

For instance, if a call option has a delta of +.50, it means that a 10 cent increase in the underlying futures will increase the option's premium by 5 cents—all else remaining equal, such as volatility, time to expiration, and interest rates. Conversely, a 10 cent decrease in futures will decrease the option's premium by 5 cents.

Sign of Delta

A positive sign is given to the delta of a long call and a short put, as these are analogous to long futures positions, and a trader will profit from an increase in the underlying futures. A negative sign is given to the delta of a long put and a short call as these are analogous to short futures positions, and a trader will profit from a fall in the underlying futures. (See Table 2–1.) To illustrate, Table 2–2 shows the profit/loss impact of a 10 cent per bushel increase in soybean futures on four different options positions.

It must be emphasized that the profits and losses in Table 2–2 are only approximations, as the analysis ignores volatility changes, time decay, and changes in delta itself. These refinements are discussed further in the sections concerning vega, theta, and gamma.

Delta Equivalents: Expressing Delta as Fractions of the Underlying Commodity

The delta of an option can be defined in the same units as the underlying commodity. Bushels are the delta equivalents of soybean, corn, and wheat options; short tons are the delta equivalents of soymeal options; pounds are the delta equivalents of soyoil options.

For example, since a corn futures contract represents 5,000 bushels of corn, a corn call option with a delta of .50 is equivalent to 2,500 bushels of corn. Thus, if corn futures rise by 10 cents per bushel, the trader long one futures contract profits by $500 (.10 • 5000), but the trader long one corn call with a .50 delta profits by $250 (.10 • 2500).

There are two reasons for using delta equivalents: First, soybean, corn, and wheat futures are traded in bushels, not contracts. Second, cash traders will find these quantities easier to understand and to manipulate for hedging purposes.

Note that, by definition, the delta of a long or short futures

TABLE 2–1 Sign of Delta

Option Position	Sign of Delta
Long call	Positive
Short call	Negative
Long put	Negative
Short put	Positive

TABLE 2–2 Option Profit / Loss with an Increase in Underlying Futures

Position	Delta (A)	Futures Change ($) (B)	Profit/Loss per Bushel ($) (A) × (B)	Profit/Loss per Contract ($)
Long 800 call	+.550	+.10	+.0550	+275.00
Short 800 call	−.550	+.10	−.0550	−275.00
Long 775 put	−.325	+.10	−.0325	−162.50
Short 775 put	+.325	+.10	+.0325	+162.50

contract is always +1 or −1, respectively. It follows that the delta equivalent of a long or short futures contract is the quantity of commodity defined in the contract times +1 or −1—for example, −5,000 bushels for a short wheat future or +100 short tons for a long soymeal future.

The soybean option deltas in Table 2–2 are expressed in terms of bushel equivalents in Table 2–3. Given a 10 cent per bushel increase in soybean futures and the bushel equivalents in Table 2–3, the reader should obtain the same profit/loss impact per contract as in Table 2–2.

Delta as a Measure of Probability

Delta can also be thought of as the probability that an out-of-the-money option will become an in-the-money option or that an in-the-money option will stay in-the-money. Ignoring signs for the moment, as an option moves from deep out-of-the-money to deep in-the-money, its delta increases from close to zero to close to one (see Table 2–4).

The rationale behind this pattern lies in probability. If the underlying futures move ten cents toward the strike price of a deep out-of-the-money call option, should that option's premium also rise by ten cents if it is now, say, 50 cents out-of-the-money versus 60 cents before the move? Certainly not, since the probability of the futures

TABLE 2–3 Bushel Equivalents

Position	Delta (A)	Bushel Equivalent (A) × (5,000)
Long 800 call	+.550	+2,750
Short 800 call	−.550	−2,750
Long 775 put	−.325	−1,625
Short 775 put	+.325	+1,625

TABLE 2–4 Value of Delta for Out-/at-/in-the-Money Options

Option	Associated Delta
Deep out-of-the-money	Close to 0
Out-of-the-money	Greater than 0, less than .50
At-the-money	Equals .50
In-the-money	Greater than .50, less than 1
Deep in-the-money	Close to 1

moving another 50 cents is low; therefore, the option's premium should not rise by the full amount of the futures change. It should rise by some small fraction, however, since it is indeed closer to being in-the-money than before and is thus more valuable.

Consider the at-the-money option. Assuming random price movements, the futures have a 50 percent chance of moving above or below the strike price and putting the option in-the-money or out-of-the-money. Thus, an at-the-money option has a delta of .50.

Likewise for a deep in-the-money option: The probability that it stays in-the-money is high, since to put it out-of-the-money the futures price has to move radically. The most likely conclusion is that it will remain in-the-money and so should reflect a large proportion of any change in the underlying futures.

Figure 2–1 shows the sign-correct relationship for a long and a short 775 call while Figure 2–2 shows the same for a long and a short 800 put.

FIGURE 2–1

Relationship of 775 Soybean Call Delta to Futures

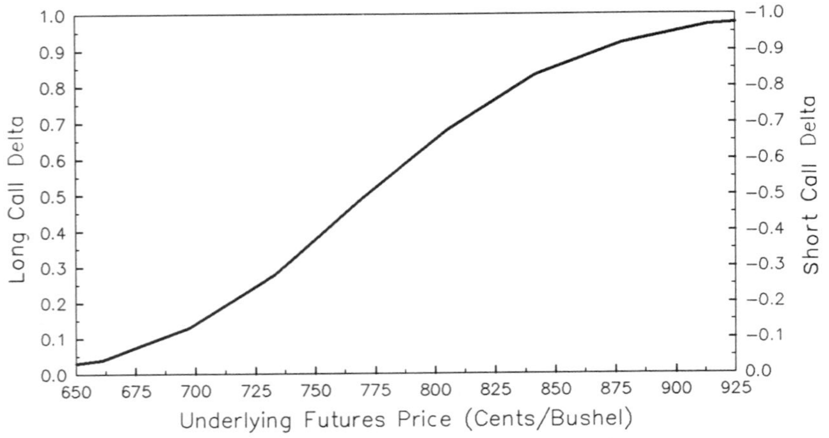

FIGURE 2–2

Relationship of 800 Soybean Put Delta to Futures

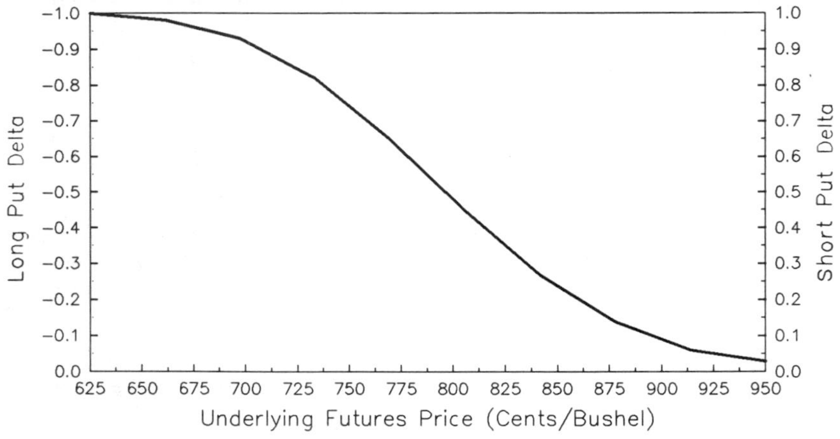

Delta Neutral Positions

A trader who buys one futures contract and sells two call options (each with a −.50 delta), is defined as being **delta neutral**. That is, all else remaining equal, any change in the futures price will be offset by the two short calls (and vice versa). Delta neutral positions are not limited to positions between options and futures; they can also consist of options in combination with other options (for example, long calls and long puts). As long as the total deltas of the position sum to zero, the position is considered delta neutral.

To calculate the number of option contracts for a delta neutral position, a simple formula called the **hedge ratio** can be used:

$$\text{Hedge ratio} = 1/(\text{Delta})$$

If a put has a delta of .12, then the number of puts that offsets the price movements of one futures contract is 1/(.12) or 8.3 or approximately 8 put contracts.

How Delta Changes: Gamma

Figures 2–1 and 2–2 demonstrate that delta is not a static concept; that is, as a call option goes from out-of-the-money to in-the-money, its delta will change from less than .50 to greater than .50. The way to anticipate the degree of change in delta is through the concept of **gamma**. Mathematically, gamma is the ratio of the change in delta versus the change in futures:

$$\text{gamma} = \frac{\text{change in delta}}{\text{change in futures price}} = \frac{\Delta D}{\Delta F}$$

The formula for calculating gamma from the Black equation is given in Appendix A.

For example, if a soybean call option has a gamma of +.003 and a delta of +.50, what will be the value of delta if the underlying futures rally 30 cents (one limit move)? From the formula for gamma, we can calculate the approximate change in delta:

$$(\text{gamma}) \cdot (\Delta F) = \Delta D$$
$$(.003) \cdot (30) = .09.$$

Therefore, the new delta will be close to .59:

$$.5 + .09 = .59$$

Conversely, if futures were to fall 30 cents, the new delta would be approximately .41:

$$.50 - .09 = .41$$

Note that gamma provides only approximate changes in delta. This is because gamma also changes as futures move up or down, and unless one is prepared to calculate changes in gamma, a close approximation of the new delta will have to suffice.

Sign of Gamma: How Delta Can Expand and Contract

Long Calls and Long Puts

As the futures price increases, the delta of a long call expands and its delta equivalent position becomes longer, while the delta of a long put contracts and its delta equivalent becomes less short. When the futures price declines, the delta of a long call contracts and its delta equivalent position becomes less long, while the delta of a long put expands and its delta equivalent position becomes shorter. (Confirm this from Figures 2–1 and 2–2 using the left axes). Table 2–5 demonstrates these phenomena for a long wheat call and put.

Because these are direct relationships (increasing futures result in longer or less-short delta equivalents; decreasing futures result in

TABLE 2–5 Expansion and Contraction of Delta for Long Options Positions

Futures (cents/bu.)	Long 330 Wheat Call		Long 330 Wheat Put	
	Delta	Bushel Equivalents	Delta	Bushel Equivalents
300	+.16	+800	−.84	−4200
320	+.38	+1900	−.62	−3100
340	+.65	+3250	−.35	−1750

shorter or less-long delta equivalents), the gamma of a long call or a long put is positive.

> *MATHEMATICS REVIEW*
> A direct relationship means that two variables (such as futures and delta) move in tandem. When one variable increases (decreases), the other variable increases (decreases). Consequently, the relationship between them (in this case, gamma) is termed positive.

Short Calls and Short Puts

As the futures price increases, the delta of a short call expands, and its delta equivalent position becomes shorter, while the delta of a short put contracts, and its delta equivalent position becomes less long. When the futures price declines, the delta of a short call contracts, and its delta equivalent position becomes less short, while the delta of a short put expands, and its delta equivalent position becomes longer. (Confirm this from Figures 2–1 and 2–2 using the right axes.) Table 2–6 demonstrates these phenomena for a short wheat call and put.

TABLE 2–6 Expansion and Contraction of Delta for Short Options Positions

Futures (cents/bu.)	Short 330 Wheat Call		Short 330 Wheat Put	
	Delta	Bushel Equivalents	Delta	Bushel Equivalents
300	−.16	−800	+.84	+4200
320	−.38	−1900	+.62	+3100
340	−.65	−3250	+.35	+1750

Because these are inverse relationships (increasing futures result in shorter or less-long delta equivalents; decreasing futures result in longer or less-short delta equivalents), the gamma of a short call or short put is negative.

> *MATHEMATICS REVIEW*
> An inverse relationship means that two variables (such as futures and delta) move opposite to each other. When one variable increases (decreases), the other variable decreases (increases). Consequently, the relationship between them (in this case, gamma) is termed negative.

The sign of gamma (see Table 2–7) is critical to an understanding of profit/loss considerations. When the futures price moves favorably for the trader long puts or calls, the trader makes money at an increasing rate, since the delta equivalent position is expanding. When the futures price moves unfavorably, the trader loses money at a decreasing rate, since the delta equivalent position is contracting.

Conversely for the trader short calls or puts: The trader makes money at a decreasing rate as futures prices move favorably, since the delta equivalent position is contracting. When futures prices move against the trader, he or she loses money at an increasing rate, since the delta equivalent position is expanding. This phenomenon is called **convexity**.

Nonetheless, before concluding that long option positions are always better than short option positions, the reader should consider the merits and demerits of long and short options. The merit of a long call or put option is the leverage it offers the trader; that is, for a small premium the trader can ultimately control a large amount of the underlying commodity if prices move favorably. Furthermore, the trader's risk is predefined, as the trader can lose no more than the premium paid.

The demerit of the long call is that market volatility may not be sufficient during the life of the option to allow leverage to work. That is, the statistical odds are often against the option long. (This will be discussed further in the sections on volatility and time decay.)

TABLE 2–7 Sign of Gamma

Option Position	Sign of Gamma
Long call	Positive
Long put	Positive
Short call	Negative
Short put	Negative

For a short call or put option, the merit is the ability to generate income upfront upon writing the option, and then earning that income through time decay. The demerit is unlimited risk if futures move unfavorably.

Putting Gamma Risk in Perspective

For small options positions, a slight shift in delta has a negligible impact, but for large positions it can be significant. Consider the previous example of a soybean call option with a delta of .50 and a gamma of .003.

If a trader is short 200 of these calls, he or she is short the delta equivalent of 500,000 bushels:

$$(-.50) \cdot (5000) \cdot (200) = -500{,}000 \text{ bushels.}$$

With a limit-up move in futures, however, the trader will be short an additional 90,000 bushels:

$$\underbrace{(-.003) \cdot (30)}_{\Delta D} \cdot (5000) \cdot (200) = -90{,}000,$$

and so on with each limit move.

A trader with a growing short position in a strong up market may want to reconsider his or her strategy or cover aggressively.

Variation of Gamma with Underlying Futures

It is important to understand that gamma is highest for at-the-money options and lowest for deep in-the-money and deep out-of-the-money options (see Figure 2–3). This is true for both puts and calls and can be explained in terms of probabilities. Since deep in-the-money or deep out-of-the-money options have only a small probability of becoming out-of-the-money or in-the-money options respectively, their gammas are low and their deltas change little with shifts in futures. At-the-money options have the highest probability of moving in one or the other direction, so their gammas are high, and their deltas shift rapidly with changes in the underlying futures.

Relation between Gamma and Time to Expiration

Another point to consider from Figure 2–3 is that gamma is highest for options near expiration and lowest for options far from expiration (especially for at- and near-the-money options). This phenomenon is further shown in Figure 2–4. For near-the-money call and

FIGURE 2–3

Relationship of 750 Soybean Call Gamma to Futures

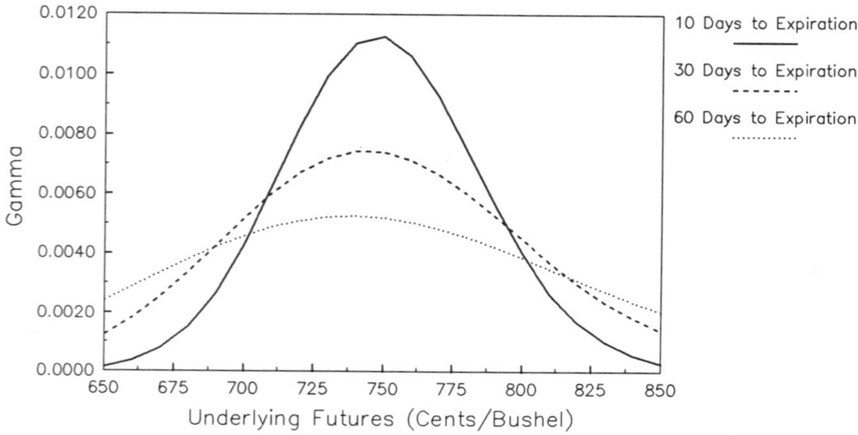

put options, gamma begins increasing exponentially about 30 to 40 calendar days before expiration. As a corollary, the farther in- or out-of-the-money an option is, the more stable its gamma.

Again, for large positions consisting of near-the-money options, the trader will find that gamma exposure increases rapidly from day to day as expiration nears. Consequently, small changes in the underlying futures will have large impacts on the trader's delta equivalent position. For example, assume a trader is long futures and short near-

FIGURE 2–4

Relationship of Gamma to Time to Expiration

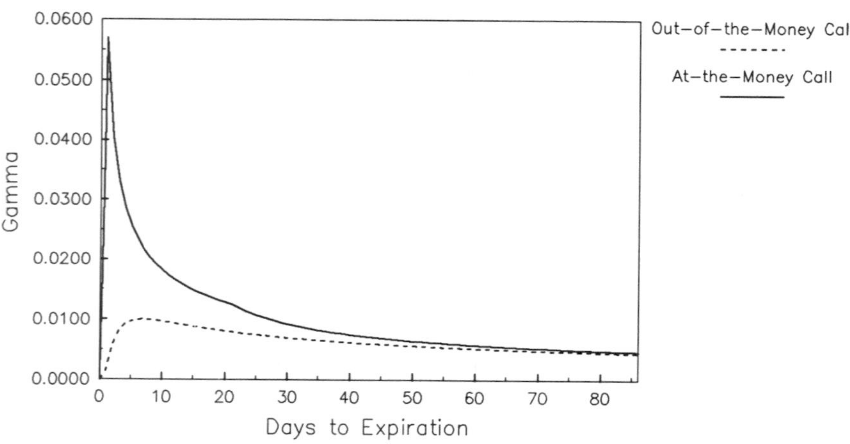

the-money calls such that his net bushel equivalent is 100 thousand bushels long. The trader can easily go from a delta equivalent of 100 thousand bushels long to 100 thousand bushels short with a small rise in futures due to the gamma effect. Note, however, that this will not occur if the position consists of deep in- or out-of-the-money options.

Gamma Equivalents: Expressing Gamma as Fractions of the Underlying Futures

Just as delta can be expressed in equivalents (bushels, tons, pounds), so can gamma. Nevertheless, the trader must define the unit of change in the underlying futures that allows him or her to interpret gamma exposure easily. For example, in the case of soybeans, corn, and wheat, it is convenient to determine gamma equivalents on the basis of a one cent increase or decrease in the underlying futures.

Take the previous example of a soybean call option with a delta of .50 and a gamma of .003. If a trader is long 100 of these options, the delta equivalent is

$$(+.50) \cdot (5000) \cdot (100) = +250{,}000 \text{ bushels.}$$

The gamma equivalent per one cent increase in soybean futures is

$$(+.003) \cdot (5000) \cdot (100) \cdot (1) = +1{,}500 \text{ bushels.}$$

That is, for every one cent increase in futures, the delta equivalent position is longer by 1,500 bushels; conversely, for every one cent decrease in futures, the delta equivalent of the position is less long by 1,500 bushels.

Position Delta and Position Gamma

For positions involving different combinations of long calls, short calls, long puts, and short puts, the individual delta and gamma equivalents can be added to obtain the net delta and gamma equivalents of the position. *This effectively defines all potential sources of flat-price risk for the trader.*

Table 2–8 shows one possible format to use for a soybean options position. The reader should calculate the delta and gamma equivalents as an exercise. The net position in Table 2–8 shows that the trader is net long 502,000 bushels of soybeans and that each one cent increase in soybean futures will decrease that long by 2,328 bushels; alternatively, each one cent drop in futures will increase that

TABLE 2–8 Delta and Gamma Equivalents of a Soybean Options Position

Position	Number of Contracts	Delta	Gamma	Delta: Bushel Equivalents	Gamma: Bushel Equivalents
Long 750 put	75	−0.50	0.0109	−187,500	+4,088
Short 775 put	170	0.73	−0.0085	+620,500	−7,225
Long 750 call	60	0.50	0.0111	+150,000	+3,330
Short 775 call	60	−0.27	−0.0084	−81,000	−2,520
Net position:				+502,000	−2,328

Note: 5,000 bushel contract

long by 2,328 bushels. This is due to the large amount of short puts in the position.

Examples of Trading Problems Using Delta and Gamma Concepts

1. A trader is short eight 850 soybean calls. The 850 soybean call has a delta of .38. If the trader anticipates a rally in futures and wants to cover the short (that is, be delta neutral) how many soybean futures should the trader buy against the short options contracts?

   ANSWER: Bushel equivalent of 1 short 850 call = (−.38) • (5000) = −1900 bushels. Trader is short eight contracts = (8) • (−1900) = −15200 bushels. Since one soybean futures contract is 5000 bushels, the trader needs to buy 15,000 bushels of soybeans or three futures contracts.

2. Assume the same problem as in Question 1 except that the trader decides to sell out-of-the-money puts to even up the short call position instead of futures. The trader feels that selling the 775 put is a good alternative to buying futures. The 775 put has a delta of .30. How many puts should the trader sell?

   ANSWER: Bushel equivalent of 1 short 775 put = (.30) • (5000) = +1500 bushels. Total bushels short with 850 call = (−.38) • (8) • (5000) = −15200 bushels. Put contracts needed to be delta neutral = (−15200)/(1500) = −10.13 or sell ten 775 puts.

   Notice the difference in profit outcome between selling puts and buying futures. Assume the premium of the 850 call is 10 cents. By hedging the short calls delta neutral, the trader has the potential to earn a 10 cent profit, or $4,000 over eight contracts;

however, if the trader sells ten 775 puts with a premium of 12 cents, the total return will increase by $6,000 to $10,000 if both options expire out-of-the-money (futures price stays between 775 and 850). The latter alternative, although high in profit, may be more risky due to volatility effects, as will be shown in the next section.

3. The trader in Question 1 also wants to be protected from a limit-up move in futures (30 point move in soybeans), since a limit-up move would increase the delta of the short calls and put the trader shorter than desired (for example, the trader would be trading against the trend). If the gamma of the 850 calls is .011, how many extra 775 puts should the trader sell to remain delta neutral in a limit-up move?

ANSWER: A limit-up move increases one 850 call delta by (30) • (−.011) = −.33. This puts the trader shorter by (−.33) • (5000) • (8) = −13200 bushels. Thus the number of extra 775 puts to sell is (−13200)/(1500) = −8.8 or approximately 9, for a total sale of 19 puts.

Note that if the anticipated limit-up move occurs, the sale of the additional puts buffers the trader's losses on the short calls; however, it does not insure that the position will be delta neutral when futures are 30 cents higher because the delta equivalent of the short puts will change due to gamma (the short put position becomes less-long). Hence, the trader may have to adjust further once the anticipated move occurs. Secondly, if the opposite occurs (a sharp fall in prices) the trader suffers greater loss due to the extra sale of puts.

4. A trader is long one hundred 800 soybean calls with a delta of .54. What loss should the trader anticipate with a limit-down move in futures (all other factors remaining equal, that is, volatility and time decay)?

ANSWER: Anticipated dollar move in option premium = (+.54) • (−.30) = −.162. Total profit/loss impact: (−.162) • (5000) •(100) = −$81,000.

Nevertheless, assuming implied volatility is unchanged, the $81,000 loss is *overstated*. Due to the convexity phenomenon, the call's delta will decrease as the market moves downward (due to gamma) and thus decelerate losses. If the gamma of the 800 call is +.0054, the delta will change by (+.0054) • (−30) = −.16 after the limit-down move in futures. The resulting delta of (+.54 + −.16) = .38 implies a loss of (+.38) • (−.30) •

(5000) • (100) = −$57,000. This result *understates* the actual loss; thus, the actual loss is less than −$81,000 but greater than −$57,000. Some traders would simply take the average (−$69,000). Although this is a good rough guess, it assumes that delta changes linearly, which it does not.

Option Premium and Volatility

Complete books have been written on the volatility aspect of option pricing, which only demonstrates the importance of this variable to the options trader. Yet many traders initiate options trades and strategies without considering volatility implications. Equipped solely with an understanding of delta, many of these traders will make money, but in the long run the vast majority will lose.

The presentation here is meant only to define volatility and to enable a trader to define volatility risks; this is ninety-five percent of the job. Traders are encouraged to consult some of the books in the bibliography for more detailed discussions of volatility and the statistical concepts associated with it.

The necessity of understanding volatility for the agricultural commodities trader is even greater, as most of these commodities have seasonal volatility trends in addition to day-to-day volatility fluctuations. Therefore, a separate chapter of this book (Chapter 3) is devoted to outlining seasonal volatility for some of the major agricultural commodities.

Basic Concepts

Volatility is simply a measure of the *annual* price fluctuations in the market. Over the course of a year, a soybean market moving up or down by 15 or 20 cents a day is more volatile than a market moving up or down in 3 or 5 cent daily increments. When volatility is quoted as 27 percent, it means that over the course of the year soybeans currently trading at $7.85 could trade between $7.85 ± $2.12 ($7.85 • .27 = $2.12) with a reasonably high probability (to be exact, a 68 percent probability).

It is intuitive that all options—both puts and calls—will have greater value in a market moving up or down daily by 15 to 20 cents than in a market moving in 3-to-5-cent daily increments, since there is a greater probability that individual options will come into-the-money. A trader who sells out-of-the-money options in a market that is moving at 20 to 30 cents a clip must rationally demand a higher premium.

Historical Volatility versus Implied Volatility

Historical volatility is a statistically computed measure of the variation in the underlying futures price. Traders and analysts ordinarily apply the statistical concept of standard deviation to a price series of futures to calculate historical volatility. Nonetheless, if we assume that prices cannot be zero or negative, we must use the log-normal probability distribution, which entails some data manipulation before we can calculate standard deviation (see Table 2–9).

The volatility of 22.6 percent is simply the standard deviation of the log-normal series of price ratios adjusted by 256 trading days to

TABLE 2–9 Sample Calculation of Historical Volatility Using Soybean Meal Futures

Date	Futures Settle (P_t)	Price Ratios[1] $\left(\frac{P_t}{P_{t-1}}\right)$	Natural Log of Ratios[2] $\text{Ln}\left(\frac{P_t}{P_{t-1}}\right)$	$\left[\text{Ln}\left(\frac{P_t}{P_{t-1}}\right) - \text{Average}\right]^2$
14-Oct	259.70			
17-Oct	263.70	1.015	0.015	0.00024
18-Oct	261.20	0.991	−0.010	0.00009
19-Oct	261.20	1.000	0.000	0.00000
20-Oct	255.10	0.977	−0.024	0.00055
21-Oct	250.70	0.983	−0.017	0.00029
24-Oct	245.20	0.978	−0.022	0.00048
25-Oct	245.70	1.002	0.002	0.00001
26-Oct	248.70	1.012	0.012	0.00015
27-Oct	245.60	0.988	−0.013	0.00015
28-Oct	249.60	1.016	0.016	0.00027
31-Oct	253.20	1.014	0.014	0.00021
01-Nov	254.10	1.004	0.004	0.00001
02-Nov	261.40	1.029	0.028	0.00082
03-Nov	261.60	1.001	0.001	0.00000
04-Nov	262.20	1.002	0.002	0.00001
07-Nov	265.20	1.011	0.011	0.00014
08-Nov	264.90	0.999	−0.001	0.00000
09-Nov	263.50	0.995	−0.005	0.00003
10-Nov	258.50	0.981	−0.019	0.00036
Number of data points:	20		Average: −0.00024	Sum: 0.00380
Historical volatility	=	$\sqrt{\frac{(.0038)}{(20 - 1)} \cdot 256}$		= 22.6%

[1]Day's price divided by day before price.
[2]Take natural log to assume log-normal distribution.

FIGURE 2–5

Soybean Historical Volatility

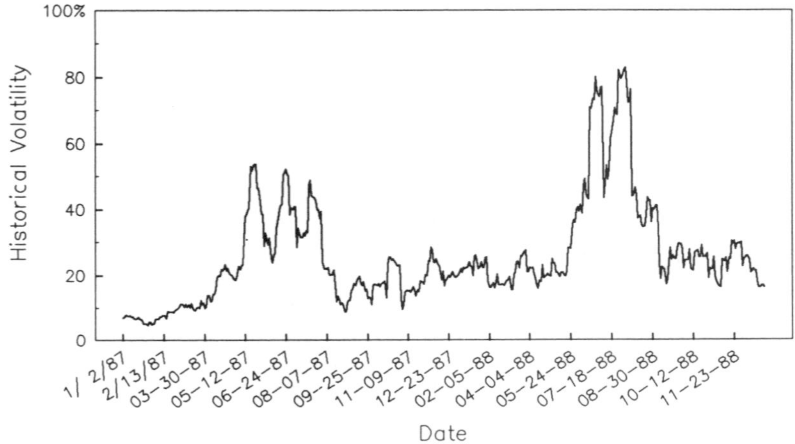

make it an annual statistic (consult Appendix A if there is any difficulty with the above). Twenty data points were chosen because it was felt that price changes over this 20-day period reflect market volatility. More or fewer data points can be chosen; however, it is best to have at least a 15-to-20-day sample for the results to be statistically useful.

Figures 2–5, 2–6, and 2–7 show a long-term chart of the historical volatility of soybeans, corn, and wheat, respectively.

FIGURE 2–6

Corn Historical Volatility

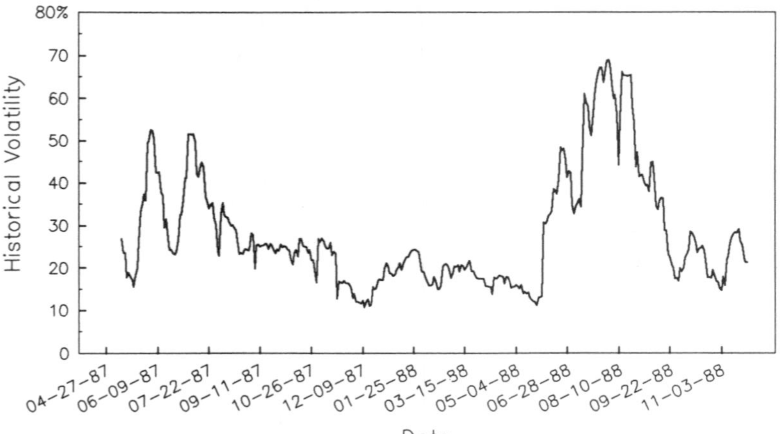

FIGURE 2–7

Wheat Historical Volatility

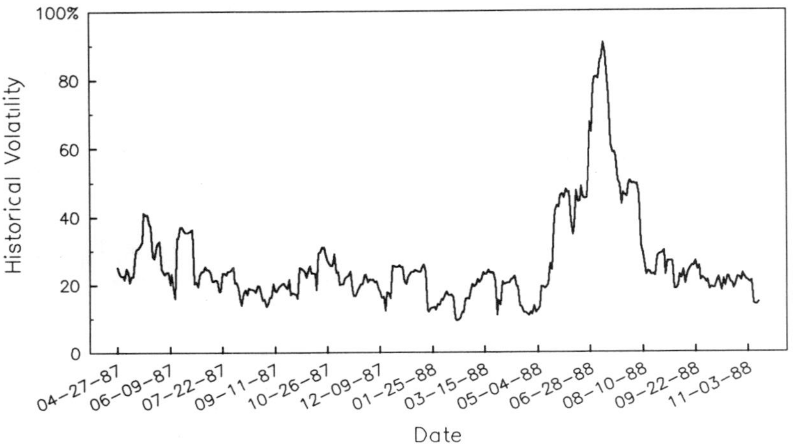

Implied Volatility

In contrast, **implied volatility** is the market volatility suggested by an option's premium. A trader will take an option pricing model such as the Black model, plug in the strike price, futures price, days to expiration, and interest rate, and then adjust the volatility input until the theoretical Black premium equals the premium currently trading in the market. *The volatility that equates the market premium with the theoretical premium is the implied volatility of that option.*

An example will help: A trader wants to know the implied volatility of an 875 soybean call trading at a premium of 6.75 cents. The underlying futures are at 812.5 cents per bushel and there are 36 days to expiration. The current yield of a T-Bill maturing around the expiration of the option is 7 percent. For volatility, the trader decides to evaluate the Black model at four levels: 20 percent, 25 percent, 30 percent, and 35 percent. The trader calculates the corresponding theoretical premiums as shown in Table 2–10. Table 2–10 shows that the implied volatility of the 875 call option is around 25 to 26 percent; that is, the market's estimate of futures price volatility with respect to this 875 call option is 25 to 26 percent. Analysts will do this calculation for every option trading in a particular class (for example, November calls) and then assign a weight to each strike according to its volume traded to come up with an implied volatility estimate for the entire class. Thus, traders will often say, "November calls are trading at 23 percent volatility."

Figures 2–8 and 2–9 show a continuation chart of implied vola-

TABLE 2–10 Approximation of Implied Volatility for a Call Option

Volatility Estimate	Theoretical Premium	Current Market Premium
20%	3.25	
25%	6.25	↔ 6.75
30%	10.00	
35%	14.00	

tility of the nearby soybean and corn option contract, respectively. (Note: these are given as examples; a more complete analysis of the behavior of implied volatility over time is given in Chapter 3).

It should be made clear that there is no formula that one can use to calculate implied volatility. The complexity of the Black formula does not permit solving for implied volatility. Instead implied volatility must be approximated as in the previous example or determined by means of a computer software package.

Implied versus Historical Volatility

Beginning traders are often confused about which volatility to focus on, implied or historical. In general, it is best to focus on implied volatility, as this is the volatility consensus of market participants (of course, the market participants can be wrong, and this is

FIGURE 2–8

Soybean Implied Volatility: 1987–1988

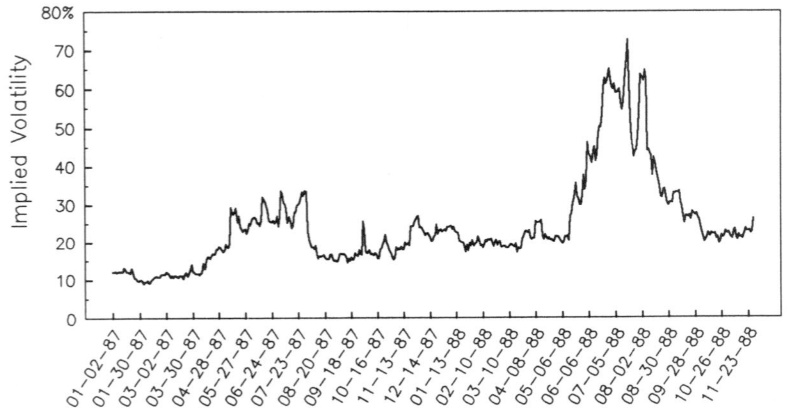

FIGURE 2–9

Corn Implied Volatility: 1987–1988

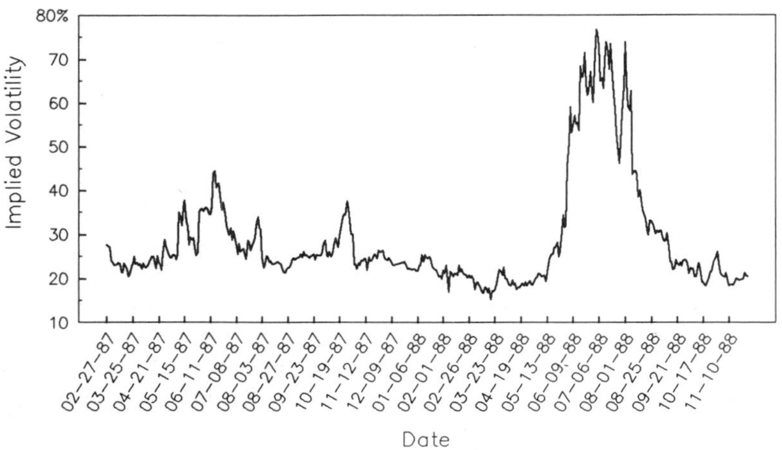

precisely where profitable opportunities exist). In addition—and perhaps more importantly—implied volatility is what affects a trader's daily profit/loss, so he or she must focus on it to define this aspect of risk.

Nevertheless, traders should always keep apprised of historical volatilities as well, especially when historical volatility radically diverges from implied volatility. Many traders take these divergences as signals to sell options when implied volatility is above historical volatility and to buy options when implied volatility is below historical volatility.

Optimally, a trader should analyze volatility divergences on a case-by-case basis, because often it is not obvious which indicator is leading or lagging behind the other. (The first two case studies in Chapter 6 will bear this out.) Indeed, there may be a good reason why market participants are bidding up implied volatility over the historical measure (for instance, in anticipation of seasonal factors such as drought).

Profit/Loss Impacts from Implied Volatility Shifts

From Chapter 1, we know that rising volatility increases the value of both puts and calls while falling volatility has the opposite effect, all other factors (futures price, time decay, and interest rate) remaining constant. To that extent, implied volatility is a trader's guide to how cheap or expensive an option is. To illustrate, examine Table 2–11.

TABLE 2–11 Relationship between Implied Volatility and Call and Put Premiums

Underlying soybean futures constant at 812.5. 36 days to expiration. Interest rate at 7%.		
Implied Volatility	**825 Call Premium**	**775 Put Premium**
20%	15.00	6.50
25%	19.75	10.00
30%	24.50	14.75
35%	30.25	19.25

One can intuit from Table 2–11 that a trader will make money when he or she is long options (puts or calls) and volatility is rising, or when he or she is short options and volatility is falling. If simultaneously the price outlook for the underlying futures was correct, the trader's profit will be greater than the delta suggested; if wrong, the losses will be less than the delta suggested.

Conversely, a trader loses money when long options and volatility is falling or when short options and volatility is rising. Again, if simultaneously the trader's price outlook for the underlying futures was correct, the gains will be less than the delta suggested; if wrong, the losses will be greater than the delta suggested.

To summarize: *A trader who buys option premium is long volatility; a trader who sells premium is short volatility.*

Quantifying Profit/Loss from Volatility Shifts: Concept of Vega

The objective for any trader should be to define volatility risk in dollar terms. The indicator used to accomplish this is called **vega**. Mathematically, vega is the ratio of change in the option premium versus the change in volatility, or:

$$\text{vega} = \frac{\text{change in option premium}}{\text{change in volatility}} = \frac{\Delta P}{\Delta V}$$

The formula for calculating vega from the Black equation is given in Appendix A.

Sign of Vega

Given the profit/loss impacts of implied volatility fluctuations described in the Option Premium and Volatility section, Table 2–12 shows the sign of vega corresponding to different options positions.

TABLE 2–12 Sign of Vega

Position	Sign of Vega
Long calls	Positive
Long puts	Negative
Short calls	Positive
Short puts	Negative

There are many computer software programs that enable a trader to calculate the vega of an option. Often they convert this number into dollar terms such as dollars lost/gained with a one percent shift in implied volatility.

For example, what is the dollar impact of a one percent increase in volatility of one short 800 soybean call with a vega of -162?

Answer:

$$\Delta P/\Delta V = -162 = \Delta P/.01$$

$$\Delta P = (.01) \cdot (-162) = -1.62 \text{ cents, or per contract:}$$

$$(-.0162) \cdot (5000) = -\$81.00$$

Note: The vega was calculated from inputs that were given in cents so that the vega is also in terms of cents.

This means that with a one percent increase in volatility, a trader who is short this call will lose $81 even if the futures remain unchanged. To hedge delta neutral with futures does not help the trader either as there was no flat-price change.

In this case the only way the trader could have diluted the risk would have been to be long another call option at a different strike. Accordingly, one good reason for spreading options (for example, short the lower strike long the upper strike or vice-versa) is to maintain a flat price bias while diluting volatility risk. Such tactics will be elaborated in Chapter 4.

Relationship of Vega to Underlying Futures, Vega to Implied Volatility, and Vega to Time to Expiration

As shown in Figure 2–10, the options most sensitive to implied volatility shifts are the at- or near-the-money options and options far from expiration. To further isolate these phenomena, Figure 2–11 examines vega's relation to implied volatility for in-/out-/at-the-money options, and Figure 2–12 demonstrates the effect of the number of days to expiration on vega.

FIGURE 2–10

Relationship of 750 Soybean Call Vega to Futures

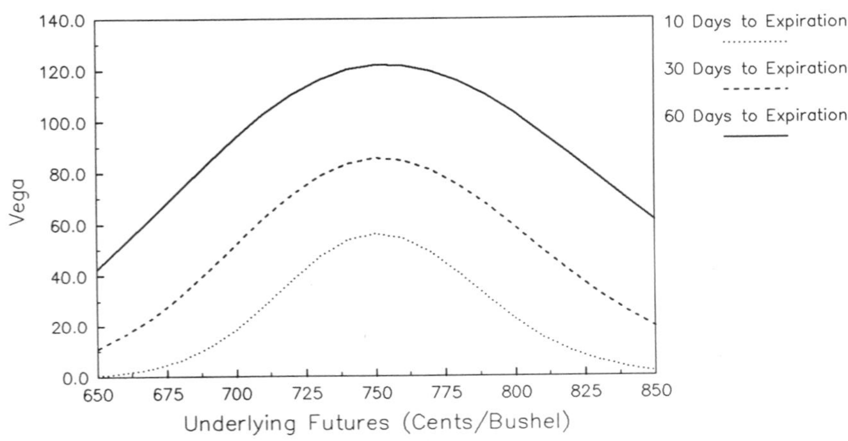

Figure 2–11 shows that although at- and near-the-money options show the greatest absolute sensitivity to volatility shifts, this sensitivity is *stable* over a wide range of volatilities. This is not the case, however, for in- and out-of-the-money options. *In- and out-of-the-money options display increasing sensitivity to volatility as volatility rises and decreasing sensitivity as volatility declines.*

Thus, the volatility profits and losses of at- and near-the-money options (long or short) are relatively constant. But for in- and out-of-the-money options, there are different implications for long options

FIGURE 2–11

Relationship of Vega to Implied Volatility

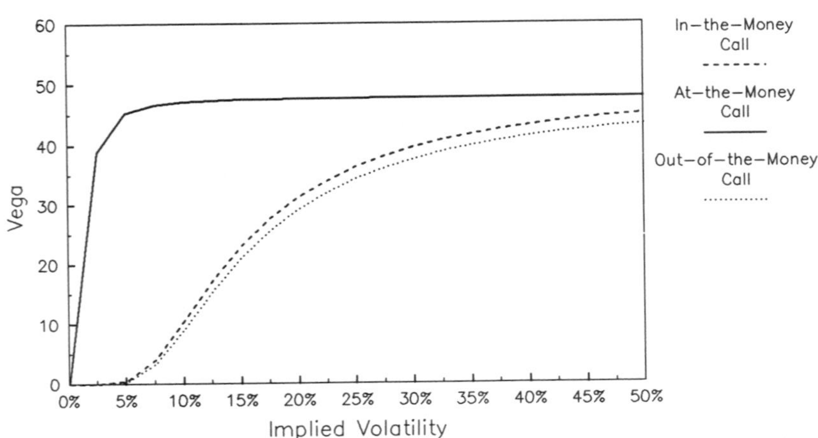

FIGURE 2–12

Relationship of Vega to Time to Expiration

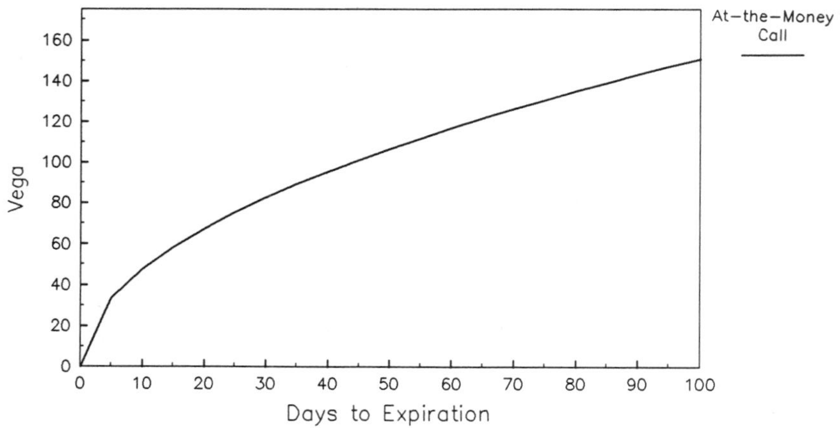

and short options. The long in- or out-of-the-money option yields increasing volatility profits as volatility moves favorably and decreasing losses as volatility moves unfavorably. Conversely, the short in- or out-of-the-money option yields decreasing volatility profits as volatility moves favorably and increasing losses as volatility moves unfavorably. Note the similarity to the convexity phenomenon discussed earlier.

Figure 2–12 isolates the relationship of vega to time to expiration. With 40 days or more to expiration, the decrease in vega is nearly linear; however, with less than 40 days to expire, vega declines at a faster rate. Consequently, the option becomes increasingly insensitive to fluctuations in volatility as expiration approaches. The trend is similar for in-, out-, and at-the-money options.

Option Premium and Time Value

As we have seen from Table 2–11, extrinsic value changes with volatility; that is, it goes up with increases in volatility and drops with decreases. Nevertheless, extrinsic value is also a function of time: Options far away from expiration should be worth more than options near expiration, since a greater amount of time allows for a greater probability that the option will gain or add intrinsic value. Again, this assumes all else remains equal, such as strike price, futures price (no carrying charges or inverses), volatility, and interest rates.

This becomes intuitive if we look at the range of possible futures prices implicit in volatility. Assume that we can be one hundred percent assured that price volatility in the corn market over the course of the year will remain constant, for example, at 25 percent. If December futures are trading at 250 cents per bushel, the possible *annual* range in prices is 250 ± 62.5 cents. But what is the possible range during the next day? The next two weeks? The next three months? To calculate that, one must adjust the annual volatility by the square root of the trading period in question, as shown in Table 2–13.

Table 2–13 is almost self-explanatory: With corn futures at 250 cents per bushel, an out-of-the-money March 280 call with 60 trading days before expiration should be worth more than an out-of-the-money December 280 call with 10 days left to expiration, because the March call is within the range of probable prices that can occur in the next 60 days. This does not mean that an extraordinary futures price move cannot occur in the next ten days to put the December call in-

TABLE 2–13 Calculating Volatility over Different Time Periods

Price range over 1 day:	$\dfrac{25\%}{\sqrt{\dfrac{256}{1}}} = 1.56\%$ (0.156) · (250) = 4.0 250 ± 4 cents
Price range over 10 days:	$\dfrac{25\%}{\sqrt{\dfrac{256}{10}}} = 4.94\%$ (.0494) · (250) = 12.25 250 ± 12.25 cents
Price range over 60 days:	$\dfrac{25\%}{\sqrt{\dfrac{256}{60}}} = 12.1\%$ (.121) · (250) = 30.25 250 ± 30.25 cents

To summarize:

Trading Period	Price Range
1 day	± 4 cents
10 days	± 12.25 cents
60 days	± 30.25 cents
256 days	± 62.5 cents

TABLE 2–14 Time Value of In-/At-/Out-of-the-Money Options

January Soybean Options	Futures	Premium	Time Value = Extrinsic
725 call	775	50.50	0.50
750 call	775	31.00	6.00
775 call	775	19.50	19.50
800 call	775	10.00	10.00
825 call	775	5.75	5.75
850 call	775	3.25	3.25

the-money; it only means that within the range of likely outcomes, the March call has a better chance over time of going into-the-money than the December call.

The use of volatility to explain time value should indicate to the reader that there is a connection between the two; indeed, the interrelationship among the underlying futures price, volatility, and time should start to become clearer.

Options with the Greatest Time Value

Within any type and class of options, the option with the greatest amount of time value is the at-the-money option (see Table 2–14).

The concept of probability has been stressed repeatedly in option pricing, and there is no exception when discussing time effects. The at-the-money option has the greatest likelihood of going into-the-money and thus carries the greatest extrinsic value. Notice also from the previous discussion that the at-the-money option is the option most sensitive to changes in its delta (via gamma) and volatility shifts (see Figures 2–3, 2–4, 2–10, and 2–11).

Therefore, the profit/loss potential of at- and near-the-money options is high, and these options deserve the greatest amount of analysis before they are traded. Faced with a matrix of time values as in Table 2–14, many traders would opt to sell the at-the-money premium, as it has the highest time value, only to be devastated by gamma or volatility fluctuations.

Profit/Loss Impacts from Time Decay: The Concept of Theta

It has been shown that there are risks and rewards associated with time decay just as there are with shifting futures prices and volatilities. For example, if the market price in Table 2–14 stayed at 775 until expiration, the trader short any of these options would earn the full amount of time value. Conversely, the trader long any of these options would lose the full amount of time value. Thus, time decay works to the benefit of any shorts (puts or calls) and to the detriment of any longs (puts or calls). *Notice that this is the opposite of the volatility effect.*

Quantifying Profit and Loss from Time Decay

The indicator used to quantify a trader's exposure to the passage of time is **theta**. Mathematically, theta is the ratio of change in the option premium versus the change in time:

$$\text{theta} = \frac{\text{change in option premium}}{\text{change in time}} = \frac{\Delta P}{\Delta T}$$

The formula for calculating theta from the Black equation is given in Appendix A. *Important:* The change in time is always defined as the ratio of the number of days passing versus 365 days in a year, so one day would be expressed as 1/365, or .00274; 7 days as 7/365, or 0.1917; and so on.

Sign of Theta

Given the profit/loss impacts from time decay just described, Table 2–15 gives the signs of theta corresponding to different options positions.

Just as with vega, there are many option software programs that will compute thetas. From there, the trader must define the period of time to analyze profit and loss, although it is usually standard to define it as dollars earned or lost in one day.

For example, a 775 soybean put has a theta of 114.2. What is the profit/loss impact of one day's passage of time for a trader who is short 150 of these contracts? Here is the answer:

$(\Delta P/\Delta T) = +114.2$

$\Delta T = (1/365) = .00274$

$\Delta P = (114.2) \cdot (.00274) = .3129$ cents per bushel per day, or per contract:

$(.003129) \cdot (5000) = \$15.65$ per contract per day, and over 150 contracts:

$(150) \cdot (\$15.65) = \$2364.75$ per day

TABLE 2–15 Sign of Theta

Position	Sign of Theta
Long calls	Negative
Long puts	Positive
Short calls	Negative
Short puts	Positive

At first glance this seems amazing: $2,364.75 per day for simply writing options. Remember, however, that a trader short options is also short volatility (negative vega) and is exposed accordingly. There is flat-price exposure as well if the position is not delta neutral.

Second example: A trader is long 100 contracts of 850 calls with a theta of 65.9 and short 75 contracts of 875 calls with a theta of 50.2. What is the net dollar impact of one day's passage of time on this position?

$$
\begin{aligned}
\text{Net theta} &= (100) \cdot (-65.9) = -6590 \\
& \quad (75) \cdot (50.2) = 3765 \\
& \quad (-6590) + (3765) = -2825 \\
\text{Net impact per day} &= (-2825) \cdot (.00274) \\
&= -7.75 \text{ cents} \\
\text{Net dollar impact} &= (-.0775) \cdot (5000) \\
&= -\$387.03
\end{aligned}
$$

This position is only slightly susceptible to time decay. The trader has managed to spread the time risk (theta) by spreading into the 875 call.

Relationship of Theta to Underlying Futures and Time to Expiration

The relationship of theta to the underlying futures is given in Figure 2–13. The graph demonstrates that at-the-money options decay at a higher rate than in-the-money or out-of-the-money options. More importantly, options close to expiration decay at a faster rate than options far from expiration.

This phenomenon is further isolated in Figure 2–14. The theta of an at- or near-the-money option begins increasing exponentially 30 to 40 days before expiration; accordingly, time decay is rapid during this period. Also, the further in- or out-of-the-money an option is,

FIGURE 2–13

Relationship of 750 Soybean Call Theta to Futures

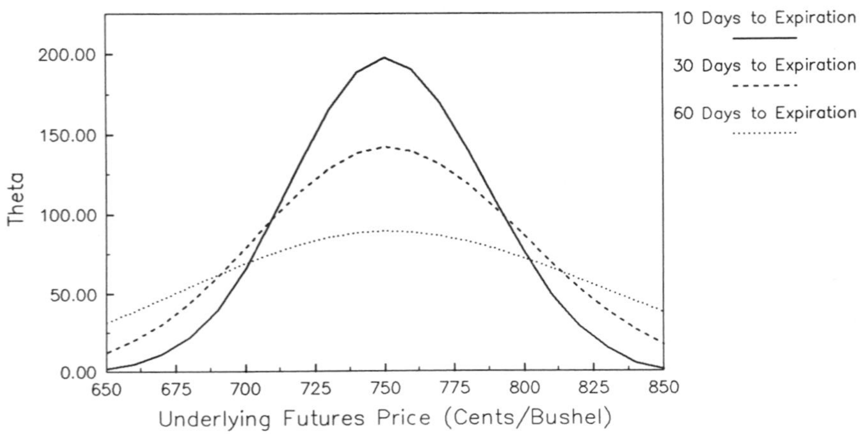

the less sensitive theta is to the passage of time; hence, time decay proceeds more linearly.

There is clearly a 30-to-40-day period before the expiration of at- or near-the-money options where gamma, vega, and theta change rapidly. Specifically, gamma and theta (time decay) increase while vega decreases; that is, at- or near-the-money options shed their option-like characteristics and act more like futures.

The trader who can predict a calm market during this period

FIGURE 2–14

Relationship of Theta to Time to Expiration

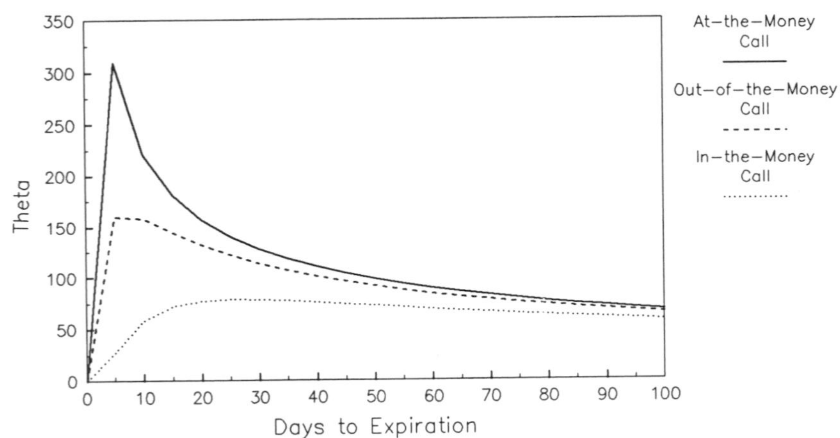

TABLE 2–16 Summary of Signs for Delta, Gamma, Vega, and Theta Corresponding to Different Options Positions

	Delta	Gamma	Vega	Theta
Long calls	+	+	+	–
Long puts	–	+	+	–
Short calls	–	–	–	+
Short puts	+	–	–	+

will profit by writing options, as decaying extrinsic value will rapidly accrue to his or her account. There is still the problem of an expanding delta risk (via gamma), but a calm market allows a trader to easily hedge this risk with futures or simply to ignore it. The market rises and the market falls, but essentially it goes nowhere.

Putting It All Together: Delta, Gamma, Vega, and Theta

An Example

A trader gives you the following problem: 160 soybean call options with a strike price of 750 were bought at the previous day's closing price of 10 cents per bushel; futures settled at 652 cents per bushel. Subsequently, futures rallied 11.25 cents to close at 663.25 cents per bushel the following day; however, the 750 call premium settled unchanged at 10 cents. The trader asks why no money was made if long calls are the correct strategy for a bullish market outlook.

Steps to solution: (1) Calculate the implied volatility of the option for both days based on the closing prices (assume 52 days to expiration). (2) Calculate the delta, gamma, vega, and theta of the 750 call as of the previous day's close. The calculations should result in the following numbers:

	PREVIOUS DAY	FOLLOWING DAY
Delta	+.20	
Gamma	+.0028	
Vega (cents/1%)	+.6820	
Theta (cents/day)	–.2531	
Implied Volatility	39.72%	36.84%

	PREVIOUS DAY	FOLLOWING DAY
Futures (cents/bu.)	652.00	663.25
750 Call Premium	10.00	10.00

By using the formulas in this book, identify the dollar profit/loss characteristics of each aspect of the option's price:

Delta Profit/Loss	=	(+.20)(+.1125)(5000)(160) =	+$18,000.00
Gamma Profit/Loss	=	(+.0028)(+.1125)(5000)(160) =	+$252.00
Vega Profit/Loss	=	(+.006820)(−2.88)(5000)(160) =	−$15,713.20
Theta Profit/Loss	=	(−.002531)(1)(5000)(160) =	−$2,024.80
Total Profit/Loss	=		+$514.00

The 2.88 percent drop in implied volatility cancelled out the profit from delta and gamma. Note that a small positive amount is left as a residual ($514). This results from calculating delta, gamma, vega, and theta at one point (previous day) and extrapolating profit/loss impacts when in fact the flat price had changed. Since the 750 call is closer to the money after the 11.25 cent rally, its vega and theta are higher, and this erases all profit in actuality.

Summary

a. Delta should be a straightforward concept for most traders, as it links the option's value with movements in the underlying futures.

b. Gamma measures the change in delta given a change in the underlying futures. It should not be a concern for small positions, but it must be monitored closely for large positions consisting of at- or near-the-money options with less than 30 to 40 days to expiration.

c. Vega quantifies the impact of volatility changes on an option's premium. Theta quantifies the impact of time decay on an option's premium. Vega and theta have a definite interrelationship: Longs and shorts cannot have it both ways, as longs benefit from increases in volatility but are hurt by time decay, and vice-versa for shorts.

d. Vega and gamma vary inversely for at- and near-the-money options as expiration nears; that is, gamma gains and vega falls.

e. Theta and gamma vary directly for at- and near-the-money options as expiration nears; time decay increases exponentially and the option becomes more futures-like.

It has been demonstrated that options approaching expiration undergo a great amount of change in their delta, gamma, vega, and theta characteristics and that the greatest concentration of change is in the at- or near-the-money option. In the following two sections, the trading implications of these phenomena are examined. A complete trading approach is presented in Chapter 4.

Buying At- or Near-the-Money Options Close to Expiration

Traders buy at- or near-the-money options that are close to expiration (that is, 30 to 40 days to expiration) for two reasons: (1) they offer an exponential increase in leverage (the gamma effect; see Figure 2–4), and (2) they are cheap vis-à-vis deferred options.

Nonetheless, the vega of an at- or near-the-money option close to expiration is low (see Figure 2–12). Therefore, what these traders are implicitly counting on is a sharp price movement in their favor concurrent with an extraordinary increase in market volatility to sustain that movement. If the "big move" does not occur, and the odds suggest it will not, these traders will lose a good portion of their premium to time decay. Indeed, time decay—as will be seen in the next section—is the real reason these options are cheap.

Therefore, when the trader has less conviction in a sudden and volatile price move, the long at- or near-the-money option is better placed in a deferred month, because deferred options are more sensitive to volatility changes (higher vega), and they decay slowly (more on time decay in the next section).

But how far out in time should the trader place a long? The trader must weigh the trade-off between leverage (gamma) and vega, since the farther one goes out in time, the lower the gamma and the higher the vega. As a rule of thumb, the trader is better off trading one contract month out from the nearby (for example, if the May options are near expiration, the July options should be traded), because the liquidity of the deferred options beyond two contract months is generally poor.

Selling At- or Near-the-Money Options Close to Expiration

Just as there are traders buying at- or near-the-money options close to expiration with the idea of cashing in on exponentially increasing leverage (gamma; see Figure 2–4), so there are traders selling at- or near-the-money options with the idea of earning exponentially increasing time decay (see Figure 2–14). But the simultaneous increase in both gamma and theta at 30 to 40 days to expiration is no coincidence. What is a benefit for the long is a drawback for the short, and vice versa.

How does one trade this if there is no apparent edge to being long or short? The answer lies in one's outlook on market behavior during the last 30 to 40 days to expiration. Will the market be calm or volatile? In agricultural options, a partial answer is provided by the seasonal patterns of implied volatility; the rest of the solution—like much in trading—is a matter of one's conviction. The importance of seasonal volatility patterns is such that it is treated separately in the next chapter.

However, another clue is provided by the relationships between gamma and implied volatility and theta and implied volatility. Figures 2–15 and 2–16 show the effect of volatility on a call option's gamma with 30 days and 7 days to expiration, respectively. One phenome-

FIGURE 2–15

Relationship of Gamma to Implied Volatility
30 Days to Expiration

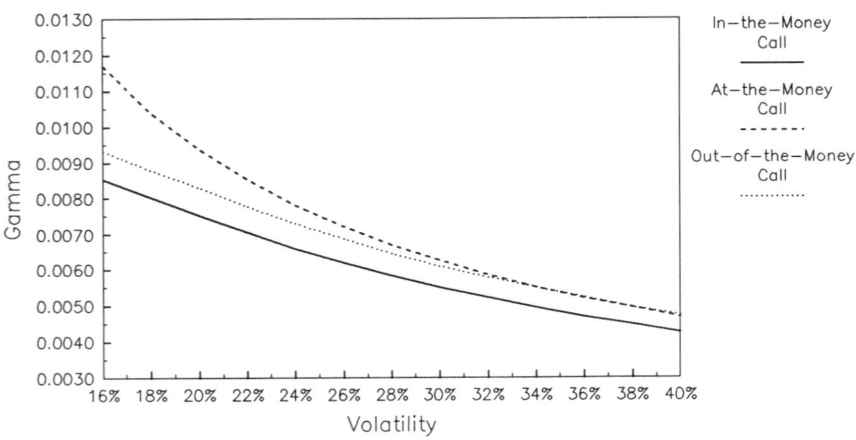

FIGURE 2–16

Relationship of Gamma to Implied Volatility
7 Days to Expiration

0.0250
0.0225
0.0200
0.0175
0.0150
0.0125
0.0100
0.0075
0.0050
Gamma
16% 18% 20% 22% 24% 26% 28% 30% 32% 34% 36% 38% 40%
Volatility
In–the–Money Call
At–the–Money Call
Out–of–the–Money Call

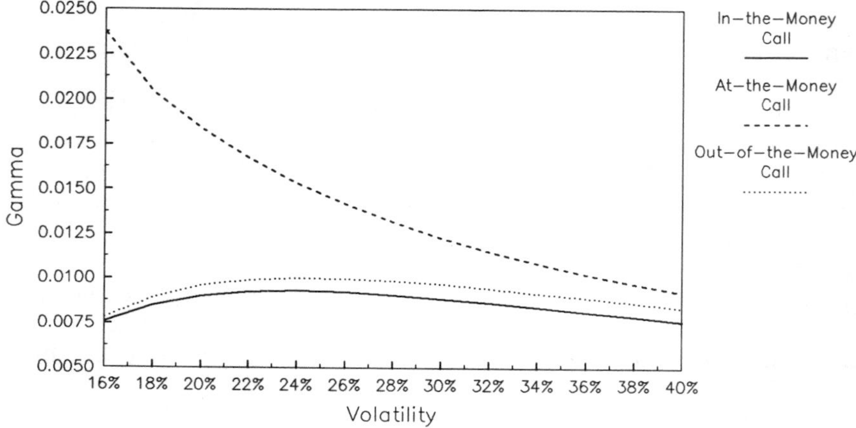

non stands out: The gamma of an at-the-money option is more elastic with respect to volatility than the gamma of in- or out-of-the-money options; and the divergence of elasticities becomes more pronounced as expiration nears.

Therefore, in a market where implied volatility is fluctuating erratically between 20 and 35 percent (volatility is volatile), the seller of at-the-money options has a distinct disadvantage. In the opposite

FIGURE 2–17

Relationship of Theta to Implied Volatility
30 Days to Expiration

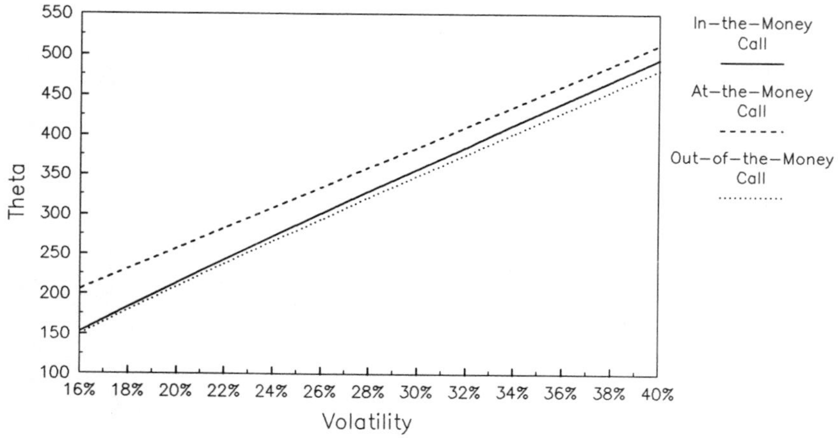

550
500
450
400
350
300
250
200
150
100
Theta
16% 18% 20% 22% 24% 26% 28% 30% 32% 34% 36% 38% 40%
Volatility
In–the–Money Call
At–the–Money Call
Out–of–the–Money Call

FIGURE 2–18

Relationship of Theta to Implied Volatility
7 Days to Expiration

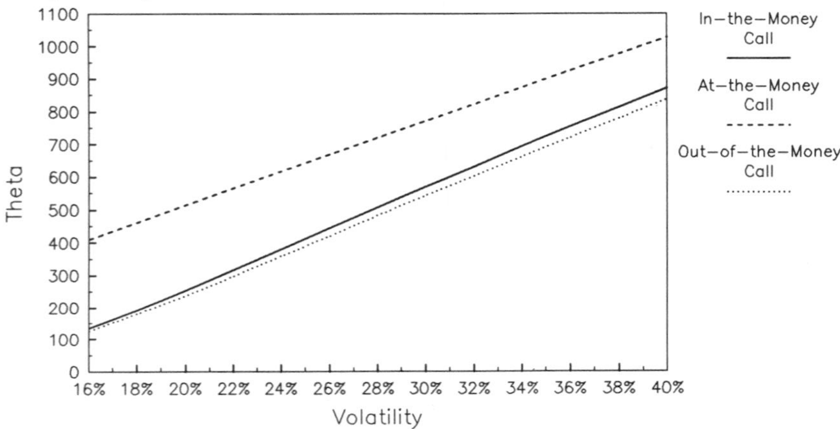

case, where volatility is stable or when it moves in a narrow band, a selling strategy is preferred.

For instance, if a trader's strategy is to sell at-the-money options and hedge delta neutral using futures, the amount of adjustments to maintain delta neutrality will be high if volatility is erratic; the delta becomes a moving target. Profit slippage will result and transaction costs will be high. The trade is not worth it, and the long side is preferred because of the high leverage of the at-the-money option at every volatility level. Again, traders of agricultural options can anticipate these volatility fluctuations based on seasonal factors.

Figures 2–17 and 2–18 demonstrate the relationship between theta and volatility: Theta increases linearly as implied volatility increases. As one would expect, at-the-money options decay at a faster rate at every volatilty level vis-à-vis in- and out-of-the-money options. This reinforces the conclusions above: If implied volatility is expected to fluctuate over a small range (for example, between 18 and 24 percent), the at-the-money option always represents a better sale, because its rate of time decay is superior to that of the in- or out-of-the-money option.

Summary

The last two sections support the conclusion that if market volatility is expected to increase suddenly, one should buy the nearby at- or near-the-money option. At the very least, one should avoid selling it. Conversely, the at- or near-the-money option becomes an attractive short only as one's market expectations call for stable or declining volatility. These decisions—given one's market expectations—are clear-cut.

But what about in- and out-of-the-money options? Under what circumstances does one want to buy or sell those options? These questions are discussed next.

Buying and Selling In- and Out-of-the-Money Options

When trading out-of-the-money and in-the-money options, there are two interrelationships to consider in more detail: The effect of time on delta and the effect of volatility on delta (see Figures 2–19 and 2–20). These relationships demonstrate some of the most critical points in options trading—especially for out-of-the-money options, since both buyers and sellers tend to gravitate towards them.

If a trader expects volatility to increase or remain stable and thus wants to go long options (puts or calls), he or she should buy out-of-the-money options that are far from expiration (for example, more than 30 to 40 calendar days). However, if market volatility is expected to decline—and the trader still wants to probe the long side—he or she should buy in-the-money options that are near expiration.

In the first case, the trader avoids a decaying out-of-the-money option whose delta is highly susceptible to declines in volatility. In

FIGURE 2–19

Relationship of Delta to Time to Expiration

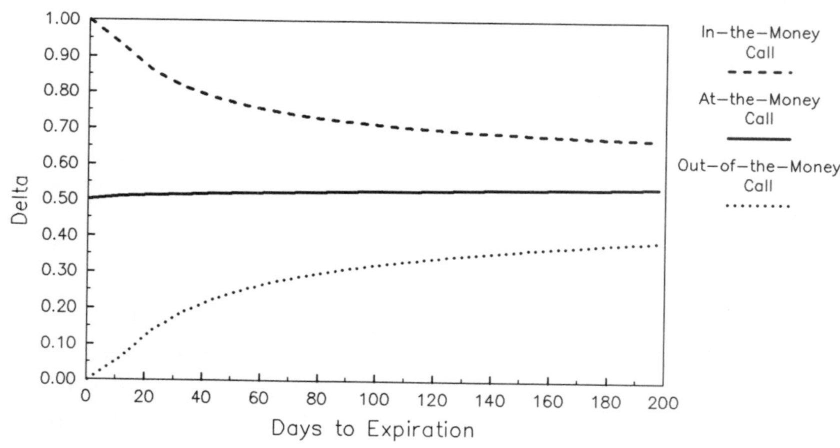

FIGURE 2–20

Relationship of Delta to Volatility

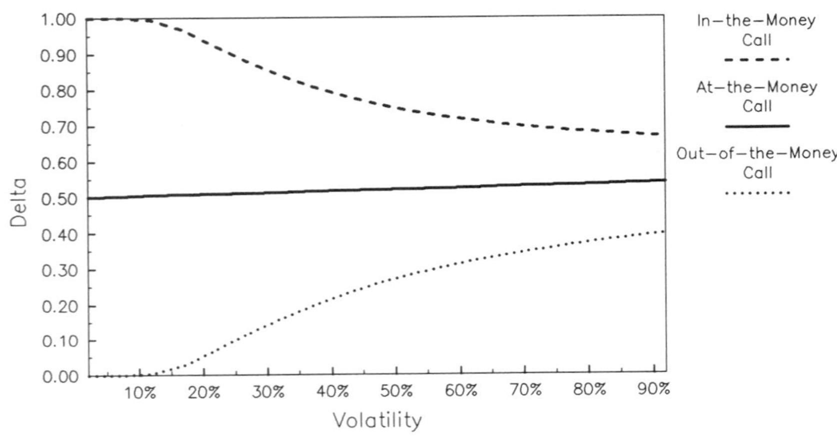

the latter case, the trader invests in intrinsic value and exploits the positive effects of volatility declines on the delta of an in-the-money option.

If a trader expects volatility to decrease or remain stable and thus wants to go short options (puts or calls), he or she should sell out-of-the-money options that are near expiration (for example, less than 30 to 40 calendar days). But if market volatility is expected to increase—and he or she still wants to probe the short side—the trader should sell in-the-money options that are far from expiration.

In the first case, the trader exploits the negative effect of declining volatility on delta and gains income from a decaying out-of-the-money option. In the second case, the trader exploits the negative effect of increasing volatility on the delta of an in-the-money option and still sells some extrinsic value.

A concise summary of the last three sections is given in Table 2–17.

Other Parameters That Influence Option Prices: Interest Rates and Market Liquidity

Interest Rates

In the short term, traders should not be overly concerned with the impact of changing interest rates on commodity option values, because it is negligible. Nevertheless, the impact of falling or rising rates should be understood.

TABLE 2–17 Trading Decisions Based on Expectations of Market Volatility and Proximity to Expiration

Option	Trading Decision	
	Buy If	**Sell If**
In-the-money	You expect volatility to decrease and there are less than 20 to 30 days to expiration	You expect volatility to increase and there are more than 20 to 30 days to expiration
At- or near-the-money	You expect volatility to increase greatly and there are less than 20 to 30 days to expiration	You expect volatility to be stable or decrease and there are less than 20 to 30 days to expiration
Out-of-the-money	You expect volatility to increase and there are more than 20 to 30 days to expiration	You expect volatility to decrease and there are less than 20 to 30 days to expiration

When an option is bought, the full amount of the premium must be paid; that is, the buyer cannot purchase options on margin; accordingly, margin funds cannot be invested in interest-bearing assets such as T-Bills. When an option is sold, however, the premium is credited to the seller's margin account; in turn, these margin funds can be held as T-Bills to earn interest. Therefore, opportunity costs are involved in buying and selling options, and option premiums should be looked at as investments that must price themselves attractively vis-à-vis other investments.

In an environment of high interest rates, there is less reason for investors to buy options when they can invest in high-yielding and relatively riskless alternative instruments; but there is greater incentive for sellers to write options and invest the premium earned at the high interest rate. Consequently, the combined actions of buyers and sellers during periods of high interest rates tend to put pressure on option premiums.

In periods of low interest rates, the opposite holds: Investors seek a higher rate of return than what is offered in T-Bills, CDs, and so on, and thus they invest in highly leveraged instruments such as options. Sellers have less of an incentive to sell, because their writing income earns a low rate of return when credited to their margin account. Again, the combined action of buyers and sellers during periods of low interest rates works to raise premiums.

Increasing interest rates thus work to the detriment of longs and to the benefit of shorts, and falling interest rates have the opposite effect; but again, the effect is generally small and works over the longer term.

What is more interesting is the effect that changing interest rates may have on investors' allocation of money between commodities and financial markets. Although there is a lack of empirical evidence to substantiate this, it seems that when interest rates are low and the stock and bond markets are in a bullish mode, speculative money flows out of commodity markets and into financial markets. Prices and liquidity in financial markets then strengthen, while those in commodities sag. This seems especially true when broad measures of commodity price activity—such as the Commodity Research Bureau (CRB) Index—are historically low.

What Is the Appropriate Interest Rate to Use in the Black Model?

Since interest rates do not make or break one's option strategy or determine profit/loss results in commodity options per se, traders should not be overly concerned about whether they are using the "correct" rate (for example, T-Bills versus CDs, or Prime Rate versus Broker Rate, and so on). In most cases, one cannot go wrong by using the rate of a T-Bill maturing around the expiration day of the option. The appropriate calculation is given in Appendix A.

Market Liquidity

Table 2–18 shows open interest data for several commodities at the Chicago Board of Trade for November 21, 1988. In general, it

TABLE 2–18 Option Open Interest as a Percentage of Futures Open Interest

	Options	Futures	Options Open Interest as a Percentage of Futures Open Interest
Soybeans	453.7	558.7	81%
Corn	326.8	1,189.6	27%
Wheat	109.4	360.1	30%
Soymeal	924.3	7,876.6	12%
Soyoil	377.3	4,923.6	8%

Note: Soybeans, corn, and wheat in millions of bushels. Soymeal in thousand tons. Soyoil in millions of pounds.

reflects the hierarchy of market liquidity in commodity options during the last few years. Open interest in options is defined here as the sum of puts and calls multiplied by the units of the underlying futures contract (for example, bushels, tons, and pounds).

Table 2–18 demonstrates that the soybean market is the most liquid market of the agricultural options. Corn and wheat run second, with soymeal and soyoil making a poor showing. Accordingly, traders can expect bid/ask spreads to correlate with Table 2–18, that is, best for soybean options, worst for meal and oil options.

Figures 2–21, 2–22, and 2–23 demonstrate that, in general, open interest has been increasing in soybean, wheat, and corn options since the inception of trading in these instruments. The weather market of 1988 also increased the trading activity, although it remains to be seen whether or not speculator and commercial interest will continue to grow.

Caution should be exercised in trading soymeal and soyoil options, as the open interest (Figures 2–24 and 2–25, respectively) makes entry and exit in those markets potentially costly. There is money to be made in these markets (as in other illiquid markets), but large speculative positions or complex hedging strategies are best executed by using soybean options as a proxy.

Figure 2–26 compares open interest in soybean options with open interest in treasury bond options in order to show the difference in magnitude of the two markets. Although on a relative basis

FIGURE 2–21

Soybean Call Option Open Interest
Since Inception of Trading

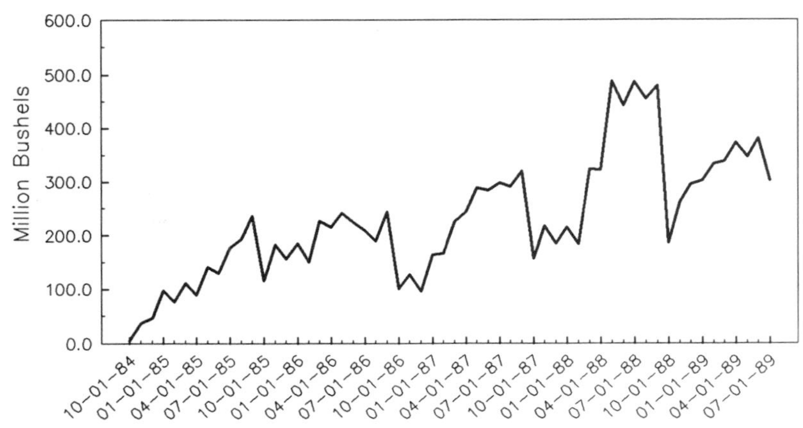

FIGURE 2–22

Wheat Call Option Open Interest
Since Inception of Trading

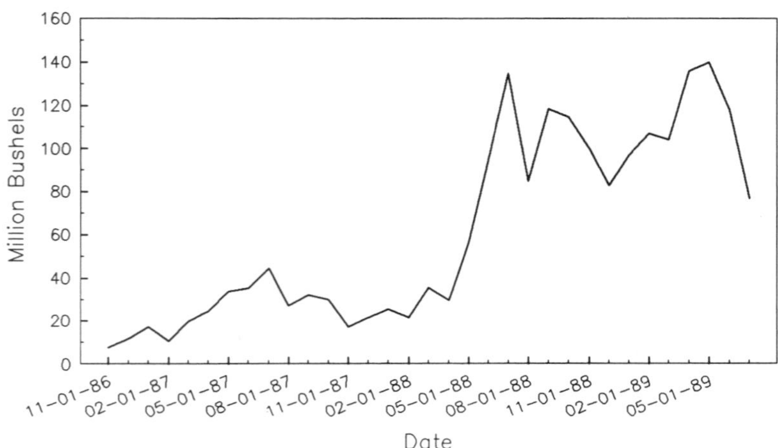

FIGURE 2–23

Corn Call Option Open Interest
Since Inception of Trading

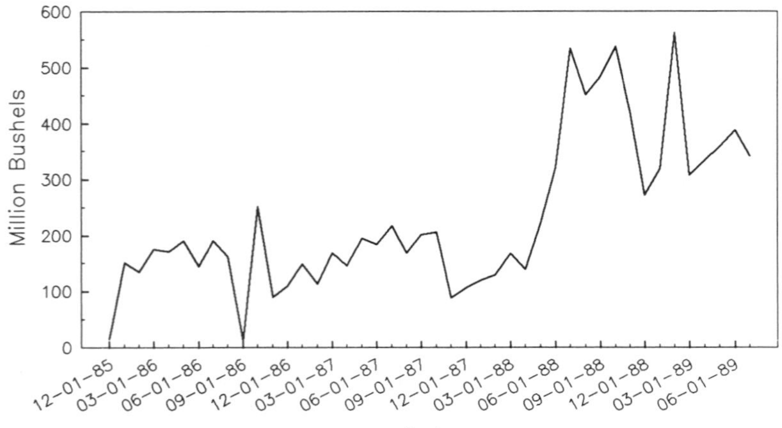

FIGURE 2–24

Soymeal Call Option Open Interest
Since Inception of Trading

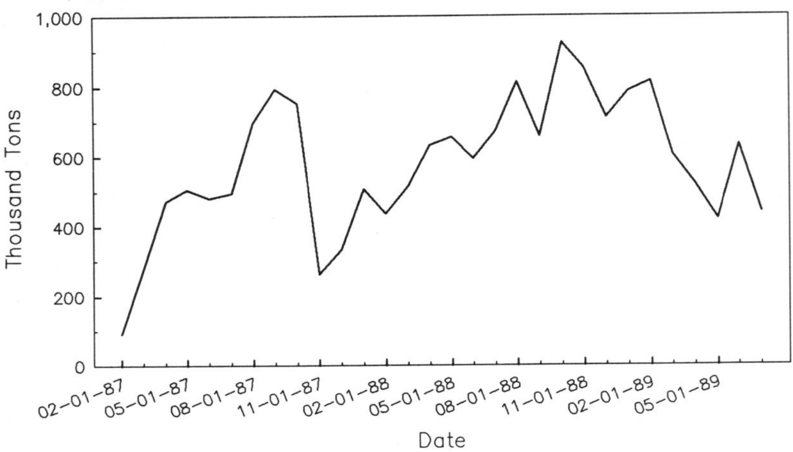

FIGURE 2–25

Soyoil Call Option Open Interest
Since Inception of Trading

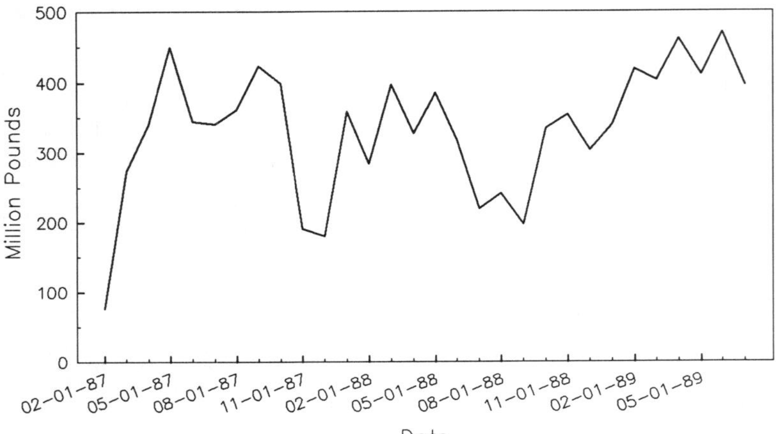

FIGURE 2–26

Soybean Option Open Interest versus Treasury Bond Option Open Interest

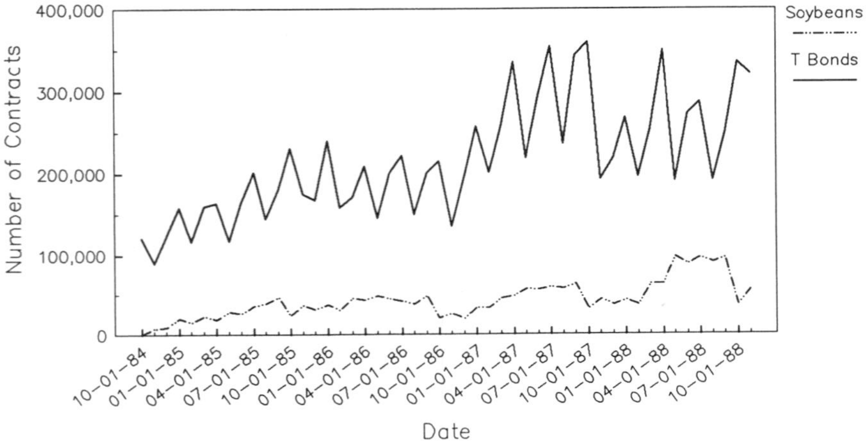

soybean options compare well with T-Bonds (soybean and T-Bond puts and calls both cover 75 to 80 percent of their futures open interest), the sheer magnitude of the T-Bond option market ensures easier entry and exit as well as smaller bid/ask spreads.

Put/Call Volume Ratios

The ratio of put volume traded to call volume traded has two implications regarding the value of put and call option premiums: (1) It indicates the flat-price bias of the market participants and thus how they are valuing put premiums relative to call premiums, and (2) it can possibly indicate imminent flat-price trend reversals and thus represent situations where "undervalued" premiums can be bought and "overvalued" premiums sold.

The standard wisdom concerning the put/call ratio is as follows: Since it is commonly assumed that there tends to be a long bias in the options markets (for example, the public tends to purchase rather than sell options), an increasing put/call ratio indicates a rising bearish sentiment while a decreasing put/call ratio indicates a rising bullish sentiment. Traders then use this as a contrarian tool: A high put/call ratio is a signal to buy calls or sell puts; a low put/call is a signal to buy puts or sell calls. What is meant by "high" and "low" is determined by looking at long-term charts of the put/call ratio (see Figures 2–27, 2–28, and 2–29).

FIGURE 2–27

Put/Call Ratio in Soybean Options
Sept. 87 to Nov. 88

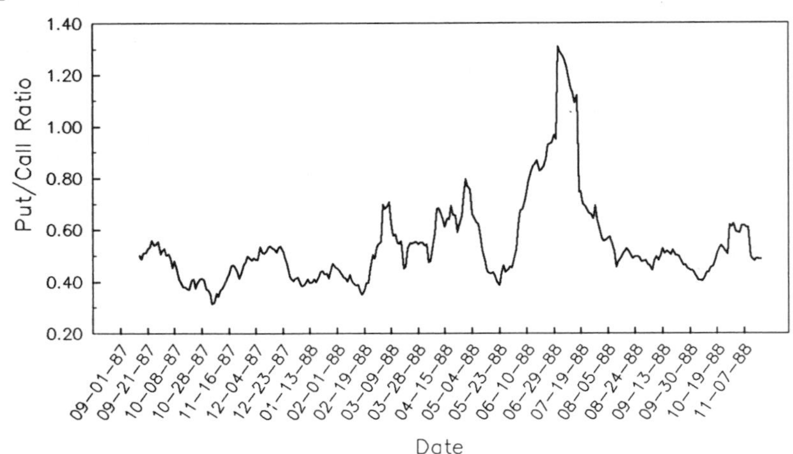

FIGURE 2–28

Put/Call Ratio in Corn Options
Sept. 87 to Nov. 88

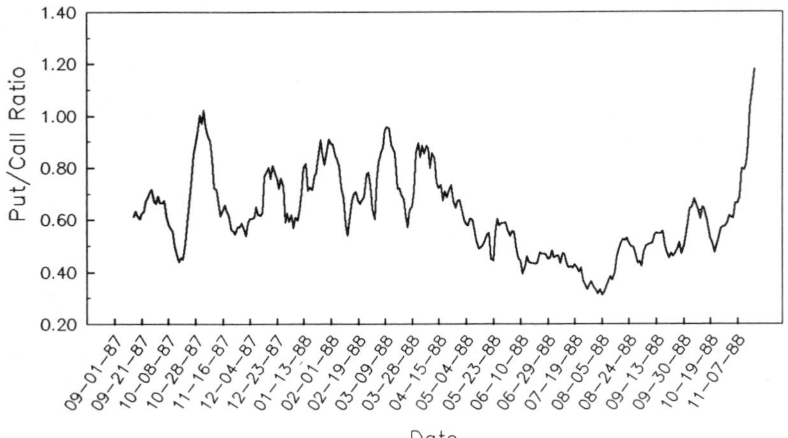

FIGURE 2–29

Put/Call Ratio in Wheat Options
Sept. 87 to Nov. 88

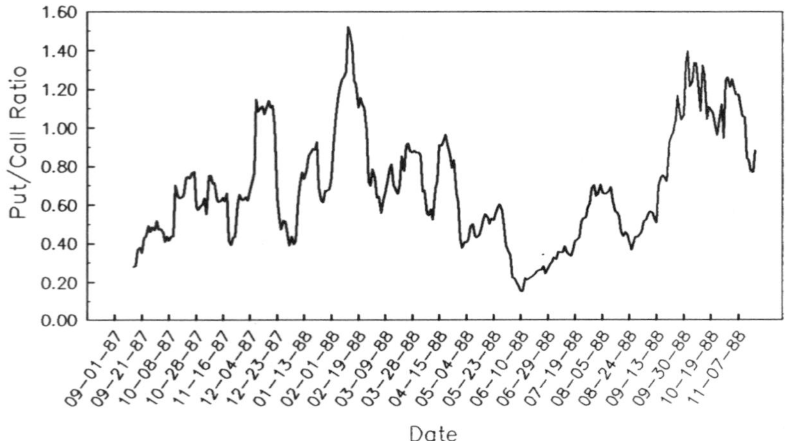

In the first place, the decision to buy and sell options is not so easy (as has been shown in the discussion of option pricing). Furthermore, it is simply not true that a long options bias always exists. Nonetheless, if used on a case-by-case basis and in conjunction with the other technical indicators, the put/call ratio can be a powerful tool. In highly overbought markets, a high put/call ratio should signal the trader to buy puts or sell calls, as a market may be near a top. In oversold markets, a high put/call ratio may signal the trader to buy calls or sell puts, as a market may be near a bottom. Again, a "high" or "low" ratio is determined by historical reference.

In the case of overbought markets, a high put/call ratio is usually a signal that traders have been selling large quantities of out-of-the-money puts with the expectation that those options will expire worthless. Conversely, traders have been reticent about selling calls in the face of a raging bull market. At some point, this tactic gets overdone, as the bull market cannot continue forever. When the crash finally—and inevitably—occurs, the put sellers scramble to cover their exposure; selling short puts then loses its appeal and many traders resurface as sellers of calls.

Accordingly, this chain of events leads to a downward adjustment in the put/call ratio. Any traders astute enough to be long puts or short calls at that point will reap the benefits of their fellow traders' folly. First, before the price crash, put premiums were probably cheap relative to call premiums, since traders were selling more puts than calls. Second, after the crash, put premiums will be bid up beyond the level implied by the flat-price collapse, since traders are scrambling to get out of their positions: Volatility is bid up.

The opposite situation holds in oversold markets. The prevalence of a high put/call ratio most likely signals that traders are heavily long puts and are avoiding the purchase of calls. This situation is less common, but it would imply that traders should consider evening up their positions if they are still short after a large price collapse; or they should consider probing the long side by buying calls.

Actually, it is more common to find a low put/call ratio in highly oversold markets, because traders turn to shorting calls vis-à-vis buying puts. Again, the idea is that these options will expire worthless if the bear trend continues (the reverse situation of the bull trend and market top example given earlier). In this case, it may be advantageous to either sell puts or buy calls. Alternatively, a low put/call ratio in an overbought market suggests a strategy of selling calls and buying puts.

Notice that these analyses of the put/call ratio are more flexible than the prevailing wisdom. But in the final analysis, the put/call ratio is best used as a supplementary indicator in options trading; its value rests in pointing to possible market extremes.

Put/Call Parity

Put/call parity conveys the fact that the difference between the call and put premium of options with the same strike price should be equal to the difference between the underlying futures price and the options' strike price, or:

$$(\text{Call premium} - \text{Put premium}) = (\text{Futures price} - \text{Strike})$$

Note: An interest rate factor is involved as well. It would be a small adjustment to this equation, but it only detracts attention from the basic relationship and so is not included.

For example, with soybean futures trading at 754 cents per bushel and a 775 put and call premium at 27.75 and 6.75 cents per bushel respectively, the put/call parity relationship holds:

$$(6.75 - 27.75) = (754 - 775)$$
$$-21 = -21$$

But what if the 750 call was valued at 8 cents per bushel while all other prices (put premium and futures) remained unchanged? In that case, an arbitrage profit could be earned equal to the difference in the put/call parity relationship:

$$(8.00) - (27.75) = -19.75$$
$$(754) - (775) = -21.00$$
$$\text{Difference:} = 1.25$$

Thus, a 1.25 cent per bushel riskless profit can be earned by selling the call, buying the put, and buying futures. If at expiration the futures settled at 750 cents per bushel, a 4 cent loss results from the futures purchase, an 8 cent gain results from the sale of the 775 call, and a loss of 2.75 cents results from the put purchase (25 − 27.75), for a net profit of 1.25 cents:

	PROFIT/LOSS
Futures trade: bought at 754; sold at 750	−4.00
Call trade: sold at 8; expires at 0	+8.00
Put trade: bought at 27.75; expires at 25.00	−2.75
Net profit:	+1.25

The practical value of the put/call parity relationship is in situations where futures are not trading but options are trading (for example, during limit-up or -down moves). Under those circumstances, a trader can use the put/call parity equation to determine the level at which futures would be trading if they were allowed to fluctuate beyond their daily limits.

For example, on January 16, 1989, March soybean futures closed down the limit at 785.25 cents per bushel. The 775 put and call option settled at 19.5 cents and 23 cents, respectively. By rearranging the put/call parity equation, one can solve for the level at which March futures would have been trading had they been able to trade beyond their daily limits:

$$\text{Futures price} = (\text{Call premium}) - (\text{Put premium}) + (\text{Strike})$$
$$\text{Futures price} = (23.00) - (19.50) + (775)$$
$$\text{Futures price} = 778.50 \text{ cents/bu.}$$

Chapter **3**

The Limits, Boundaries, and Seasonality of Implied Volatility in Agricultural Options

Before discussing how the knowledge of option prices and risk can be applied in trading strategies, it is necessary to understand how implied volatility behaves in agricultural options. Indeed, a trader's expectation of volatility must dictate his or her strategy, since the flat-price outlook can be traded from either a long or short volatility perspective. Again, what beginning option traders often fail to realize is that, more often than not, *it is the correct volatility perspective that determines the success or failure of options trading, not the correct flat-price outlook.*

Intuitively, just as there is seasonality in the *level* of agricultural prices, there is seasonality in the *movement* of agricultural prices. After a three- or four-month growing period in the United States, crop production will either be abundant or deficient, and prices must adjust accordingly during that short period. Therefore, weather is the overwhelming determinant of price volatility, though volatility will rise or fall due to other isolated events. The Chernobyl nuclear accident in the Soviet Union in May 1986 is one example of this type of isolated event. These phenomena are unpredictable and common to all options markets, however; they are not our concern here.

Agricultural options have been traded during periods of both abundant crops and drought; therefore, options traders effectively have their volatility boundaries defined, as well as a clear picture of the seasonality of volatility. From this, a partial solution to the long volatility/short volatility quandary alluded to in Chapter 2 is obtained.

Soybean Implied Volatility: Historical Trends

If one disregards the 1988 drought (May–August 1988), Figures 3–1 and 3–2 demonstrate that soybean option implied volatility has averaged about 20 percent from 1985 to 1988.[1] Distinct boundaries are recognized above and below this average: 30 percent as the upper boundary and 10 percent as the lower boundary. Drought scares did occur in 1986 and 1987, but with large stocks in the hands of farmers and the government, large price adjustments were not necessary, and thus volatility had trouble maintaining the 30 percent level.

In the summer of 1988, however, the severity of the drought, combined with an earlier drawdown of stocks, called for radical price adjustments. Volatility broke through the 30 percent level and reached an average high of 72 percent in July 1988. In fact, in some strike prices, implied volatility went over 100 percent.

This was because exchange rules allowed nearby futures contracts to trade without limits, and these contracts were subjected to price moves on the order of fifty cents to a dollar (that is, more than

FIGURE 3–1

Soybean Implied Volatility: 1985–1987

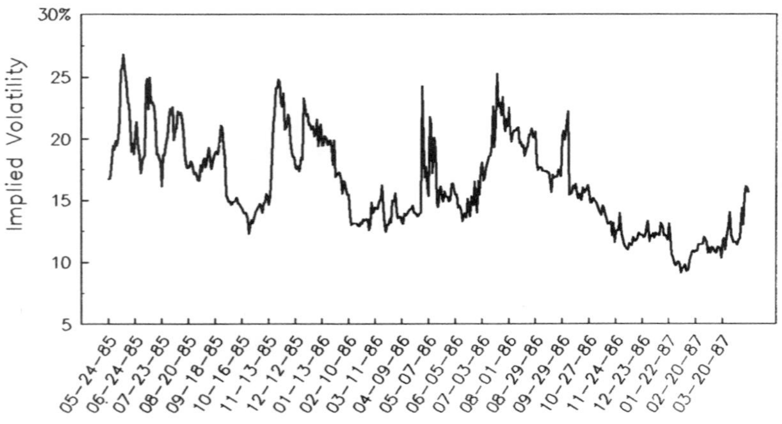

1. Implied volatility as defined here is the average of the implied volatility of the at-the-money option and the implied volatility of the first in- and out-of-the-money option.

FIGURE 3–2

Soybean Implied Volatility: 1987–1989

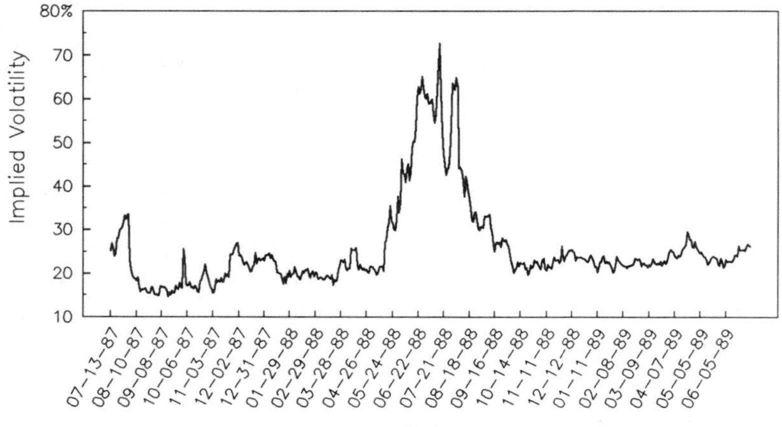

Mean of First–In, First–Out, and At–the–Money Put and Call Implied Volatility

three normal limits). In addition, since futures contracts were often locked-limit while options continued to trade, traders used the options pit to offset risk or to initiate new trades, which caused volatility to be bid up accordingly.

Corn, Wheat, Soymeal, and Soyoil Implied Volatility

Because the fundamentals of other agricultural commodities were similar to those of soybeans during the period in question (1985–1988), they tended to follow the same implied volatility pattern, as Figures 3–3 to 3–7 show. Again, ignoring the 1988 drought for the moment, corn option implied volatility has averaged 20 percent; its lower boundary is 10 percent, and its upper boundary has reached 35 to 40 percent. The 1988 drought caused a breakout above the upper boundary to a high of 75 percent. The upper boundary for wheat option implied volatility is 30 percent, and its drought breakout reached 60 percent. Soymeal and soyoil option implied volatility are nearly identical to that of soybeans.

Trading Conclusions

Three important trading implications can be drawn from the situation just described. First, lower boundaries are similar across commodities

FIGURE 3–3

Corn Implied Volatility: 1985–1987

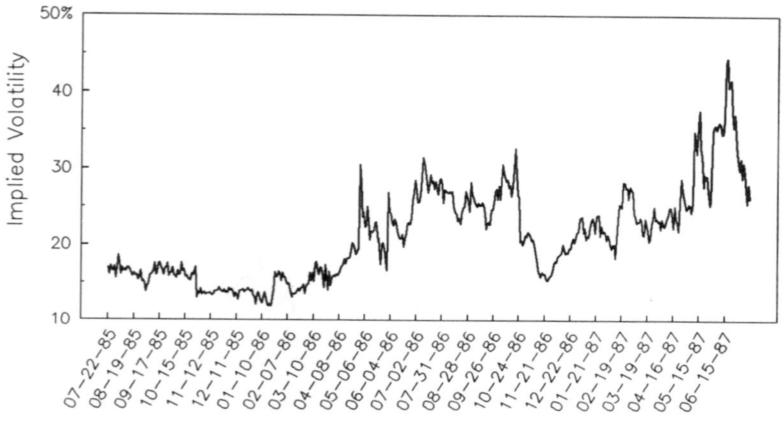

and tend to be solid; that is, they represent opportunities to buy volatility. Specifically, the area between the average and the lower boundary (10 to 20 percent) is generally a buying opportunity, especially when implied volatility is expected to increase from a seasonal standpoint (more on seasonality later).

Second, upper boundaries are usually firm and represent oppor-

FIGURE 3–4

Corn Implied Volatility: 1987–1989

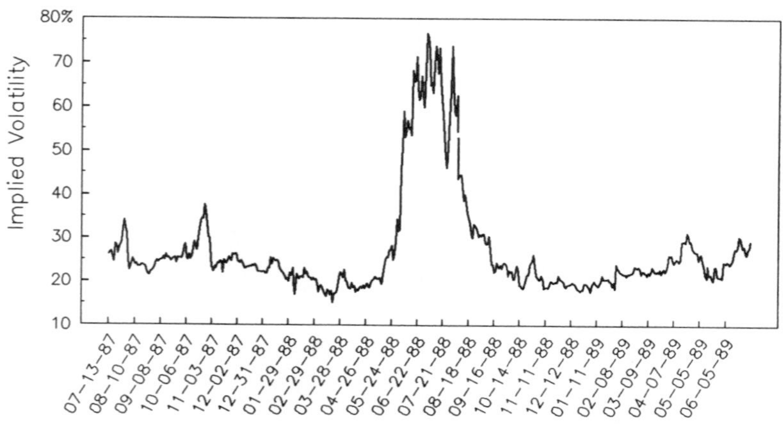

FIGURE 3–5

Wheat Implied Volatility
Nearest At–the–Money Call

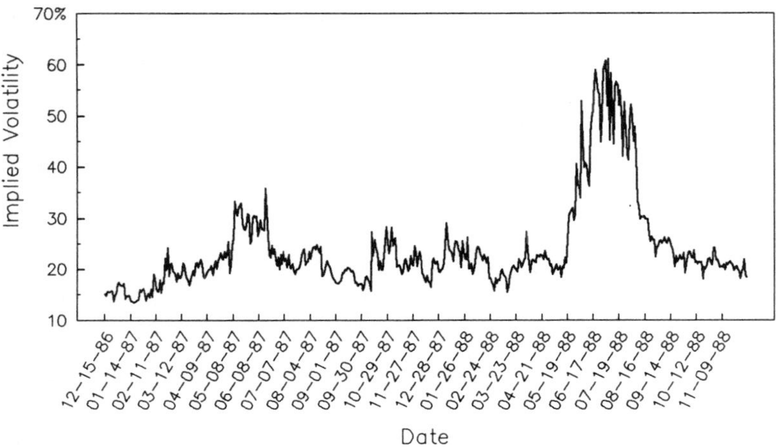

tunities to sell volatility; again, especially when a seasonal decline is expected. Finally, when implied volatility breaks out above upper boundaries and stays there, traders should give serious thought to exiting or to adjusting short volatility trades—especially those that have deltas with signs opposite to that of the price move; for exam-

FIGURE 3–6

Soyoil Implied Volatility
Nearest At–the–Money Call

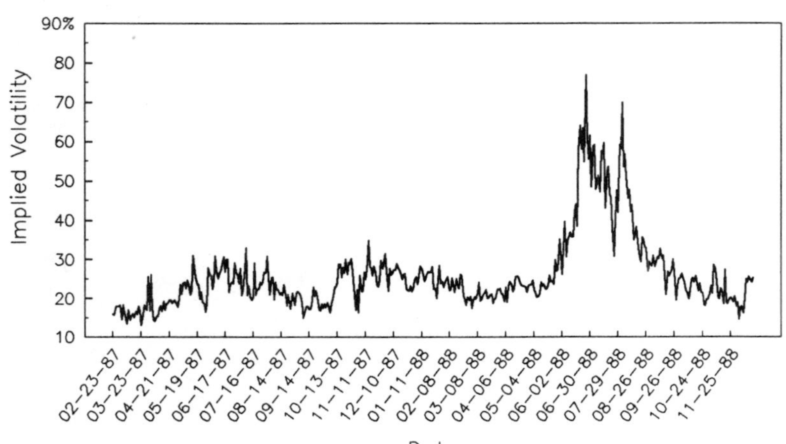

FIGURE 3–7

Soymeal Implied Volatility
Nearest At–the–Money Call

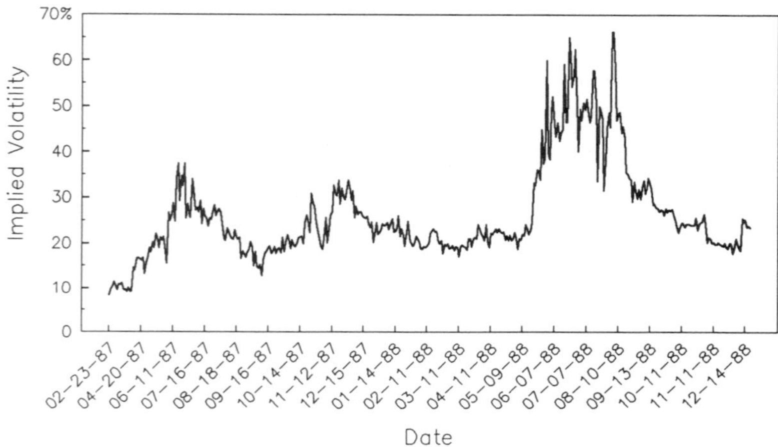

ple, when the market starts a rapid upward adjustment and a trader is short calls.

At that point, the market should be reanalyzed both fundamentally and technically to establish the significance of the volatility breakout. As a rule of thumb, however, if such a breakout occurs at the beginning of summer during a short crop year, the bias will be for further movement upward. If the breakout occurs during any other time of year—especially in a fundamental background of abundant stocks or sluggish demand—the move should be suspect.

Case in Point: The 1988 Drought

The soybean and corn option trading environment during the 1988 drought is an excellent example of these points. Tables 3–1 and 3–2

TABLE 3–1 Soybean Implied Volatility

	Calls		Puts	
Contract	**Low**	**High**	**Low**	**High**
May	18%	30%	17%	30%
July	19%	80%	17%	60%
August	19%	90%	20%	75%
November	22%	50%	22%	60%

TABLE 3–2: Corn Implied Volatility

Contract	Calls Low	Calls High	Puts Low	Puts High
May	17%	26%	15%	28%
July	18%	85%	17%	65%
September	20%	80%	19%	90%
December	18%	58%	19%	55%

show the lows and highs of the different option contracts traded during that period (April 1988 to August 1988).

Observations

In the case of both soybeans and corn, the area between the average and the lower boundary (10 to 20 percent) tends to hold; that is, low volatility does not go much lower, and it represents an opportunity to be long volatility. Note also that the 20 percent historical average for soybeans and corn held fairly well before the May/July leap in implied volatility.

The highs seem to have no limit once they break out of their long-term upper boundaries. There are exceptions: The May soybean and corn options never passed their historical upper boundary and represented a shorting opportunity. This is because from a seasonal

FIGURE 3–8

Soybean Implied Volatility
August 88 Calls versus November 88 Calls

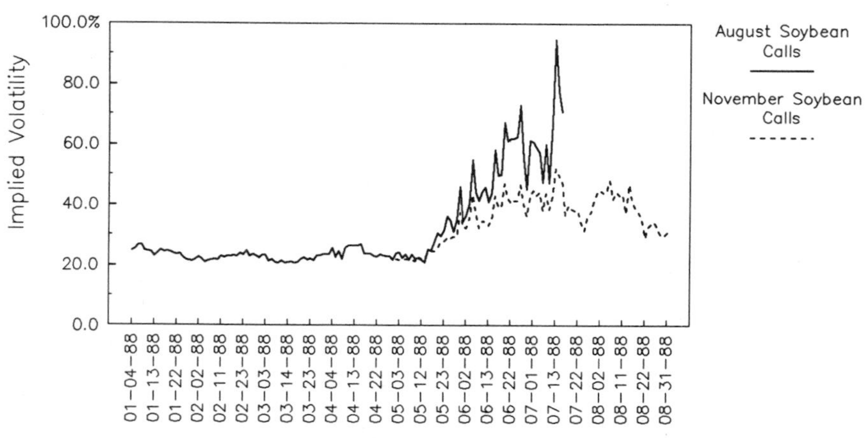

FIGURE 3–9

Corn Implied Volatility
September 88 Calls versus December 88 Calls

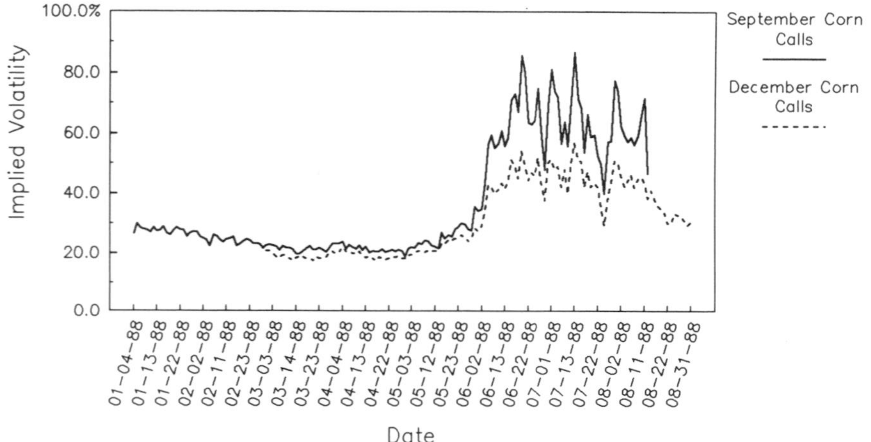

standpoint the upside in implied volatility of the May option was limited, as it expired in April. For the rest of the option months, buying the breakout in implied volatility would have been the correct strategy.

One final observation is that both the deferred soybean and corn option volatility (November and December, respectively) lagged behind the front options (see Figures 3–8 and 3–9). In addition, the deferred months' volatility was less volatile; that is, its peaks and valleys were not as pronounced as the front-end options. These two facts combined to make the deferred soybean and corn options excellent shorting opportunities during the seasonal volatility high in late July and early August of 1988.

Seasonality in the Implied Volatility of Agricultural Options

Table 3–3 and Figures 3–10 to 3–14 show the seasonal highs and lows of implied volatility among agricultural commodities.

It should be noted that the graphs represent the average of implied volatility during each month for each commodity in question. No effort was made to construct indices, because indices would not add to the illustration. In fact, they would distract attention from the absolute numbers that effectively define seasonal boundaries. Again, a distinction must be made between price level and price movement:

TABLE 3–3

Commodity	Volatility Lows	Volatility Highs
Soybeans	February	July
Corn	February	July
Wheat	December	July
Soymeal	February	June
Soyoil	March	July

It is the latter, not the former, with which we are concerned here. Thus, there is nothing preventing the price of soybeans from going to 20 dollars, but it would be surprising to see price movements greater than those of the summer of 1988.

The seasonal patterns in Table 3–3 and the accompanying graphs indicate the general trading strategies outlined in Table 3–4.

Of course, each of the seasonal strategies shown in the table must be undertaken in the light of a market outlook; for example, it may be logical to sell both puts and calls in July or only puts, or only calls, depending on the fundamentals that govern at the time. The important point is that traders use these approaches as a general guideline for being net long or short volatility while constructing their strategy to reflect a flat-price bias.

For example, a trader who is bearish at the beginning of the summer is most likely better off buying puts than selling calls. Or, if

FIGURE 3–10

Average Monthly Soybean Implied Volatility
Nearest At–the–Money Call

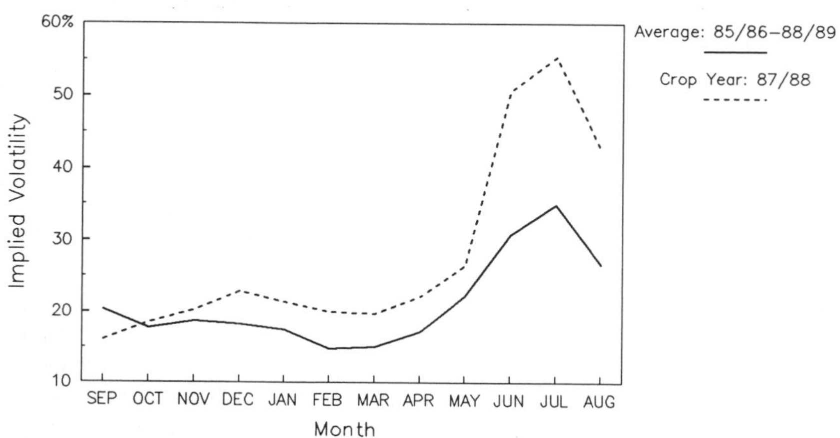

FIGURE 3–11

Average Monthly Corn Implied Volatility
Nearest At–the–Money

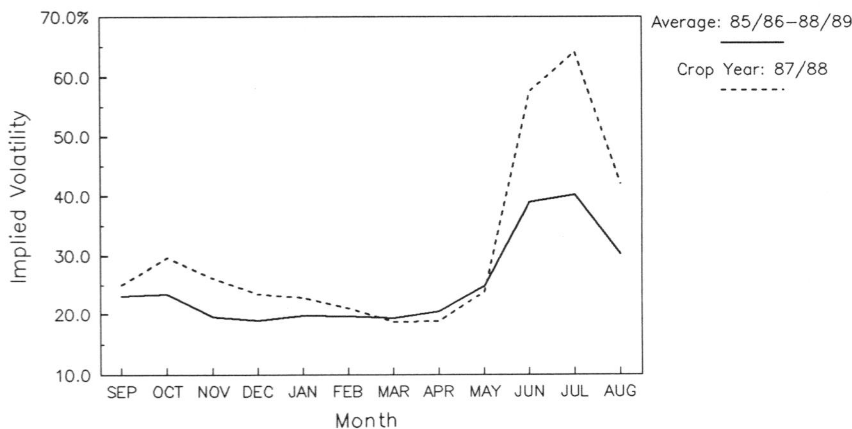

FIGURE 3–12

Average Monthly Wheat Implied Volatility
Nearest At–the–Money Call
1986–1988

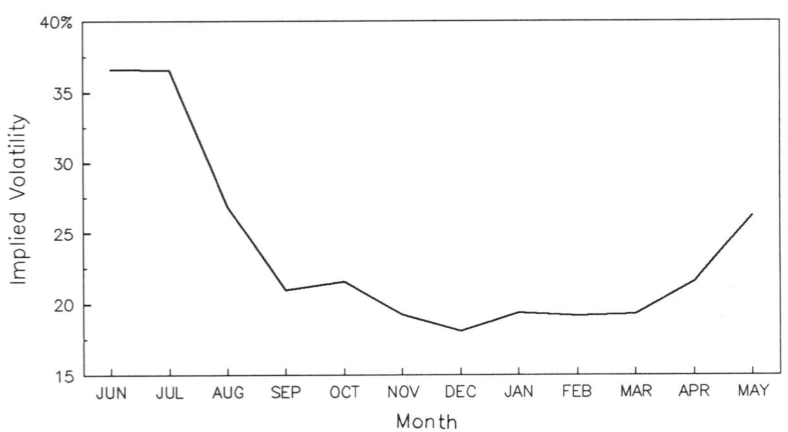

FIGURE 3–13

Average Monthly Soyoil Implied Volatility
Nearest At–the–Money Call
1987–1988

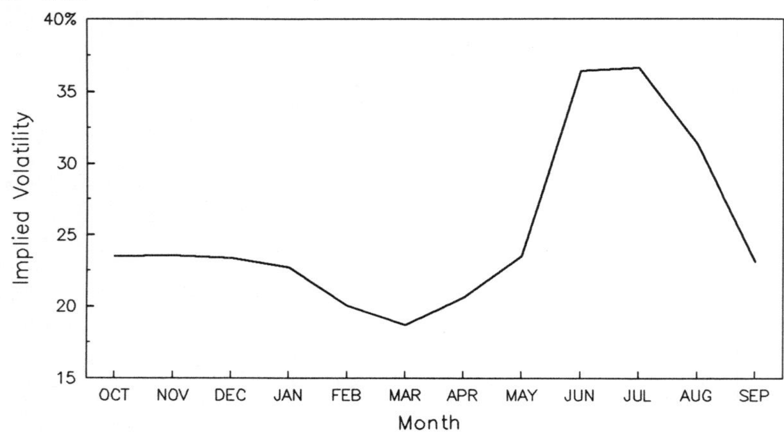

FIGURE 3–14

Average Monthly Soymeal Implied Volatility
Nearest At–the–Money Call
1987–1988

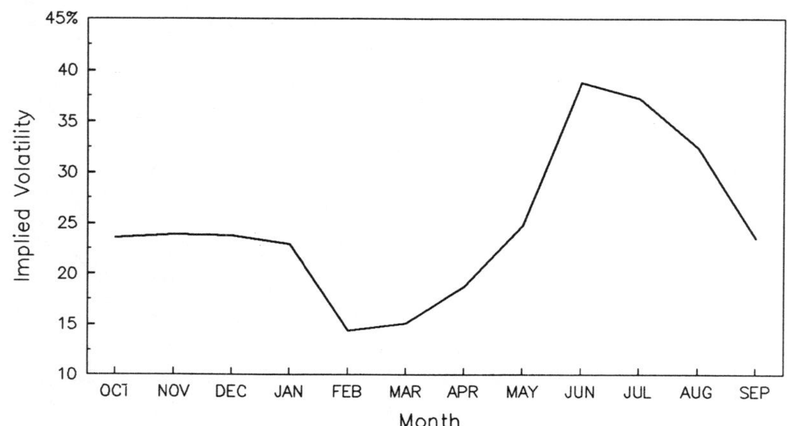

TABLE 3–4

Trading Period	Trading Approach
January to March	1. Nondirectional time and expiration strategies. 2. Sell volatility on the upper boundary. 3. Buy volatility on the lower boundary.
March to May	1. Buy volatility on the lower boundary. 2. Sell volatility on the upper boundary.
May to July	1. Buy volatility with the price trend. 2. Sell volatility with the price trend.
July to December	Sell volatility in general, but look for opportunities to: 1. Buy volatility on the lower boundary. 2. Sell volatility on the upper boundary.

the trader insists on selling calls, it is more rational to spread the short volatility risk by purchasing a higher strike call simultaneously (more on spreading in the next chapter).

Simply stated, it is one thing to be wrong on one's flat-price outlook, but it is even worse to lose more money because one's volatility assumptions were also incorrect—especially when this might have been avoided by a better understanding of seasonal fluctuations. The reverse—and probably more humiliating—situation is when the trader's flat-price analysis was correct but the trader failed to make money due to volatility considerations. These two situations cause many traders to vow never to touch these instruments again.

There is one caveat to this analysis: the increasing importance of South American soybean, corn, and wheat production. Up to 1990, there has been no discernable influence on the seasonality of implied volatility by weather scares during the South American planting and growing season, which is roughly between December and March. In fact, from the graphs it is evident that implied volatility tends to *decline* into March. This situation may not be expected to continue, as shortfalls in the United States must be increasingly recouped in Brazil and Argentina. Only future developments will bear out this observation, but at the minimum it underscores the importance of being apprised of domestic (U.S.) and world market fundamentals at all times.

Seasonality of Implied Volatility and Plant Water Use

Some analysts associate the seasonal rise in implied volatility with the rise in plant water use from early summer to mid-summer.

For instance, the peak in the corn plant's water usage is about seventy to ninety days after planting, while the peak in the soybean plant's water usage occurs about one hundred days after planting. This puts the peak water use for both corn and soybeans in mid-July to mid-August, or, coincidentally, right at the seasonal highs of corn and soybean implied volatility.

This reasoning is neither intellectually sound nor intuitively appealing. First, water use simply conveys the idea that corn and soybean crops use more water at certain times and less at others. If that is supposed to convey the fact that corn and soybean plants are sensitive to adverse weather during specific periods of the growing cycle, we already know that from the seasonal graphs of implied volatility (Figures 3–10 to 3–14). This reasoning also fails to guide our volatility positions during the remainder of the year when weather is not a factor.

Consequently, it is more logical to focus on those factors that affect water use—temperature and rainfall, for instance—rather than water use itself. If temperatures are ideal and rainfall is adequate, prices will fall. In that case, one should be long volatility (puts) with the price trend or short volatility (calls) with the price trend (see Table 3–4).

This underscores the fact that our knowledge of the seasonality of implied volatility does not remove the burden of making trading decisions; it only narrows the choices. The rest is a matter of conviction regarding the variables at hand (such as weather). To recommend only long volatility positions based on a rising water use chart or only short volatility positions based on a falling water use chart is dogmatic trading. At the very least, dogmatic trading is boring; at the extreme, it leads to losses.

Differences Between In-/At-/Out-of-the-Money Option Volatility

Figure 3–15 shows the seasonal pattern of soybean option implied volatility for in-, at-, and out-of-the-money options. In general, the seasonal pattern is the same but the level of implied volatility is different; specifically, out-of-the-money options are valued at a volatility 5 to 10 percent higher than in-or at-the-money options. Technically, this means that the statistical distribution of prices is something other than normal; that is, there is a higher probability that out-of-the-money options will come into the money than is suggested by the normal probability distribution; thus, market participants assign a higher volatility to these options.

FIGURE 3–15

Average Monthly Soybean Implied Volatility
1986–1988

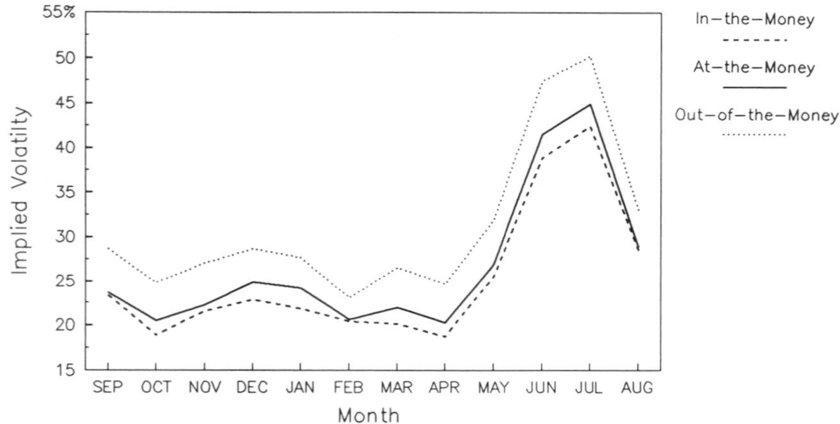

A less elegant but equally plausible explanation is that there is a tendency on the part of option buyers and sellers to focus on the out-of-the-money options. Buyers like the out-of-the-money options for the leverage they can command; sellers also like out-of-the-money options because it seems a safe bet that they will be able to keep the writing income. Sellers, however, expose themselves to open-ended risk, so an added inducement is needed. Therefore, between buyers' eagerness to buy and sellers' reticence to sell, out-of-the-money option volatility is bid up, and with it, premiums.

The implications for trading are straightforward. Traders should be cautious about selling out-of-the-money volatility at lower volatility boundaries or before seasonal volatility up-trends are expected, because these are the options that buyers will flock to at the first sign of an imminent price move. Conversely, buyers should be cautious about buying out-of-the-money volatility at higher volatility boundaries or before seasonal volatility down-trends are expected, because these are precisely the options that sellers will short with a vengeance. The reader will note that these conclusions are in line with the general volatility strategies outlined in Table 3–4.

Implied versus Historical Volatility

This controversy was introduced in Chapter 2: Should a trader follow implied volatility, historical volatility, or both? And which leads or lags behind the other? Figure 3–16 provides some guidance: In general, if historical volatility remains flat (for example, the period between January and May in Figure 3–16), implied volatility will be conditioned by historical volatility. Implied volatility may be at a premium to the historical measure—as buyers and sellers may be expecting an imminent price move—but it will not diverge radically from the historical measure. As a collorary, once historical volatility moves up or down, the implied figure follows.

Therefore, for trading purposes, it is best to use historical volatility as a constant check against movements in implied volatility; that is, if historical volatility is flat, then any divergent moves in implied volatility should be suspect. For the trader short volatility, this may provide a substantive reason to hold on to a position despite a one- or two-day adverse move in implied volatility. The same is true for the volatility long: If historical volatility does not move, there is no reason to abandon a long volatility position because of a random adverse move in implied volatility (although a trader may want to continually reassess the probability that his or her position will gain value as time to expiration approaches).

Finally, historical volatility is often a valuable indicator by itself. If a historical volatility chart is unusually flat, it often portends a radical move in futures prices. Traders who have open positions with paper profits should consider liquidating and going to the bank with profits. Others who plan to initiate option trades should enter from the long side of volatility or use option spreads.

FIGURE 3–16

Soybean Implied Volatility versus Historical Volatility

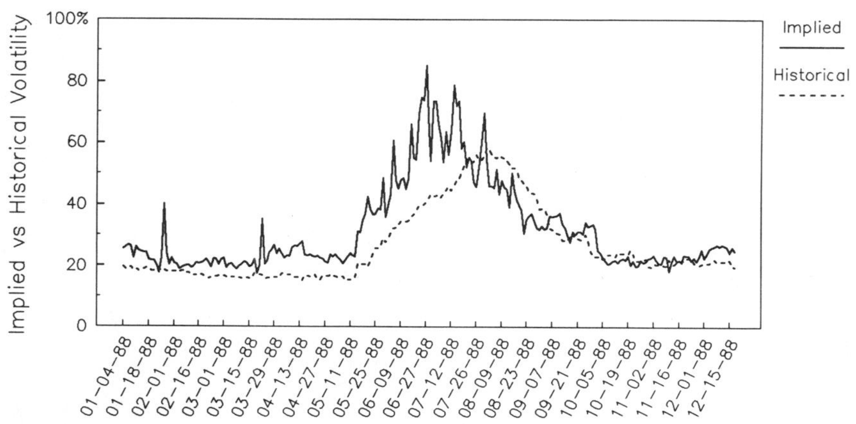

The Spread between Call and Put Volatility

Figure 3–17 shows the spread between call and put implied volatility. In normal market situations, the spread is very narrow; however, in abnormal situations (such as the drought of 1988) the disparity between put and call volatility increases. This is important for three reasons.

First, wide disparities between call and put volatility seem to be indicative of market tops; that is, the market is moving wildly in one direction, which eventually calls for a reaction in the opposite direction. Note that in June 1988, call volatility wildly outpaced put volatility as the market reached new heights. In July, however, put volatility outpaced call volatility as the market plummeted; eventually, call and put volatilities came back into line.

Second, from a money management standpoint, option strategies during these periods should be limited to those of predefined risk such as spreads (more on this in the next chapter), because naked buying or writing strategies leave a trader open to costly swings in implied volatility.

Third, it should be emphasized that when implied volatility is fluctuating wildly above its upper boundary, anything is possible. For example, traders who consider 50 percent or 75 percent volatility as a good sale should understand that in extraordinary situations, implied volatility can easily double from those levels. This was exactly the case during the 1988 drought. Eventually, volatility will come back to normal levels and call/put volatility spreads will come back into line, but the pain inflicted in the short term can be severe.

FIGURE 3–17

Spread between Soybean Put and Call Volatility

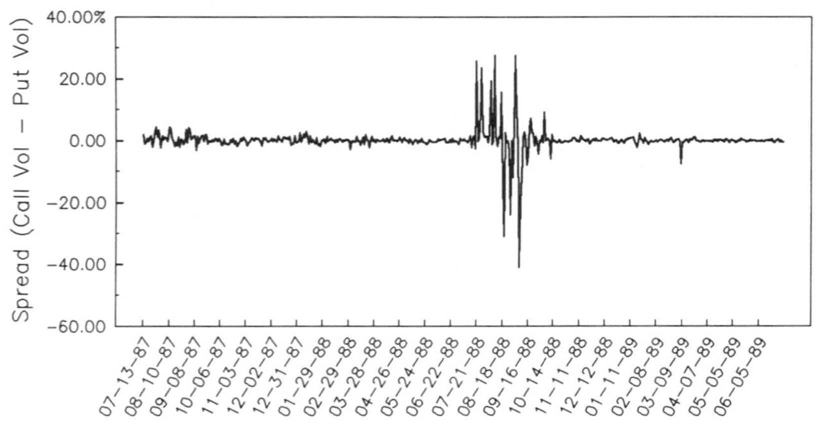

Chapter **4**

Options Strategies: Formulation and Analysis

Most books take one of two approaches to options strategies. The first involves simplistic cookbook-like recipes; the second, complicated mathematical analyses. The goal here is to create, somewhere between these two extremes, a style of options trading that is neither devoid of logic and creativity nor overly rigorous in theory. But first a few comments on the standard approaches.

Option Cookbooks

The problem with the cookbook format—in which the trader is presented with a series of strategy choices to fit a flat-price bias—is the relentless focus on flat-price trading. This is myopic, because option premiums also reflect market volatility and time value: *A comprehensive options strategy always integrates volatility and time decay in its formulation in order to add profit or minimize loss.* Thus, the trader who uses options as surrogates for futures does not fully exploit profit and exposes himself or herself to unnecessary risk, or both.

In this manner, cookbooks promote sloppy and uncreative trading, because they offer readymade answers rather than forcing the trader to make difficult decisions regarding flat-price direction, volatility, and time decay exposure. Furthermore, cookbooks encourage indecisiveness. Their strategies are usually couched in terms such as "slightly bullish," "slightly bearish," or "neutral." But is the trader's outlook really slightly bullish, slightly bearish, or neutral? Or is the trader just undecided? If it is a case of indecision, the trader is better off not trading.

A case in point is the so-called neutral strategy in which a trader sells or buys both a put and a call at the same strike or at different strikes. Traders should only do this if they have very strong opinions regarding flat-price behavior, volatility, and time decay, not because they have no opinions on these issues. Nonetheless, traders are drawn to such strategies because cookbooks often present them as no-lose opportunities involving little risk (and little thought).

Finally, a good options trader considers profit and loss exposure from day to day, not just at expiration. Accordingly, he or she reduces, adds to, or exits a position based on how much profit remains and how much risk has grown or diminished.

The Mathematical Approach to Options

The mathematical approach to options trading is preferable to the options cookbook, as it is more analytically rigorous and thus forces the trader to think through all aspects of the trade. Nevertheless, what it makes up for in analytical rigor, it loses in speed and facility of use.

Although computers have given traders the ability to solve complex equations quickly, they will never replace that element of trading that requires split-second decisions to exploit profitable opportunities. A trader must learn to intuit such opportunities and must have the conviction and fortitude to act on them. This does not mean that the trader throws theory out the window; rather, it means he or she should put it in its proper perspective.

From the viewpoint of the pragmatic trader, *the proper theoretical perspective is the ability to discern relationships rather than to calculate absolutes.* Such skill adds to a trader's conviction. Thus, a trader has more power if he or she knows the relationship of delta to the underlying futures than if he or she knows the absolute value of delta or the formula to calculate it. Indeed, a good guess of the absolute value can be accurately made if the relationship is understood. This also holds for all the other variables about which options traders are concerned, that is, gamma, vega, theta, and volatility.

Again, during a more reflective moment, the trader can always sit down and analyze the absolute numbers. As was outlined step by step in Chapter 2, a good options trader will quantify all sources of risk and reward in terms of dollars and cents—both during and after each trading session. At that point the trader can fine-tune his or her position; however, the absolute numbers will offer no major suprises if the trader bought and sold according to knowledge of option price and risk relationships.

The math of options is a tool like any other. In the right hands it is useful, in the wrong hands dangerous. If a trader wants to buy a call with the idea that volatility will increase ten percent, the trader can factor this bias into the Black model and obtain a theoretical premium. At that point, all market premiums look cheap compared to the theoretically "correct" value. This amounts to using a theoretical model to objectify subjective views. Subjective views are guesses—sometimes educated, sometimes not—and dressing them in theoretical jargon does not add finesse; it only encourages self-delusion.

In short, the market could care less about one's mathematical edge. The only edge that counts is one's knowledge of risk and the ability to deal with it. If a trader can learn just that much, there will be a greater possibility of profit.

Preliminaries: Option Cash Flow

Before beginning the discussion of option strategies, some basic definitions regarding the cash flow of option buying, selling, profit, and loss should be reviewed. Many traders are overwhelmed by strategy mechanics because they have not absorbed these simple concepts, not because the strategies themselves are complicated.

When an option is bought, the cash outflow from the trader's account is termed a debit. If a trader buys a 270 corn put for 3 cents per bushel, the debit is 3 cents per bushel or a cash outlay of $150 per option contract ($.03 • 5000). By definition, this is the option buyer's maximum risk.

Conversely, the trader who sold the corn put takes a 3 cent per bushel credit or a cash inflow of $150. To the extent that the option writer has additional margin funds to cover the short put (and any other positions), he or she can withdraw the $150 and invest it elsewhere. But if the put increases in value, the trader will be asked to deposit additional monies into the account; that is, the trader receives a margin call.

When strategies consist of combinations of short and long options, traders determine their net debit and net credit by summing over all individual option credits and debits. Consider the trader who sells 150 contracts of 450 wheat puts for 13 cents per bushel and buys 150 contracts of 440 wheat puts for 7.5 cents per bushel. The net outcome is a credit of 5.5 cents per bushel (13 − 7.5) or $41,250 on the basis of 150 contracts (.055 • 5000 • 150). The trader is now ready to calculate the profit/loss profile at expiration over a range of futures prices as shown in Table 4–1.

Traders should get into the habit of calculating such "back-of-

TABLE 4–1 Long 440 Put/Short 450 Put; Position Value at Expiration

Futures at Expiration	Long 440 Put	Short 450 Put	Initial Net Credit	Net	$ Profit/Loss: 150 Contracts
430	+10	−20	+5.5	−4.5	−$33,750
435	+ 5	−15	+5.5	−4.5	−$33,750
440	0	−10	+5.5	−4.5	−$33,750
445	0	− 5	+5.5	+0.5	+$3,750
450	0	0	+5.5	+5.5	+$41,250
455	0	0	+5.5	+5.5	+$41,250
460	0	0	+5.5	+5.5	+$41,250

Note: 5000 bushel contract.

the-envelope" profit and loss expiration profiles, because this allows them to get a snapshot of a strategy's profit range and cash flow.

Preliminaries: Bull, Bear, and Non-Directional Strategies

Option strategies are termed bullish, bearish, or non-directional depending on the sign of the net delta of the strategy; that is, if the net delta is positive (negative), the strategy is termed bullish (bearish). If the net delta is zero or near zero the strategy is defined as neutral, non-directional, or technically delta neutral. Again, net delta refers to the sum of all the deltas of the position (see Chapter 2, the first section). Table 4–2 gives some examples of soybean option strategies.

There are three types of non-directional strategies. Using the first type of strategy, a trader *sells puts and calls* with the expectation

TABLE 4–2 Net Delta of Different Options Strategies

Strategy	Deltas	Net Delta	Strategy Classification
1. Long 1 750 Call	+.44	+.44	Bullish
2. Long 1 800 Put Short 1 775 Put	−.75 +.48	−.27	Bearish
3. Long 1 800 Call Long 1 750 Put	+.23 −.26	−.03	Non-directional

Note: Examples 2 and 3 are option spreads; spreads are a unique class of strategy and are treated separately.

TABLE 4–3 Examples of Different Non-Directional Trades

Strategy	Deltas	Net Delta	Strategy Classification
1. Short 1 775 Call Short 1 775 Put	−.44 +.48	+.04	Non-directional, sideways market
2. Long 1 800 Call Long 1 750 Put	+.23 −.26	−.03	Non-directional, breakout expected
3. Short 4 800 Call Long 1 Future	−.92 +1.00	+.08	Non-directional, covered call write
4. Short 10 725 Put Short 1 Future	+1.00 −1.00	.00	Non-directional, covered put write

that the futures prices will trend sideways. If the trader is correct, he or she will earn all or part of the initial credit by expiration.

The second type of strategy involves *the purchase of puts and calls* when a trader anticipates a violent bullish or bearish move. Using this strategy allows one option to gain value so that the initial debit is recouped plus a profit.

The final type of strategy is called *covered writing*. Using this strategy, a trader sells a put or a call and hedges delta neutral with futures in order to earn the extrinsic value of the initial credit. If futures and thus volatility are stable, the hedging adjustments should be few and time decay will be earned easily. Otherwise, profit slippage occurs due to over- or under-adjusting the futures hedge. (This type of trade is analyzed in detail in the first case study in Chapter 6.) Examples of each type of non-directional trade are given in Table 4–3.

Non-directional strategies are the trades that most beginners gravitate toward because they appear to be no-lose propositions. Although it seems that a certain amount of weight is taken off the trader's flat-price conviction, *this weight is simply relegated to either gamma, vega, or theta risk.*

Actually, non-directional strategies require greater conviction, forethought, and monitoring than strategies involving bullish or bearish flat-price bias. The use of the word *neutral* or *non-directional* to describe these trades belies their complexity. It can also be debated whether or not any weight is taken off one's flat-price conviction, because it often takes more courage to say the market is going to move radically or not at all than to say that it will move higher or lower.

Strategy Formulation

Options strategies begin with some flat-price conviction—not a lack of one. In addition to bullish and bearish price outlooks, flat-price conviction in options trading encompasses sideways price outlooks as well as price breakout forecasts that can be either bullish or bearish. These latter outlooks are the rationale behind non-directional strategies.

When a lack of conviction prevails, traders will often buy options with the idea that they can lose no more than the premium paid, or they sell out-of-the-money strikes with the idea that the futures will never rise or fall to those strike levels. This is a sure sign of potential disaster. If the trader cannot make a flat-price decision, he or she certainly cannot be expected to make a decision regarding future volatility. The best alternative in this situation is to stand aside.

Once a trader has a flat-price outlook (bullish, bearish, or non-directional), the options trading problem is reduced to making an intelligent decision regarding volatility expectations over the life of the trade, that is, the possible extent and timing of flat-price movement over the life of the trade. This will dictate whether the strategy is traded from the long or short volatility side. The trader simply uses his knowledge of volatility limits and seasonality to decide this aspect. (This was outlined thoroughly in the last chapter.)

Note that once a flat-price and volatility expectation is formulated, the gamma and theta bias automatically falls out as a residual (review Chapter 3, Putting It All Together: Delta, Gamma, Vega, and Theta). For example, if a trader sells puts with the anticipation that futures will rise but volatility will fall, the strategy immediately has a negative gamma and a positive theta bias. To that extent, the trader must then quantify gamma and theta risk and track it daily.

The remaining strategy questions of what option month to trade, what strike price to trade, and whether or not to spread, follow from the strength of one's convictions regarding flat-price and volatility. These are the issues developed throughout the rest of this chapter. Table 4–4 provides a summary of the steps to strategy formulation.

TABLE 4–4 Five Steps to Strategy Formulation and Analysis

1. Formulate flat-price bias.
2. Formulate volatility bias.
3. Understand gamma and theta implications given 1 and 2.
4. Decide option month, strike, and spreading tactics.
5. Monitor delta, gamma, vega, and theta on a daily basis.

Three Final Decisions in Strategy Formulation: Contract Month, Strike Price, Spreading

The following are three final decisions that a trader must make before implementing an options strategy. An elaboration of each point will follow.

1. ***Contract Month:*** The greater the conviction that a large flat-price and volatility change is *imminent or not imminent,* the greater the focus on trading the nearby contract month. If a long-term view on flat-price and volatility prevails, the greater the focus on trading the first deferred contract month or beyond, depending on the time frame involved and market liquidity considerations.

2. ***Strike Price:*** The greater the conviction that a flat-price and volatility change is *imminent or not imminent,* the greater the focus on trading the at-the-money or near-the-money strike price. The less conviction regarding flat-price and volatility changes, the greater the focus on trading out-of-the-money options.

3. ***Spreading:*** A trader spreads in order to dilute (enhance) his or her flat-price, volatility, or time decay risk (profit). Accordingly, spreading allows the trader to subtract or add one degree of conviction to the strategy without adjusting the contract month or strike price.

Contract Month

As was shown in Chapter 3, options with 30 to 40 days to expire are subjected to very rapid and powerful changes in their gamma, vega, and theta characteristics. Therefore, the nearby month is suitable for market outlooks where all *or* nothing is expected to happen; that is, either some extreme price move occurs and the trader long options profits greatly (via gamma and vega), or nothing happens and the trader short options earns all or part of time decay (via theta).

Consequently, traders who expect imminent flat-price changes and volatility increases should purchase these options as they offer the greatest leverage effect for the lowest cost. Nonetheless, the problem is how to define imminent: Is it two days? Five days? The trader long options must be concerned with this, as time decay is constantly working against him or her. As a rule of thumb, the trader's definition of imminent should be dictated by the number of days left to expiration; that is, with 30 to 40 days to expiration, imminent could be 2 to 10 days; with 15 days to expiration, imminent could be 2 to 5 days, and so on.

Nevertheless, this is purely arbitrary, and the more technically correct approach is to calculate the position's net theta and translate that into the number of dollars lost each day due to time decay. Once the theta risk is quantified, the trader who is long options can decide how many days he or she is willing to lose a certain amount of dollars if the outlook proves incorrect.

Conversely, the trader who expects no imminent flat-price change should focus on selling the nearby option month, especially with 30–40 days to expiration. This is the power of theta. Traders are often bewildered by this recommendation: Why should they sell low premiums in the nearby month when they can earn fat premiums in the deferred? This is a problem of understanding probability: If the trader's flat-price and volatility conviction proves correct, he or she has a greater probability of keeping writing income from the nearby month vis-à-vis the deferred (review Chapter 2, Option Premium and Time Value). But probabilities notwithstanding, short option strategies are always conditioned by seasonal considerations (See Chapter 3).

Finally, when the trader's expectations of flat-price and volatility take on a long-term perspective (for example, 40 to 60 days), the greater the emphasis should be on trading deferred contract months. For the trader who wants to buy options, this offers greater protection against theta exposure as the rate of time decay proceeds slowly for deferred options (review Chapter 2, Profit/Loss Impacts from Time Decay: The Concept of Theta and Figure 2–13). For the trader who wants to sell options, the deferred contracts offer a greater amount of time value as well as greater profits if implied volatility falls.

Strike Price

Just as the greatest amount of change in an option's characteristics occurs with 30 to 40 days to expiration, the greatest concentration of change—whether it is gamma, vega, or theta—occurs in the at- or near-the-money options.

Therefore, if traders' flat-price and volatility convictions are strong, they should trade the at- or near-the-money option, as it offers the greatest potential to bear out their convictions. The less their conviction, however, the more they should concentrate on trading out-of-the-money options.

Traders tend to be bewildered by this at first. "Shouldn't a trader purchase cheap far-out-of-the-money options if he or she is convinced that the underlying futures and volatility will move radically? Isn't that the way to make a huge amount of money from a small investment?"

The answer, of course, is that if the trader is convinced that the underlying futures and volatility will move rapidly, he or she should not bother with options. If futures are going to increase by a dollar, why not earn the full dollar move by buying futures rather than a third or half of it by trading out-of-the-money options? This is also why the trader should not focus on in-the-money options, since if a trader is willing to buy or sell large premiums, he or she is better off trading futures and receiving full leverage up-front. In short, the arbitrary buying and selling of out-of-the-money options is based on hope—not strong conviction—as such, hope comes cheap and earns little.

To summarize, traders who buy options should be willing to pay more the higher their conviction. If they are willing to pay more than the premium amount of an at- or near-the-money option, they should consider trading futures. If they are not willing to pay more than the premium amount of the at- or near-the-money option, traders should trade out-of-the-money options or spread (spreading is discussed in the next section). Likewise, for the options short, traders should want more premium income the higher their conviction, and thus they should trade at- or near-the-money options. Alternatively, traders should be willing to accept lower premium income if their conviction is lower, and they should sell out-of-the-money options or spread.

Option Spreading

Spreading is a tactic used to dilute risk or to enhance profit, depending on the trader's flat-price, gamma, volatility, and time decay preferences.

Spreading to Dilute Risk

The simplest strategy for a bullish flat-price bias is to buy a call; however, *the trader must quantify the extent of his or her bullishness.* Is it a 25-cent price rise? A 75-cent price rise? If it is a 75-cent rise, the preference will be to keep the strategy as a simple naked long call in order to maintain the positive gamma and volatility effects. Time decay is still a problem, but if the expected price rise occurs, the flat-price, leverage, and volatility profits will override any time decay loss.

For example, with January soybean futures trading at 768 cents per bushel, a trader who has a strong conviction that futures prices will rally 75 cents per bushel will consider buying a near-the-money January 775 call with only 14 calender days to expiration (see Table 4–5).

What if the trader expects only a 20- to 25-cent price rise? In that case, the traders should spread by selling an upper strike call. This is because volatility often falls when a small price rise occurs with no subsequent follow-through. Combined with the constant loss of time decay, traders may well find themselves with losses, rather than profits, despite a correct flat-price forecast.

This can be proven in the extreme by assuming that prices rise exactly 25 cents subsequent to the purchase of the 775 call, and then prices remain at 793 cents per bushel until expiration. Based on delta and gamma, the trader realizes an immediate profit of approximately 11.25 cents (.44 • 25 + .011 • 25), which implies a new premium of 22.50 cents. However, if the market remains flat until expiration, the trader will lose the extrinsic value of 4.5 cents. The trader still earns a net gain of 6.75 cents, but could have almost doubled that return, if he or she initially had spread by selling a call at a higher strike.

To illustrate, the trader may decide to sell the January 800 call in conjunction with the purchase of the January 775 call as shown in Table 4–6 (this strategy is known as a **vertical bull call spread**).

By comparing the net results in Table 4–6 with those in Table

TABLE 4–5 Long January 775 Call

Strike	Credit/Debit Cents/Bushel	Implied Volatility	Delta	Gamma	Vega	Theta
775 Call	−11.25	23.74%	+.44	+.011	+$30	−$25

Note: Vega is expressed as dollars earned (lost) per one percent increase in implied volatility; theta is expressed as dollars gained (lost) per day through time decay.

TABLE 4–6 Long January 775 Call/Short January 800 Call

Strike	Credit/Debit Cents/Bushel	Implied Volatility	Delta	Gamma	Vega	Theta
775 Call	−11.25	23.74%	+.44	+.0110	+$30	−$25
800 Call	+ 5.25	26.96%	−.23	−.0075	−$23	+$22
Net	− 6.0		+.20	+.0035	+$6	−$3

4–5, it is obvious that all aspects of risk—delta, gamma, vega, and theta—are reduced. Furthermore, the cost or debit of the strategy is reduced from 11.25 cents per bushel for the naked long call to 6 cents per bushel for the spread (on a contract basis, $562.50 for the naked call versus $300.00 for the spread). The trader can lose no more than the initial debit (6 cents), but the spread limits his or her maximum profit to 19 cents per bushel (see Table 4–7).

In summary, compare the profit outcome of the naked long call and the 775/800 call spread when futures rally from 768 to 793 cents per bushel (25 cents) and remain there until expiration:

	Naked 775 Call	775/800 Call Spread	
Value at Expiration with Futures at 793:	+18.00	775 Call: 800 Call:	+18.00 0
Initial Cost:	−11.25	Spread:	+18.00 −6.00
Net Profit per Bushel: Net Profit per Contract:	+6.75 +$337.50		+12.00 +$600.00

Of course, the 5.25 cent difference in the net per bushel profit was due to the sale of the 800 call for 5.25 cents. Because the 800 call expired out-of-the-money, all the time value (5.25 cents) was earned.

There is one other tactic that can be used in implementing this spread (or any other spread, for that matter), although it is much riskier. Specifically, the 775 call is purchased, but the 800 call is sold only after the price rally occurs; this is referred to as **legging into the spread.**

This has the effect of reducing the debit, since the 800 call premium will be higher after the futures price rises. For example, the

TABLE 4–7 Long January 775 Call / Short January 800 Call; Position Value at Expiration (Cents/Bushel)

Futures at Expiration	Long 775 Call	Short 800 Call	Initial Net Debit	Net	$Profit/ Loss:
725	0	0	−6	−6	−$300
750	0	0	−6	−6	−$300
775	0	0	−6	−6	−$300
800	+25	0	−6	+19	+$900
825	+50	−25	−6	+19	+$900
850	+75	−50	−6	+19	+$900

value of the 800 call could rise by 5.75 cents on a delta basis (.23 • 25), and this reduces the debit to a mere .25 cents. The risk is that the futures price may remain stationary or fall, in which case the trader obviously loses more than if he or she had used the standard spread.

Alternatively, this maneuver is more effective as a defensive measure for the trader who prefers initially to be naked long the call. In that case, the trader can reassess the market after the price rise and sell a higher struck call if his or her convictions are then less bullish.

Spreading to Enhance Profit

In the previous example, the trader's objective was to reduce vega and theta risk; in turn, the trader's profit potential was reduced (via a lower delta and gamma). There are instances, however, when traders seek to enhance gamma, vega, and theta risk because of their volatility expectations. *They are willing to take on additional risk to increase profit potential.*

For example, a trader may make the following observations in the soybean futures and options market. Implied volatility is at a lower boundary and January futures prices are trendless. Furthermore, implied volatility should remain stable on a seasonal basis; however, a government crop report will be released in two days. In this case, it is rational to conclude that the market is vunerable to unexpected news that can push prices radically *up or down* and therefore increase volatility.

With January futures trading at 768 cents per bushel, the trader decides to buy a January 775 call *and* a January 775 put with 14 calender days left to expiration as shown in Table 4–8 (this strategy is more often referred to as a **long straddle).**

Although the net delta in Table 4–8 is not exactly zero, it is very close to zero. Thus, this qualifies as a non-directional trade. Nonetheless, the net statistics show that the trade is very biased with regard to gamma, vega, and theta. If the market moves radically in one

TABLE 4–8 Long January 775 Call / Long January 775 Put

Strike	Credit/Debit Cents/Bushel	Implied Volatility	Delta	Gamma	Vega	Theta
775 Call	−11.25	23.74%	+.44	+.0110	+$30	−$25
775 Put	−17.50	23.55%	−.48	+.0111	+$30	−$25
Net	−28.50		−.04	+.0221	+$60	−$50

TABLE 4–9 Long January 775 Call/Long January 775 Put; Position Value at Expiration (Cents/Bushel)

Futures at Expiration	Long 775 Call	Long 775 Put	Initial Net Debit	Net	$ Profit/Loss: 1 Spread
700.00	0	+75.0	−28.50	+46.50	+$2325
725.00	0	+50.0	−28.50	+21.50	+$1075
746.50	0	+28.5	−28.50	00.00	$0
750.00	0	+25.0	−28.50	−3.50	−$175
775.00	0	0	−28.50	−28.50	−$1425
800.00	+25.0	0	−28.50	−3.50	−$175
803.50	+28.5	0	−28.50	00.00	$0
825.00	+50.0	0	−28.50	+21.50	+$1075
850.00	+75.0	0	−28.52	+46.50	+$2325

direction or the other, the trader is well positioned in terms of leverage (gamma) and volatility (vega) to recoup his or her initial debit and to earn a profit as well.

But if the market fails the trader's expectations and continues to move sideways, he or she will lose a good portion of the initial debit. This is evident to the extent that the trader loses 60 dollars for every one percent drop in implied volatility and 50 dollars a day due to time decay. The strategy's profit profile at expiration is given in Table 4–9.

The reader should note from Table 4–9 that the break-even points are at 775 +/− 28.5, or 775 +/− the initial debit; maximum loss occurs at 775. Quick methods of calculating break-even points and other risk/reward characteristics of spreads are given in Table 4–15.

Nevertheless, there are traders taking the opposite side of the above strategy. Their view is that the market will continue to move sideways despite a government report (many government reports are non-events). The strategy of these traders—called a **short straddle**—simply takes on opposite signs as shown in Table 4–10.

If the market behaves according to the expectations of these traders, they will earn a large part of their initial credit (28.50 cents per bushel or $1,425 dollars per spread). This is evident from the $50 the traders earn each day from time decay. But if a breakout does occur their *losses will be open-ended,* since their net gamma and vega are very high and negative (see Table 4–11).

In summary, spreading is undertaken either to deflate or inflate market convictions. In the first example (Table 4–6), traders reduced their vunerability to vega and theta risk. In the latter non-directional examples (Tables 4–8 and 4–10), traders sought to leverage up their

TABLE 4–10 Short January 775 Call/Short January 775 Put

Strike	Credit/Debit Cents/Bushel	Implied Volatility	Delta	Gamma	Vega	Theta
775 Call	+11.25	23.74%	−.44	−.0110	−$30	+$25
775 Put	+17.50	23.55%	+.48	−.0111	−$30	+$25
Net	+28.50		+.04	−.0221	−$60	+$50

convictions. But there are spreads that fall in between these two extremes; indeed, the permutations are limited only by a trader's imagination.

Witness the traders in the last example (Table 4–10). They could have reduced their vunerability to open-ended losses by buying puts and calls against their short puts and calls. For instance, they could buy a 750 put and a 800 call against the short 775 put and call. This would reduce their profit but it would also reduce their large gamma and vega exposure (see Table 4–12).

Essentially, the traders' net credit of 28.5 cents in Table 4–10 is reduced in order to purchase "insurance." If the market runs above 792.50 cents per bushel or falls below 757.50 cents per bushel by expiration, the traders' maximum loss is limited to 7.5 cents per bushel or −$375 per spread as shown in Table 4–13.

Table 4–14 provides a guide to spreading purposes, the types of spreads to use for those purposes, and the appropriate options and

TABLE 4–11 Short January 775 Call/Short January 775 Put; Position Value at Expiration (Cents/Bushel)

Futures at Expiration	Short 775 Call	Short 775 Put	Initial Net Credit	Net	$ Profit/Loss: 1 Spread
700.00	0.0	−75.0	+28.5	−46.5	−$2325
725.00	0.0	−50.0	+28.5	−21.5	−$1075
746.50	0.0	−28.5	+28.5	0.0	$0
750.00	0.0	−25.0	+28.5	+3.5	+$175
775.00	0.0	0	+28.5	+28.5	+$1425
800.00	−25.0	0	+28.5	+3.5	+$175
803.50	−28.5	0	+28.5	0.0	$0
825.00	−50.0	0	+28.5	−21.5	−$1075
800.00	−75.0	0	+28.5	−46.5	−$2325

TABLE 4–12 Long January 750 Put / Short January 775 Put; Short January 775 Call / Long January 800 Call

Strike	Credit/Debit (Cents/Bushel)	Implied Volatility	Delta	Gamma	Vega	Theta
750 Put	−6.00	22.50%	−.28	+.0099	+$25	−$20
775 Put	+17.50	23.55%	+.48	−.0111	−$30	+$25
775 Call	+11.25	23.74%	−.44	−.0110	−$30	+$25
800 Call	−5.25	26.96%	+.23	+.0075	+$23	−$22
Net	+17.50		−.01	−.0005	−$12	+$8

strikes to use when applying spreads. It should be noted that Table 4–14 excludes a special class of spreads called calendar spreads. These are spreads between different contract months; as such, they are more difficult to analyze and are given special consideration later.

Table 4–15 goes one step further by providing the tools to analyze the risk-reward relationships that are needed to choose among spreads that can accomplish the same task. For example, when to use a vertical call bull spread versus a vertical put bull spread is discussed in the next section on risk/reward analysis. Figures 4–1 to 4–16 allow the reader to visually check the profit/loss and decay characteristics of each of the spreads in Tables 4–14 and 4–15.

TABLE 4–13 Long January 750 Put / Short January 775 Put; Short January 775 Call / Long January 800 Call Position Value at Expiration (Cents/Bushel)

Futures at Expiration	Long 750 Put	Short 775 Put	Short 775 Call	Long 800 Call	Initial Credit	Net
740.00	+10.0	−35.0	0.0	0.0	+17.5	−7.5
745.00	+5.0	−30.0	0.0	0.0	+17.5	−7.5
755.00	0.0	−20.0	0.0	0.0	+17.5	−2.5
757.50	0.0	−17.5	0.0	0.0	+17.5	0.0
765.00	0.0	−10.0	0.0	0.0	+17.5	+7.5
775.00	0.0	0.0	0.0	0.0	+17.5	+17.5
785.00	0.0	0.0	−10.0	0.0	+17.5	+7.5
792.50	0.0	0.0	−17.5	0.0	+17.5	0.0
795.00	0.0	0.0	−20.0	0.0	+17.5	−2.5
805.00	0.0	0.0	−30.0	+5.0	+17.5	−7.5
810.00	0.0	0.0	−35.0	+10.0	+17.5	−7.5

TABLE 4–14

Spreading Purpose	Type of Spread to Use	Mechanics
1. Dilute flat-price, volatility, and time decay risk.	Vertical 1:1 ratio spreads:	
	a. Call bull spread	a. Buy one lower strike call option, sell one upper strike call option.
	b. Call bear spread	b. Sell one lower strike call option, buy one upper strike call option.
	c. Put bull spread	c. Buy one lower strike put option; sell one upper strike put option.
	d. Put bear spread	d. Sell one lower strike put option; buy one upper strike put option.
2. Enhance volatility and gamma profit, but maintain no initial bull or bear bias. Expectation is for flat-price breakout.	Long straddles and strangles:	
	a. Long straddle	a. Buy a put and a call with the same strike price.
	b. Long strangle	b. Buy a put at a lower strike; buy a call at an upper strike.
3. Enhance time decay profit and maintain no bull or bear bias throughout the life of the trade. Expectation is for stable or falling volatility.	Short straddles and strangles:	
	a. Short straddle	a. Sell a put and a call with the same strike price.
	b. Short strangle	b. Sell a put at a lower strike; sell a call at an upper strike.

(*continued*)

TABLE 4–14 (Continued)

Spreading Purpose	Type of Spread to Use	Mechanics
4. Enhance time decay profit and maintain a slight bull or bear flat-price bias. Expectation is for stable or falling volatility.	1:2 put or call ratio spreads: a. Call ratio spread (slight bull) b. Put ratio spread (slight bear)	a. Buy one lower strike call; sell two upper strike calls. b. Buy one upper strike put; sell two lower strike puts.
5. Enhance volatility and gamma profit and maintain a bull or bear flat-price bias.	Put or call backspreads: a. Call backspread (bull bias) b. Put backspread (bear bias)	a. Sell one lower strike call; buy two upper strike calls. b. Sell one upper strike put; buy two lower strike puts.

TABLE 4–15

Strategy	Debit/Credit	Expiration Breakeven	Maximum Profit	Maximum Risk
Long call	Premium = Debit	Strike + Debit	(Futs@Exp − Stk) @ Futs@Exp > Bkeven	Debit
Long put	Premium = Debit	Strike − Debit	(Stk − Futs@Exp) @ Futs@Exp < Bkeven	Debit
Short call	Premium = Credit	Strike + Credit	Credit @ Futs@Exp < = Stk	Futs@Exp − Bkeven
Short put	Premium = Credit	Strike − Credit	Credit @ Futs@Exp = > Stk	Bkeven − Futs@Exp
1:1 bull call spread	Prem1 − Prem2 = Debit	Stk1 + Debit	(Stk2 − Stk1) − Debit @ Futs@Exp = > Stk2	Debit
1:1 bear call spread	Prem1 − Prem2 = Credit	Stk1 + Credit	Credit@ Futs@Exp < = Stk1	(Stk2 − Stk1) − Credit
1:1 bull put spread	Prem2 − Prem1 = Credit	Stk2 − Credit	Credit@ Futs@Exp = > Stk2	(Stk2 − Stk1) − Credit
1:1 bear put spread	Prem2 − Prem1 = Debit	Stk2 − Debit	(Stk2 − Stk1) − Debit@ Futs@Exp < = Stk1	Debit
1:2 call ratio spread	(Prem2 × 2 − Prem1) = Credit or Debit	(1 Stk Fm Stk2 ± Credit/Debit)	(Stk2 − Stk1) ± Credit/Debit, @ Stk2	Futs@Exp − Bkeven

(*continued*)

TABLE 4–15 (Continued)

Strategy	Debit/Credit	Expiration Breakeven	Maximum Profit	Maximum Risk
1:2 put ratio spread	(Prem1 × 2 − Prem2) = Credit or Debit	(1 Stk Fm Stk1 ± Credit/Debit	(Stk2 − Stk1) ± Credit/Debit, @ Stk1	Bkeven − Futs@Exp
Call backspread = Sell call @ Stk1, buy 2 calls @ Stk2	Prem1 − Prem2×2= Credit or Debit	If Credit: Upper Bkeven = 1 Stk Fm Stk2 − Credit Lower Bkeven = Stk1 + Credit	If Debit: Upper Bkeven = 1 Stk Fm Stk2 + Debit	(Stk2 − Stk1) ± Debit/Credit @ Stk2
Put backspread = Sell put @ Stk2, buy 2 puts @ Stk1	Prem2 − Prem1 × 2 = Credit or Debit	If Credit: Upper Bkeven = Stk2 − Credit Lower Bkeven = 1 Stk Fm Stk1 + Credit	If Debit: Lower Bkeven = 1 Stk Fm Stk1 − Debit	(Stk2 − Stk1) ± Debit/Credit @ Stk1
Long straddle = Buy put @ Stk1 and buy call @ Stk1	Prem_Put + Prem_Call = Debit	Upper Bkeven = Stk1 + Debit Lower Bkeven = Stk1 − Debit	Futs@Exp − Upper Breakeven or Lower Breakeven Futs(@Exp	Debit
Long strangle = Buy put @ Stk1 and buy call @ Stk2	Prem_Put + Prem_Call = Debit	Upper Bkeven = Stk2 + Debit Lower Bkeven = Stk1 − Debit	Futs@Exp − Upper Breakeven or Lower Breakeven Futs(@Exp	Debit

Short straddle = Sell put @ Stk1 and sell call @ Stk1	Prem_Put + Prem_Call = Credit	Upper Bkeven = Stk1 + Credit Lower Bkeven = Stk1 − Credit	Credit @ Futs@Exp Stk1	Futs@Exp − Upper Breakeven Lower Breakeven Futs(@Exp
Short strangle = Sell put @ Stk1 and sell call @ Stk2	Prem_Put + Prem_Call = Credit	Upper Bkeven = Stk2 + Credit Lower Bkeven = Stk1 − Credit	Credit @ Futs@Exp Between Stk1 and Stk2	Futs@Exp − Upper Breakeven Lower Breakeven Futs(@Exp

Strategy	Location of Max Ris	Delta	Gamma	Vega	Theta
Long call	Futs@Exp = Strike	(+) = Bull	(+) = Profit Accelerates	(+) = Volatility Benefits	(−) = Time Decay Detriment
Long put	Futs@Exp = Strike	(−) = Bear	(+) = Profit Accelerates	(+) = Volatility Benefits	(−) = Time Decay Detriment
Short call	Futs@Exp > Bkeven	(−) = Bear	(−) = Profit Decelerates	(−) = Volatility Detriment	(+) = Time Decay Benefit
Short put	Futs@Exp < Bkeven	(+) = Bull	(−) = Profit Decelerates	(−) = Volatility Detriment	(+) = Time Decay Benefit

(continued)

TABLE 4–15 *(continued)*

Strategy	Location of Max Ris	Delta	Gamma	Vega	Theta
1:1 bull call spread	Futs@Exp < = Stk1	(+) = Bull	(+) = Profit Accelerates	(+) = Volatility Slight Benefit	(+) = Time Decay Slight Detriment
1:1 bear call spread	Futs@Exp = > Stk2	(−) = Bear	(−) = Profit Decelerates	(−) = Volatility Slight Detriment	(+) = Time Decay Slight Benefit
1:1 bull put spread	Futs@Exp < = Skt1	(+) = Bull	(−) = Profit Decelerates	(−) = Volatility Slight Detriment	(+) = Time Decay Slight Benefit
1:1 bear put spread	Futs@Exp = > Stk2	(−) = Bear	(+) = Profit Accelerates	(+) = Volatility Slight Benefit	(−) = Time Decay Slight Detriment
1:2 call ratio spread	Futs@Exp > Upper Bkeven	Bull = > Neutral	Profit Accelerates then Decelerates	(−) = Volatility Large Detriment	(+) = Time Decay Large Benefit
1:2 put ratio spread	Futs@Exp < Lower Bkeven	Bear = > Neutral	Profit Accelerates then Decelerates	(−) = Volatility Large Detriment	(+) = Time Decay Large Benefit

Call backspread = sell call @ Stk1, buy 2 calls @ Stk2	Futs@Exp between Upper and Lower Breakeven	Neutral = > Bull	Profit Accelerates Above Upper Breakeven	(+) = Volatility Large Benefit	(−) = Time Decay Large Detriment
Put backspread = Sell put @ Stk2, buy 2 puts @ Stk1	Futs@Exp between Upper and Lower Breakeven	Neutral = > Bear	Profit Accelerates Below Lower Breakeven	(+) = Volatility Large Benefit	(−) = Time Decay Large Detriment
Long straddle = Buy put @ Stk1 and buy call @ Stk1	Between @ Stk1	Neutral = > Bull/Bear	(+) = Profit Accelerates	(+) = Volatility Large Benefit	(−) = Time Decay Large Detriment
Long strangle = Buy put @ Stk1 and buy call @ Stk2	Between Stk1 and Stk2	Neutral = > Bull/Bear	(+) = Profit Accelerates	(+) = Volatility Large Benefit	(−) = Time Decay Large Detriment
Short straddle = Sell put @ Stk1 and sell call @ Stk1	Futs@Exp > Upper Breakeven Futs@Exp < Lower Breakeven	Neutral	(−) = Profit Decelerates	(−) = Volatalility Large Detriment	(+) = Time Decay Large Benefit
Short strangle = Sell put @ Stk1 and sell call @ Stk2	Futs@Exp > Upper Breakeven Futs@Exp < Lower Breakeven	Neutral	(−) = Profit Decelerates	(−) = Volatility Large Detriment	(+) = Time Decay Large Benefit

Futs@Exp = Futures price at expiration
Bkeven = Breakeven
Stk = Strike

Stk1 = Strike of lower strike option
Stk2 = Strike of upper strike option
Prem1 = Premium of lower strike option

Prem2 = Premium of upper strike option
Prem_Call = Call premium
Prem_Put = Put premium

FIGURE 4–1

Long March 750 Soybean Call
Debit = Premium = 15.50 Cents/Bushel
Breakeven = 765.50

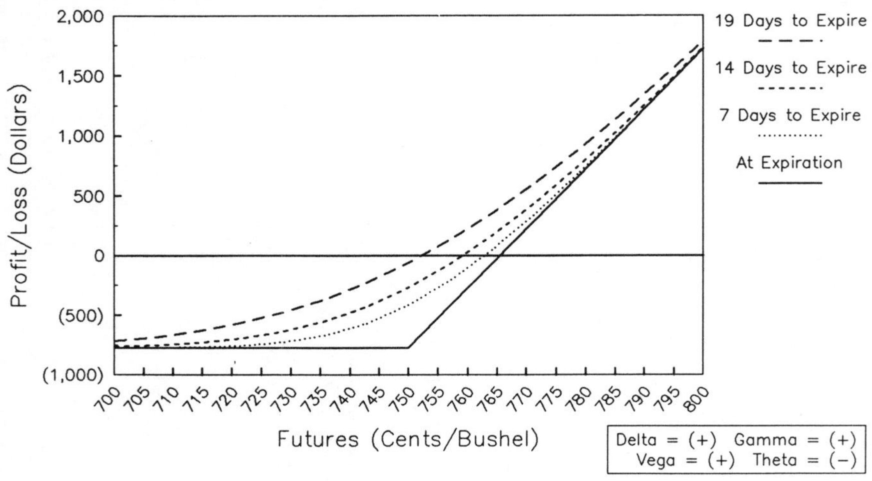

FIGURE 4–2

Short March 750 Soybean Call
Credit = Premium = 15.50 Cents/Bushel
Breakeven = 765.50

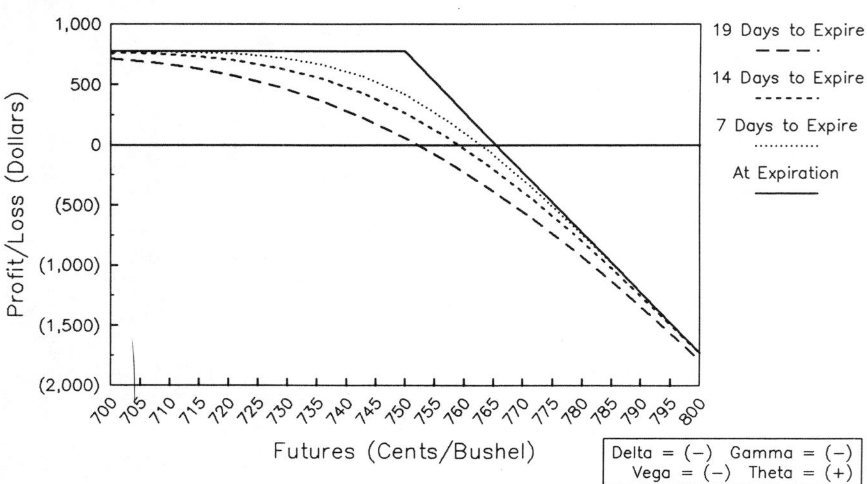

FIGURE 4–3

Long March 750 Soybean Put
Debit = Premium = 12.50 Cents/Bushel
Breakeven = 737.50

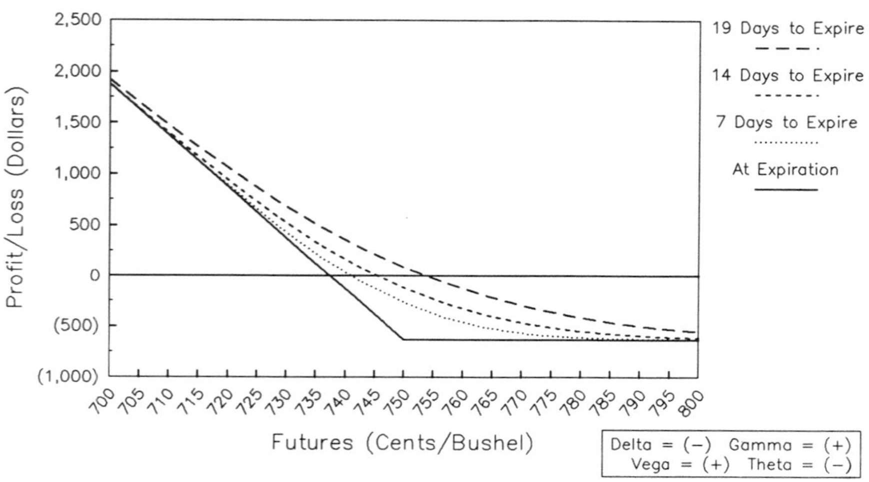

FIGURE 4–4

Short March 750 Soybean Put
Credit = Premium = 12.50 Cents/Bushel
Breakeven = 737.50

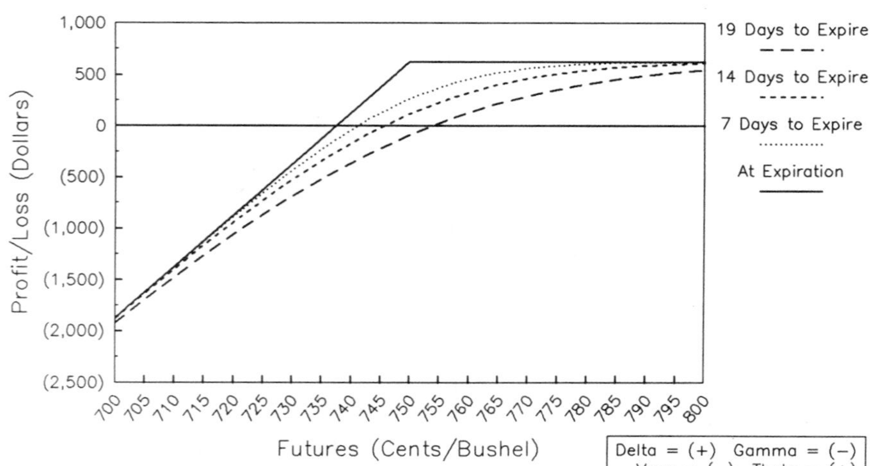

FIGURE 4–5

1:1 March 750/775 Call Vertical Bull Spread
Debit = 8.625 Cents/Bushel
Breakeven = 758.625

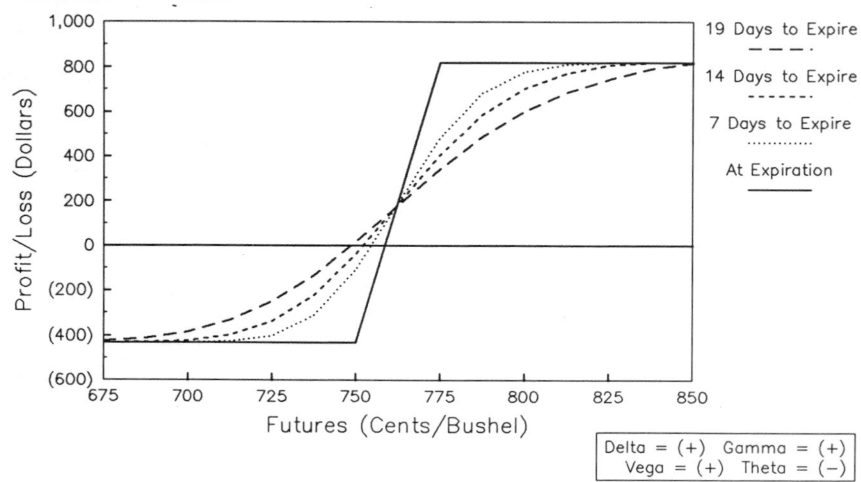

FIGURE 4–6

1:1 March 750/775 Call Vertical Bear Spread
Credit = 8.625 Cents/Bushel
Breakeven = 758.625

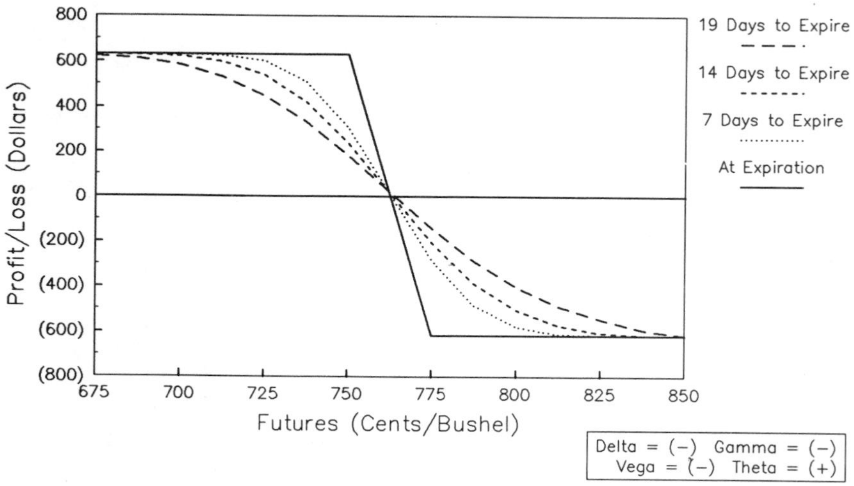

FIGURE 4–7

1:1 March 750/775 Put Vertical Bull Spread
Credit = 15.00 Cents/Bushel
Breakeven = 760.00

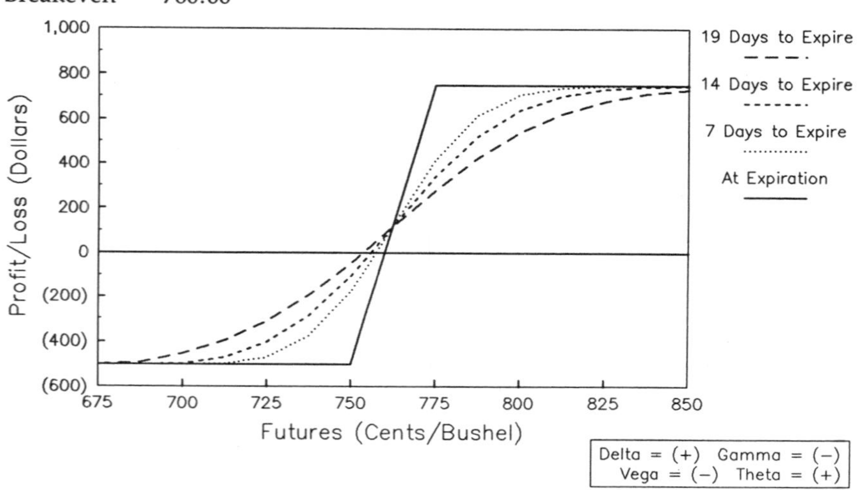

FIGURE 4–8

1:1 March 750/775 Put Vertical Bear Spread
Debit = 15.00 Cents/Bushel
Breakeven = 760.00

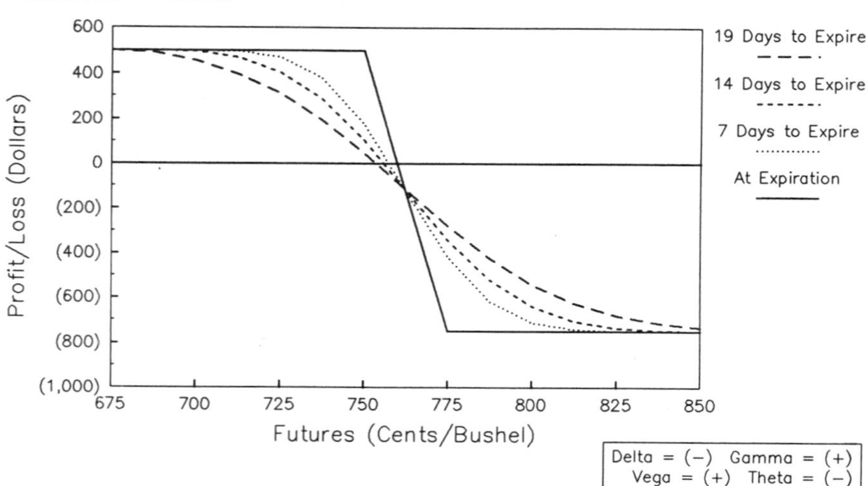

FIGURE 4–9

1:2 750/775 May Soybean Call Ratio Spread
Credit = 10.00 Cents/Bushel
Breakeven = 820.00

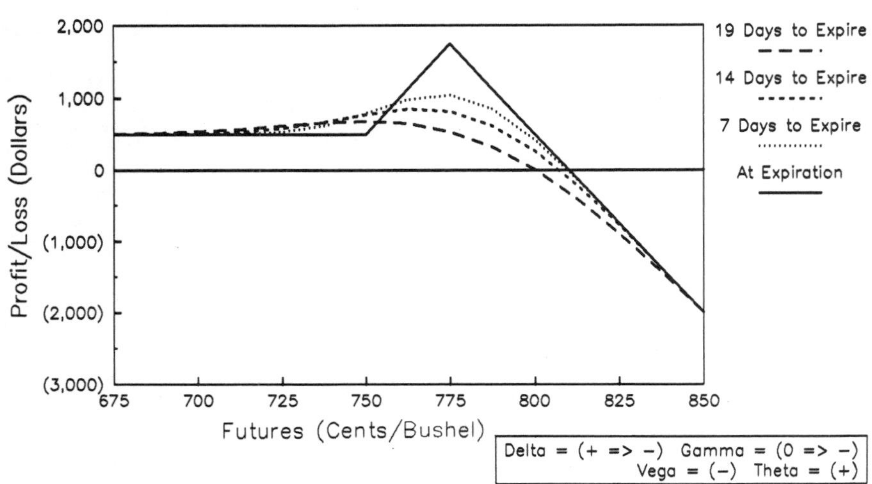

FIGURE 4–10

1:2 750/775 May Soybean Put Ratio Spread
Credit = 12.00 Cents/Bushel
Breakeven = 713.00

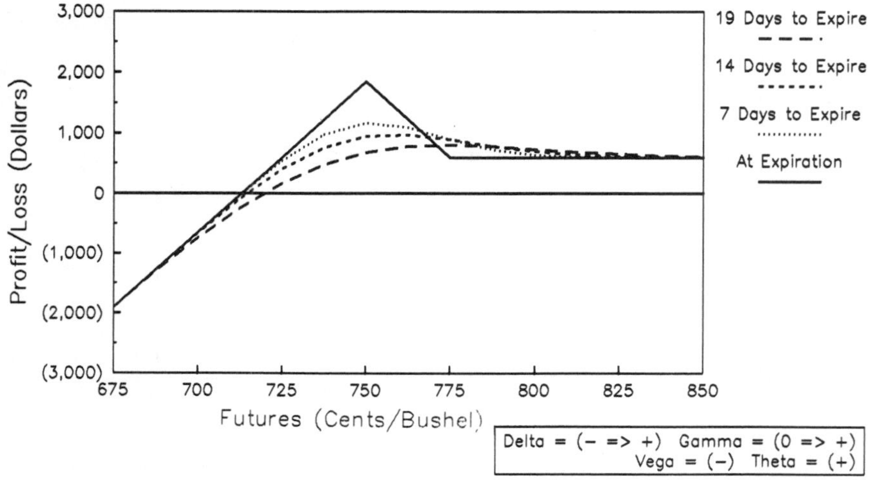

FIGURE 4–11

2:1 775/750 March Soybean Call Backspread
Credit = 2.00 Cents/Bushel
Breakeven = 752/798

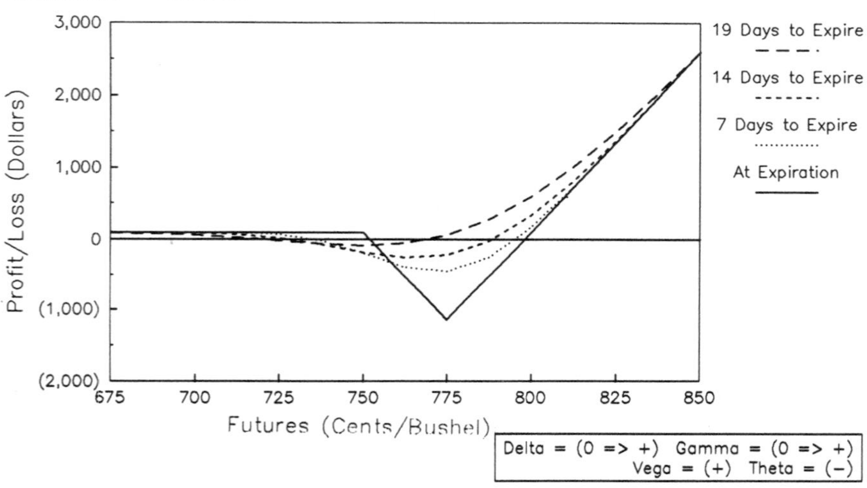

FIGURE 4–12

2:1 750/775 March Soybean Put Backspread
Credit = 2.50 Cents/Bushel
Breakeven = 727.50/772.50

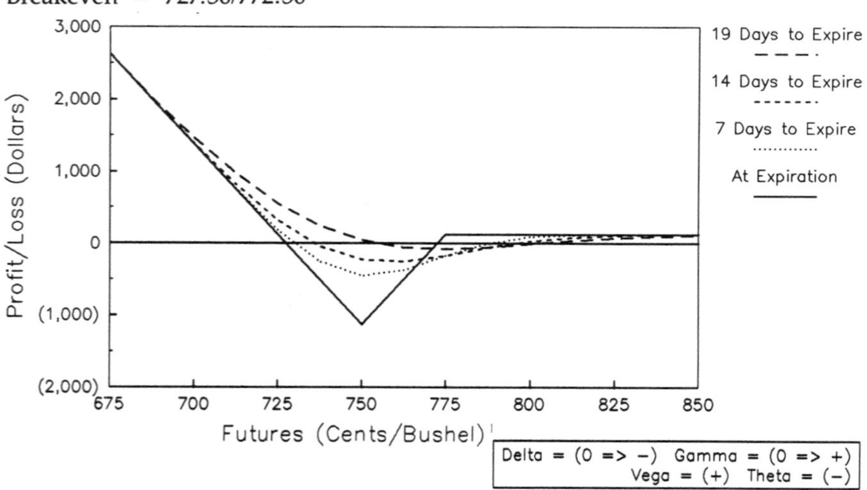

FIGURE 4–13

Long March 750 Soybean Straddle
Debit = 28 Cents/Bushel
Breakeven = 722/778

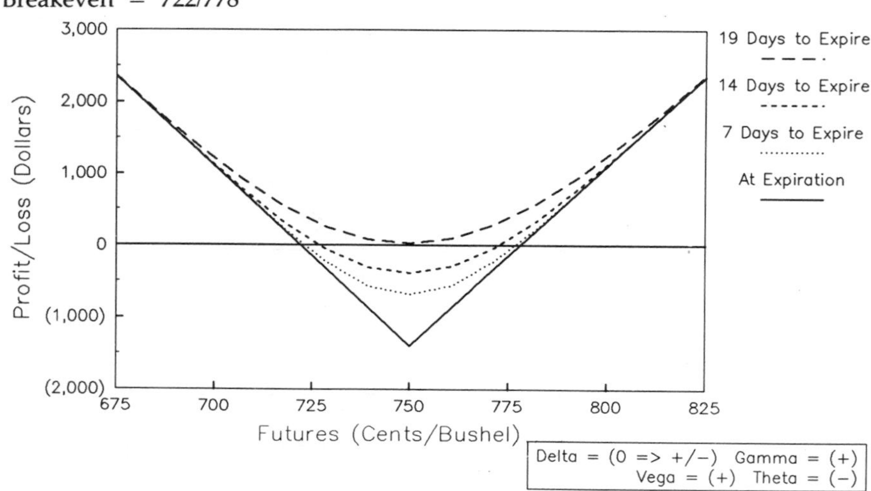

FIGURE 4–14

Short March 750 Soybean Straddle
Credit = 28 Cents/Bushel
Breakeven = 722/778

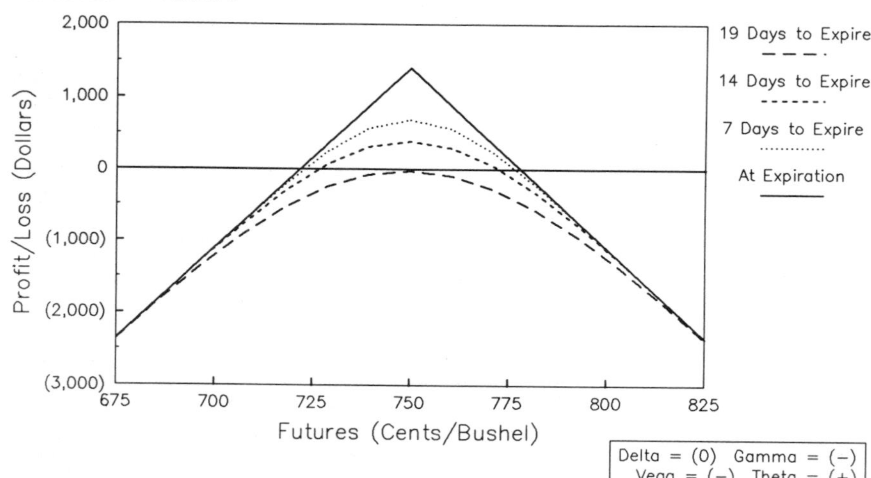

FIGURE 4–15

Long March 725/775 Soybean Strangle
Debit = 10.75 Cents/Bushel
Breakeven = 714.25/785.75

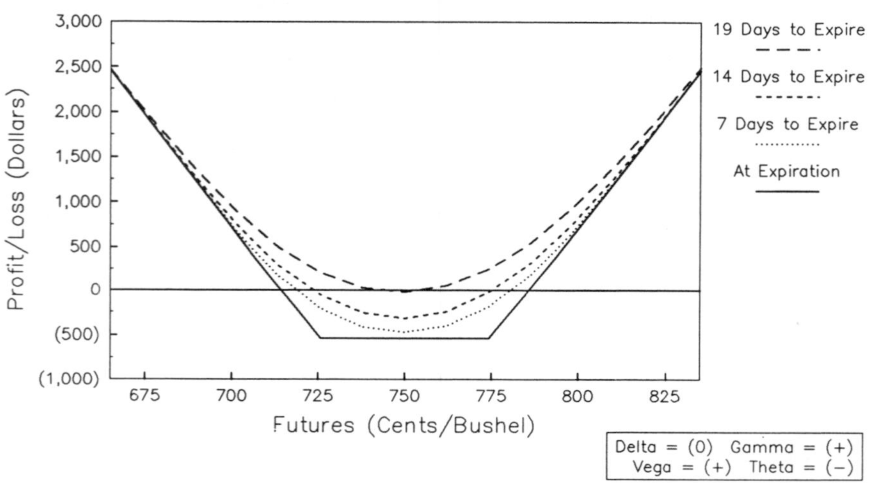

FIGURE 4–16

Short March 725/775 Soybean Strangle
Credit = 10.75 Cents/Bushel
Breakeven = 714.25/785.75

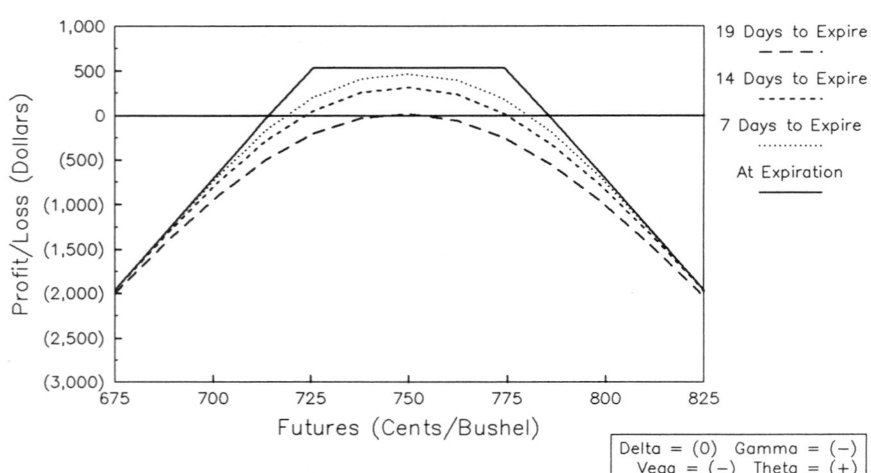

Option Spreading and Risk/Reward Analysis

The basic strategy choice for a trader with a bullish flat-price outlook for March corn is either to buy a March call or to sell a March put. If the trader's bullish flat-price conviction is high, and he or she is also bullish volatility, the optimal choice is to buy the call. The short put strategy is better if the trader foresees an orderly price rise accompanied by stable or falling volatility.

But if the trader wants to subtract one degree of confidence from his or her conviction regarding the extent of the flat-price move and the behavior of volatility, the trader should consider using a 1:1 vertical call or put bull spread in order to dilute vega and theta risk. The question then becomes how to choose between two spreads that accomplish the same task.

With March corn futures trading at 271.75 cents per bushel and 20 days left to the expiration of the March options, a trader has two possible choices: (1) buy a 270 call and sell a 280 call, and (2) buy a 270 put and sell a 280 put (see Table 4–16).

By using Table 4–15 as a guide, the maximum risk and reward can be calculated for the two strategies. The 1:1 vertical bull call spread has a maximum risk of 3.5 cents per bushel (the initial debit) or $175 per spread; its maximum reward is 6.5 cents per bushel or

TABLE 4–16 1:1 270/280 March Vertical Bull Call Spread

Strike	Credit/Debit (Cents/ Bushel)	Implied Volatility	Delta	Gamma	Vega	Theta
270 Call	−6.0	19.68%	+.56	+.0300	+$13	−$6
280 Call	+2.5	21.13%	−.29	−.0243	−$11	+$5
Net	−3.5		+.27	+.0057	+$2	−$1

1:1 270/280 March Vertical Bull Put Spread

Strike	Credit/Debit (Cents/ Bushel)	Implied Volatility	Delta	Gamma	Vega	Theta
270 Put	−4.00	18.64%	−.43	+.0323	+$13	−$6
280 Put	+10.75	21.77%	+.71	−.0242	−$11	+$6
Net	+6.75		+.28	−.0081	+$2	+$0

$325 per spread. The 1:1 vertical bull put spread has a maximum risk of 3.25 cents per bushel or $162.50 per spread; its maximum reward is the initial credit or 6.75 cents per bushel or $337.50 dollars per spread. *Obviously, the risk/reward of the bull put spread is more favorable. It is .48 (162.5/337.5) versus .54 (175/350) for the call spread.*

The put spread also has a slightly lower break-even price. From Table 4–15, the reader should calculate that the break-even for the call spread is 273.50 cents per bushel while the break-even for the put spread is 273.25.

Analyzing Neutral Strategies

It is more difficult to analyze neutral strategies because either the risk is predefined but the reward cannot be defined (long straddles and strangles), or the risk cannot be defined but the reward is predefined (short straddles and strangles). Obviously, one cannot predefine risk or reward because the exact futures price at expiration is unknown.

Thus, the analysis has to rely on the flat-price ranges that the trader views as probable or improbable during the life of the trade. The example in Table 4–17 looks at the non-directional short option strategies already introduced in Tables 4–10 and 4–12, as well as a short strangle.

The short strangle was constructed by selling the January 750 put and the January 800 call in Table 4–12; the same statistics for those options were used to compile the numbers in Table 4–12. The reader is encouraged to check the maximum profit and the upper and lower break-evens by using Table 4–15 as a guide.

From our knowledge of option prices and risk, we know that the danger of short option strategies comes from gamma and vega risk (check Table 4–15). Accordingly, Table 4–17 shows that the most attractive strategy, based on the objective of minimizing gamma and vega risk with respect to profit, is the hybrid straddle. On the other hand, the hybrid straddle offers the narrowest profit range, that

TABLE 4–17 Nondirectional Short Option Strategies; January Soybean Options

Strategy	Maximum Profit (Cents)	Breakeven		Gamma/ $ Profit	Vega/ $ Profit
		Lower	Upper		
775 short straddle	+28.50	746	804	.078	210.5
775 hybrid straddle	+17.50	757	792	.003	68.6
750/800 short strangle	+11.25	739	811	.155	426.6

is, 35 cents versus 58 cents for the straddle, and 72 cents for the strangle.

From the market environment outlined earlier (January futures at 768 cents per bushel, sideways price trend, impending crop report, and 14 days to expiration), the decision comes down to one's conviction regarding the crop report. If the crop report is extremely bullish or bearish, it is likely that all the trading ranges in Table 4–17 will be violated and open-ended losses will occur in the case of the short straddle and strangle. But if the crop report is a non-event, the market will most likely continue trading in a sideways price pattern.

Therefore, under the previous circumstances, the best strategy is the hybrid straddle, because loss is limited in case of an extreme report and the trading range of 35 cents is acceptable given seasonal volatility considerations. (Options on January soybean futures expire in mid-December; check the seasonal graphs in Chapter 3). Without the crop report, however, one degree of conviction can safely be added by using the short straddle instead of the hybrid. As Table 4–17 demonstrates, the short straddle offers better risk/reward parameters as well as a trading range that is almost as good as the short strangle.

Summary

In every risk/reward analysis, the goal is to focus on the appropriate risk for each strategy under consideration. In the case of vertical spreads, the trader focuses on maximum loss at expiration and break-even points; gamma, vega, and theta risks are diluted by definition so they are not a concern. For short non-directional strategies, the focus turns to break-even points, gamma, and vega risk. For long non-directional strategies, profit ranges and theta are the risk parameters to analyze. Table 4–15 (last column) should be consulted to isolate the risks inherent to each strategy.

Each risk is then weighed against potential profit to make it comparable to other strategies. The strategy that offers the lowest risk relative to profit is the optimal, although the trader can adjust this according to his or her knowledge of future events. In the example given in Table 4–17 the presence or absence of a crop report would have changed the trader's choice.

Calendar Spreads

Calendar spreads involve option positions taken in two separate contract months in which the nearby call (put) option is sold and the deferred call (put) option is bought. When the spread involves positions taken at the same strike price, the strategy is called a **horizontal spread.** When the spread involves different strike prices, the strategy is called a **diagonal spread.**

Horizontal Call and Put Spreads

Table 4–18 and Figures 4–17 and 4–18 demonstrate two horizontal spread strategies: The first is a **horizontal call spread** where a March 800 soybean call is sold and a May 800 soybean call is bought. The second is a **horizontal put spread** where a March 800 soybean put is sold and a May 800 soybean put is bought.

From Figures 4–17 and 4–18 and the net statistics in Table 4–18, it is obvious that the call and put horizontal spread behave much like a non-directional spread, that is, like a short straddle. The major difference is that the horizontal spread benefits from increases in volatility whereas the short straddle does not. *Consequently, a trader would use this strategy with the conviction that implied volatility will rise but that underlying futures will trade in a range.*

Indeed, the profit/loss profiles in Figures 4–17 and 4–18 were generated with the assumption that implied volatility increased from the low 20-percent range to 30-percent by the expiration of the nearby (March) contract month. Under those volatility conditions, both strategies were profitable within a 100- to 150-cent range.

TABLE 4–18 March/May Soybean Call Horizontal Spread: Short March 800 Call / Long May 800 Call

Strike	Credit/Debit (Cents/ Bushel)	Implied Volatility	Delta	Gamma	Vega	Theta
Mar 800 Call	+27.0	21.89%	−.58	−.0070	−$50	+$15
May 800 Call	−48.0	22.58%	+.61	+.0040	+$82	−$9
Net	−21.0		+.03	−.0030	+$32	+$6

March/May Soybean Put Horizontal Spread: Short March 800 Put / Long May 800 Put

Strike	Credit/Debit (Cents/ Bushel)	Implied Volatility	Delta	Gamma	Vega	Theta
Mar 800 Put	+16.25	21.89%	+.41	−.0075	−$50	+$14
May 800 Put	−29.50	22.58%	−.40	+.0039	+$82	−$10
Net	−13.25		+.01	−.0036	+$32	+$4

FIGURE 4–17

March/May Soybean Call Horizontal Spread
Short March 800 Call / Long May 800 Call
Debit = 21 Cents

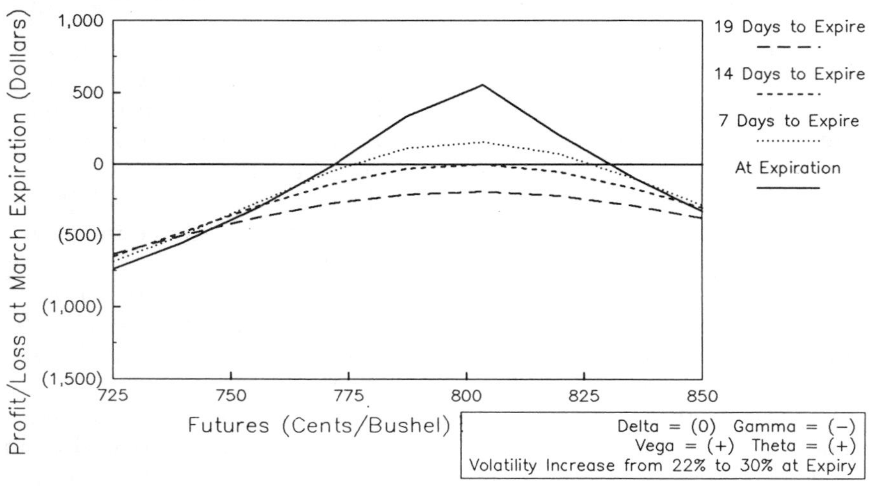

FIGURE 4–18

March/May Soybean Put Horizontal Spread
Short March 800 Put / Long May 800 Put
Debit = 13.25 Cents

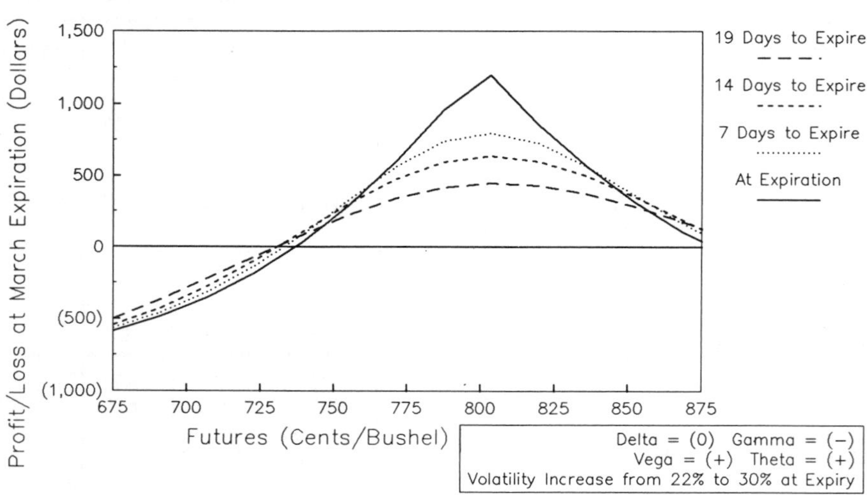

The volatility benefit is evident from the large dollar impact of vega in Table 4–18. If volatility had remained flat, the profits portrayed in Figures 4–17 and 4–18 would be much lower and the break-even range would be narrower. Conversely, if volatility had collapsed to 15 percent, the spread would have resulted in losses at every flat-price interval.

Unfortunately, the number of market situations that are suited for the call or put horizontal spread are not numerous. Usually, If volatility is increasing, the chances are that the profit range will be broken sometime before expiration; this is simply intuitive. In the soybean market, for instance, it is not unusual to break a 100-cent trading range in the course of 30 to 40 calender days.

There are situations, however, when implied volatility is being bid-up but underlying futures price is static. This usually occurs when market participants expect an impending price move. To that extent, the horizontal spread offers better profit potential than the long straddle, because the trader counts on rising volatility but not on a sharp flat-price rally or break. Note also that theta yields a slight positive dollar amount in Table 4–18; this is not true for the long straddle.

Nonetheless, such situations are usually aberrations that are eventually corrected. Either volatility collapses and the strategy loses money, or volatility rises sharply and the break-even ranges are violated.

In addition, there is also the chance that the spread relationship between the underlying futures contracts may change. All other assumptions regarding volatility and flat-price remaining equal, if the spread widens so that the deferred futures gain on the nearby, more profit or less loss will result; otherwise, if the spread narrows so that the nearby futures gain on the deferred, less profit or more loss will result. It should be emphasized that if the trader's primary goal is to profit from futures spread relationships, he or she is better off using the underlying futures.

Given that horizontal spreads profit under the paradoxical situation of rising volatility within a flat-price trading range—and that there is an additional risk that dynamic spread relationships may exacerbate loss—this strategy should only be used within a very narrow set of convictions.

Diagonal Call and Put Spreads

Table 4–19 and Figures 4–19 and 4–20 outline two diagonal spreads. In the first, a March 875 soybean call is sold and a May 825 soybean call is bought. In the second, a March 775 soybean put is sold, and a May 825 soybean put is bought.

TABLE 4–19 March/May Soybean Call Diagonal Spread: Short March 875 Call / Long May 825 Call

Strike	Credit/Debit (Cents/Bushel)	Implied Volatility	Delta	Gamma	Vega	Theta
Mar 875 Call	+5.0	24.09%	−.16	−.0040	−$31	+$10
May 825 Call	−38.0	24.06%	+.51	+.0039	+$85	−$10
Net	−33.0		+.35	−.0001	+$54	+$0

March/May Soybean Put Diagonal Spread: Short March 775 Put / Long May 825 Put

Strike	Credit/Debit (Cents/Bushel)	Volatility	Delta	Gamma	Vega	Theta
Mar 775 Put	+8.25	21.89%	+.25	−.0058	−$40	+$12
May 825 Put	−42.00	22.58%	−.50	+.0040	+$85	−$10
Net	−33.75		−.25	−.0008	+$45	+$2

FIGURE 4–19

March/May Soybean Call Diagonal Spread
Short March 875 Call / Long May 825 Call
Debit = 35.00 Cents

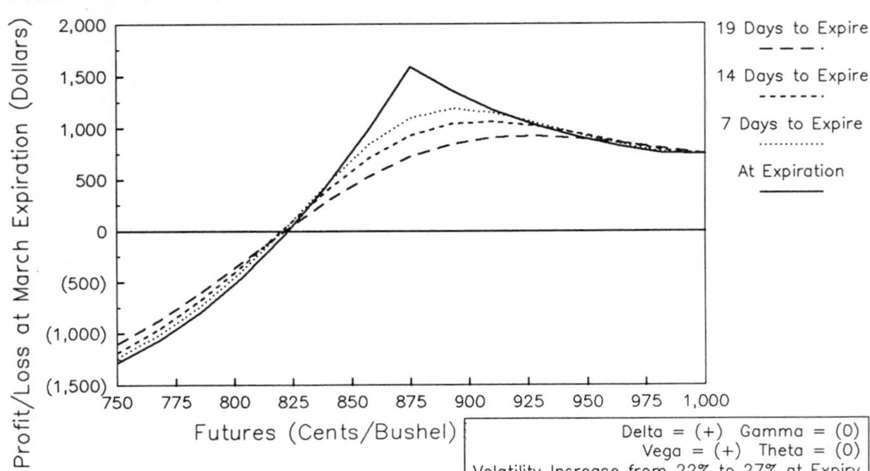

FIGURE 4–20

March/May Soybean Put Diagonal Spread
Short March 775 Put / Long May 825 Put
Debit = 33.75 Cents

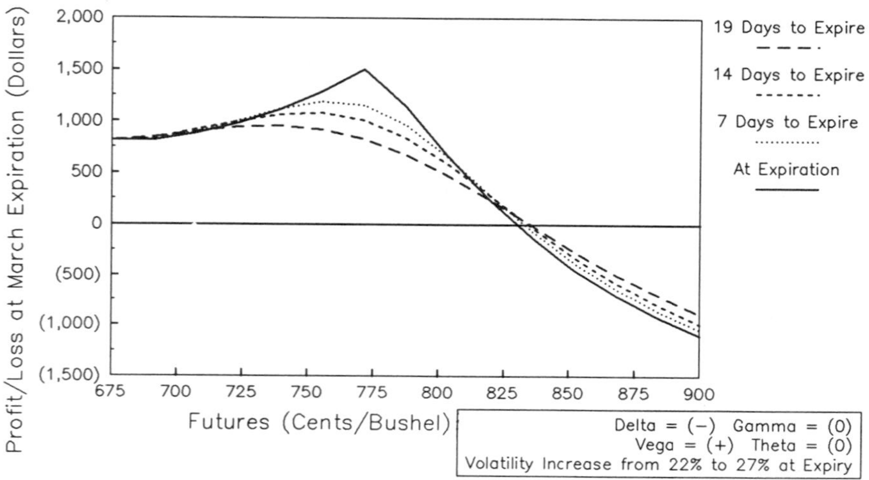

The net statistics for the diagonal call and put spreads in Table 4–19 have greater intuitive meaning for the agricultural options trader, because they are straightforward in both flat-price and volatility bias. Like the horizontal spread, the diagonal spread also profits as volatility rises; however, unlike the horizontal spread, there is a definite flat-price bias. *In agricultural markets, it is more logical to assume that flat-price rallies or collapses occur concurrently with rising volatility.*

In addition, the theta bias is close to zero, which allows the trader to work within a longer time frame without incurring time decay penalties. *Therefore, the diagonal strategy can function throughout the seasonal fluctuations of implied volatility.* For example, in anticipation of a seasonal increase in implied volatility, one could be short March calls and long May calls as in Table 4–19 or, even better, short May calls and long July calls.

Variations

Part of the problem with presenting the standard approaches to vertical or horizontal spreads is that it tends to limit the way one thinks. If a trader is told that the "correct" way to spread is 1:1 or 1:2, he or she may never think of such possibilities as 1:1.5, 1:3, and so on. Of course, there is nothing wrong with the standard spreads, and in most cases they will suffice. However, there are times when traders will want to experiment with different long and short ratios and different long and short contract months.

As an illustration, how can a trader take advantage of the seasonal decline in soybean option volatility between the months of December and March? Assume the trader has a slightly bearish flat price bias. In that case, the appropriate strategy will be very similar to a diagonal spread, with the exception that the trader will want to be net short volatility.

Creative traders will take this problem and simply reverse the standard call diagonal spread. They may also use a ratio other than 1:1. For instance, traders could sell several upper strike deferred call contracts against the purchase of a lower strike nearby call contract. By buying nearby volatility at a lower strike, the traders spread volatility risk, because if their outlook proves incorrect (for example, futures and volatility rise), the long nearby option will provide a partial gamma and vega hedge against gamma and vega risk in the short upper-strike deferred calls.

Traders may use a ratio other than 1:1, because they want to be net short both on a delta, vega, and theta basis. Therefore, traders add several degrees of conviction to their forecast that both volatility and flat-price will fall. The number of upper strike deferred calls they sell against the long nearby call simply depends on how many degrees of conviction traders want to add to their strategy.

Again, such traders have a good handle on option price and risk relationships. They understand that deferred options have higher vegas than nearby options. Thus, volatility profits will be high if their forecast bears out. They also know, however, that they can use option spreads as a device to tame adverse volatility fluctuations.

In addition, given any futures price, deferred options have lower deltas than nearby options. The traders know they will have to sell more calls in the deferred than they buy in the nearby—depending on the strike price they chose—in order to give the strategy a bear flat-price bias. Furthermore, they recognize that none of this conflicts with their outlook, convictions, or profit and risk goals. By selling more of the deferred options, their strategy automatically has a short vega and theta bias, while the negative gamma risk is partially hedged with the nearby option (remember that nearby options have higher gammas than deferred options).

As was stated earlier, when strategies are constructed with a solid knowledge of risk relationships, so that there are no conflicting goals or unquantifiable risks, there is a higher probability that profit will result.

Synthetic Futures and Options

By using different combinations of long and short futures and options, a trader can construct synthetic calls, puts, and futures. The key to these constructions lies in the put/call parity relationship (review Chapter 2, Put/Call Parity):

(Call Premium) − (Put Premium) = (Futures Price) − (Strike)

In order to facilitate the manipulation of the relationship, the following shorthand notation will be used:

Call Premium	=	C_p
Put Premium	=	P_p
Futures Price	=	F
Common Strike Price	=	S, and
Put/Call Parity:		$(C_p - P_p) = (F - S)$

If one rearranges the terms in the Put/Call Parity equation so that C_p, P_p, or F are on one side of the equation, and then multiplies by either +1 or −1 to obtain a long or short synthetic, the ingredients to any synthetic construction are easily recognized. For example, if we rearrange the put/call equation so that F is on the left side and all other terms are on the right, the following formula for a synthetic long futures is obtained:

$$F = C_p - P_p + S,$$

or alternatively,

$$F = C_p + (-P_p) + S$$

This states that a synthetic long futures consists of a long call and a short put (again, a negative sign in front of the the premium indicates the option is sold), and that it is purchased at an underlying futures price equal to the call premium minus the put premium plus the common strike price.

To obtain the ingredients for a synthetic short futures, multiply both sides of the above equation by negative one:

$$-1 \cdot F = -1 \cdot (C_p + (-P_p) + S)$$
$$-F = (-C_p) + P_p - S$$

Therefore, a synthetic short futures consists of a long put and a short call, and it is sold at an underlying futures price equal to the put premium less the call premium less the common strike price.

With similar manipulations, the reader will find the equations for synthetic long and short calls and puts are as follows:

SYNTHETIC CALLS:

Long: $C_p = P_p + F - S$

Short: $-C_p = (-P_p) + (-F) + S$

SYNTHETIC PUTS:

Long: $P_p = C_p + (-F) + S$

Short: $-P_p = (-C_p) + F - S$

Synthetic futures and options serve two basic purposes. First, they are the ingredients of arbitrage strategies. Second, they allow a trader to understand hedging applications and the prices at which these hedges are implemented.

In the arbitrage case, if traders can buy a synthetic future or option for less than what they can buy the actual future or option for in the market, they can earn a riskless profit by buying the synthetic and selling the actual. Conversely, if traders can sell a synthetic future or option for more than the traders can sell the actual future or option for in the market, they can earn a riskless profit by selling the synthetic and buying the actual.

These types of strategies often look good on paper, but they are very difficult to execute unless one is a floor trader; accordingly, the reader is referred to some of the books in the bibliography if a more in-depth study of arbitrage strategies is desired.

A more pragmatic application of synthetics lies in their use in hedging strategies. Consider a trader who buys soybean futures at 740 cents per bushel with extremely bullish convictions. Assume futures rally to 770.50 cents per bushel, but at that point, the trader's convictions of further price increases are not as strong. The trader has three choices: (1) exit the trade and take 30.5 cents of profits, (2) leave the trade alone with the risk that futures prices may collapse but with the possible reward that they may further rally, (3) create a synthetic long call by purchasing puts against the long futures position.

If the trader still wants to participate in the bull market but also wants to limit downside risk, he or she should choose the third possibility. With futures at 770.50 cents per bushel, the trader can purchase a 775 put for 15 cents; thus, the purchase price of the synthetic call is,

$$C_p = P_p + F - S$$
$$C_p = 15 + 770.50 - 775$$
$$C_p = 10.5 \text{ Cents}$$

Just like the actual call, the synthetic call has a maximum loss potential equal to the price of the premium, or 10.5 cents. Consequently, the trader locks in a 20-cent profit equal to the 30.5 cent futures profit less the price of the synthetic call. Therefore, if the market continues to rally, he or she can still profit as long as futures prices move above the break-even of the synthetic call (785.5). Alternatively, if futures prices suddenly collapse, the trader has a 20-cent profit locked in (see Table 4–20).

It should be noted that if the trader wants to lock in more than a 20-cent profit, he or she must buy a higher struck put; however, the higher strike synthetic call created has a higher break-even price. Conversely, if the trader desires less downside protection but a lower break-even, he or she should choose a lower struck put and create a lower strike synthetic call.

In short, *the less conviction the trader has regarding further price rallies, the more inclined he or she will be to use a higher strike synthetic call, because this preserves a greater part of the futures profit*. Witness the outcomes in Tables 4–21 and 4–22 using a 800 put worth 33.5 cents and a 750 put worth 5 cents. The synthetic call premiums are 4 cents and 25.5 cents for the 800 and 750 synthetic call, respectively.

TABLE 4–20 775 Synthetic Soybean Call Position: Long January 775 Put When Futures at 770.50 / Long Futures from 740

Position Value at Expiration (Cents/Bushel)				
Futures at Expiration	**Long 775 Put**	**Long Futures from 740**	**Initial Debit**	**Net**
650.00	+125	−90	−15	+20
675.00	+100	−65	−15	+20
700.00	+75	−40	−15	+20
725.00	+50	−15	−15	+20
750.00	+25	+10	−15	+20
775.00	0	+35	−15	+20
800.00	0	+60	−15	+45
825.00	0	+85	−15	+70
850.00	0	+110	−15	+95

TABLE 4–21 800 Synthetic Soybean Call Position: Long January 800 Put When Futures at 770.50 / Long Futures from 740

Position Value at Expiration (Cents/Bushel)				
Futures at Expiration	**Long 800 Put**	**Long Futures from 740**	**Initial Debit**	**Net**
675.00	+125	−65	−33.5	+26.5
700.00	+100	−40	−33.5	+26.5
725.00	+75	−15	−33.5	+26.5
750.00	+50	+10	−33.5	+26.5
775.00	+25	+35	−33.5	+26.5
800.00	0	+60	−33.5	+26.5
825.00	0	+85	−33.5	+51.5
850.00	0	+110	−33.5	+76.5
875.00	0	+135	−33.5	+101.5

There is a fourth possibility open to traders. They could exit the long futures position and simply purchase calls. For example, assuming no market inefficiency such as that the put/call parity relationship holds, the traders should be able to purchase 775 calls for 10.5 cents, which is exactly the price of the 775 synthetic call. If the traders plan to leave their position intact until the expiration of the options, they should be indifferent to using the synthetic call or the actual call. *But if the traders want more flexibility during the interim before expiration, they should use the synthetic.*

Consider the situation where traders used the synthetic 775 call

TABLE 4–22 750 Synthetic Soybean Call Position: Long January 750 Put When Futures at 770.50 / Long Futures from 740

Position Value at Expiration (Cents/Bushel)				
Futures at Expiration	**Long 750 Put**	**Long Futures from 740**	**Initial Debit**	**Net**
675.00	+75	−65	−5	+5
700.00	+50	−40	−5	+5
725.00	+25	−15	−5	+5
750.00	0	+10	−5	+5
775.00	0	+35	−5	+30
800.00	0	+60	−5	+55
825.00	0	+85	−5	+80
850.00	0	+110	−5	+105
875.00	0	+135	−5	+130

as in Table 4–20. If futures rally to 800 cents per bushel before expiration, and the traders suddenly change their conviction from bullish to bearish, they can exit the long futures position with a 60 cent profit and keep the 775 put with the idea that futures prices may fall and the put will gain in value. If traders are wrong, they still have 45 cents profit locked in and any further rallies are only opportunity costs. If correct, traders can increase their 60 cent profit depending on the extent and timing of the price collapse.

Monitoring Option Strategies and Positions

After a strategy is formulated and implemented, traders must monitor each segment of their risk—delta, gamma, vega, and theta—on a daily basis. If traders have several strategies in place, each strategy should be collapsed into one option position (or **option book**) in order to quantify overall risk. Defensive or offensive measures can then be taken to adjust risk or add profit.

Furthermore, by collapsing each strategy into one option book, any contradictions between strategies are made evident. Consider the traders who are bullish. If they collapse their strategies, they may find that their net delta equivalent is too low for their bullish convictions. They can then take action to adjust their overall position by exiting some strategies or initiating others.

Table 4–23 gives one possible construction for an options book. The trader has isolated each soybean option strategy and collapsed the positions into meaningful summary statistics. The flat-price (delta) exposure is 200 thousand bushels short. The gamma exposure is +4 thousand bushels (that is, the trader becomes less short as the market moves against him or her and shorter as the market moves in his or her favor). The vega benefit is +$3,724 for each one percent increase in implied volatility; conversely, the trader loses $3,724 for each one percent decrease in implied volatility. The trader's theta exposure is negative in that he or she loses $1,363 per day in time decay.

There are many traders who claim that daily monitoring is unnecessary as long as the break-even ranges of the strategy are known. That is, as long as the market opens and closes within the expiration range of profitability, there is no need to monitor daily risk. This is only a half truth. If a trader believes only in the expiration break-evens, what will stop him or her from implementing the trade ad infinitum? If one short straddle looks like a sure bet, why not sell 2? Or 200? Or 2,000?

The point is that every trader—because he or she is a fallible human being—needs to know (or in some cases, needs to be told)

TABLE 4–23 **Soybean Option Book**

Date: 03-Feb																
Strike	Mnth	Strat	P/C	#	Futures	Premium	Expire	Imp Vol	Delta	Bu Equiv	Gamma	Bu Equiv	Vega	$ Equiv	Theta	$ Equiv
750	H	S1	Put	150	770.50	5.00	17-Feb	21.43%	−0.25	−189	0.0099	7	48.4	$3,631	−134.9	($2,771)
725	H	S1	Put	−150	770.50	1.50	17-Feb	23.55%	−0.09	67	0.0045	−3	−24.7	($1,853)	76.5	$1,572
800	H	S2	Put	35	770.50	33.50	17-Feb	23.27%	−0.79	−138	0.0082	1	43.6	$763	−130.6	($626)
775	H	S2	Put	−35	770.50	15.00	17-Feb	21.00%	−0.55	96	0.0125	−2	−59.8	($1,047)	162.4	$779
700	K	S3	Put	60	780.40	5.00	22-Apr	21.50%	−0.12	−37	0.0026	1	74.4	$2,231	−38.5	($317)
							AVG:	22.15%	Total:	−202		4		$3,724		($1,363)

S1 = 750/725 bear put spread
S2 = 800/775 bear put spread
S3 = 700 long puts

Mnth = Contract month
Strat = Strategy
P/C = Put or call
= Number of contracts
Imp Vol = Implied volatility

Delta, thousand bu. equivalent: (#) • (5) • (Delta)
Bush equiv = Bushel equivalent
Gamma, thousand bu. equivalent: (#) • (5) • (Gamma)
Vega, $ equivalent of 1% Increase = (1%) • (#) • (50) • (Vega)
Theta, $ equivalent of 1 day = (1/365) • (#) • (50) • (Theta)

when enough is enough. Therefore, if a trader knows that his or her position stands to lose $3000 for each 1 percent increment in implied volatility, the trader can adjust the position in order to reduce the volatility risk if it is too high, or add to the risk if the trader believes he or she can afford to take more on.

In that sense, monitoring provides advance shock treatment. For instance, many traders cannot understand why their losses outstrip their flat-price (delta) exposure. However, if they know in advance all possible sources of risk and then quantify each source in order to understand its impact on the daily cash flow of their position, all elements of suprise are eliminated. There are no unexplained losses.

Chapter Summary

1. A comprehensive options strategy always integrates volatility and time decay in its formulation in order to add profit or minimize loss.

2. A good options trader considers profit and loss exposure from day to day, not just at expiration; accordingly, he or she reduces, adds to, or exits a position based on how much profit remains and how much risk has grown.

3. From the viewpoint of the pragmatic trader, the proper theoretical perspective [on options] is the ability to discern relationships rather than to calculate absolutes. When strategies are constructed with a solid knowledge of risk relationships, so that there are no conflicting goals or unquantifiable risks, there is a higher probability that profit will result.

4. When an option is bought, the cash outflow from the trader's account is termed a debit. If a trader buys a 270 corn put for 3 cents per bushel, the debit is 3 cents per bushel or a cash outlay of $150 per contract. Conversely, the trader who sold the corn put takes a 3-cent per bushel credit or a cash inflow of $150.

5. Option strategies are termed bullish, bearish, or non-directional depending on the sign of the net delta of the strategy; that is, if the net delta is positive (negative), the strategy is termed bullish (bearish). If the net delta is zero or near zero, the strategy is defined as neutral, non-directional, or technically delta neutral.

6. There are three types of non-directional strategies. The first is when the trader sells puts and calls with the expectation that futures prices will trend sideways. The second type involves the purchase of puts and calls when the trader anticipates a violent bullish or bearish move. The final type is covered writing. This is when a trader sells a put or a call and hedges delta neutral to earn extrinsic value.

7. Non-directional strategies are the trades that most beginners gravitate towards because they appear to be no-lose propositions; however, although it seems that a certain amount of weight is taken off the trader's flat-price conviction, this weight is simply relegated to either gamma, vega, or theta risk. In that sense, non-directional strategies require greater conviction, forethought, and monitoring than do strategies involving bullish or bearish flat-price bias.

8. Options strategies begin with some flat-price conviction—not a lack of one. In addition to bullish and bearish price outlooks, flat-price conviction in options trading encompasses sideways price outlooks as well as price breakout forecasts that can be either bullish or bearish.

9. Once a trader has a flat-price outlook (bullish, bearish, or non-directional), the options trading problem is reduced to making an intelligent decision regarding volatility expectations over the life of the trade, that is, the possible extent and timing of the flat-price movement over the life of the trade. This will dictate whether the strategy is traded from the long or short volatility side.

10. When a flat-price and volatility expectation is formulated, the gamma and theta bias automatically falls out as a residual.

11. The remaining strategy questions of what option month to trade, what strike price to trade, and whether or not to spread, follow from the strength of one's convictions regarding flat-price and volatility.

12. ***Contract Month:*** The greater the conviction that a flat-price and volatility change is imminent or not imminent, the greater the focus on trading the nearby contract month. If a long-term view on flat-price and volatility prevails, the greater the focus on trading the first deferred contract month or beyond, depending on the time frame involved and market liquidity considerations.

13. ***Strike Price:*** The greater the conviction that a flat-price and volatility change is imminent or not imminent, the greater the focus on trading the at-the-money or near-the-money strike price. The less conviction regarding flat-price and volatility, the greater the focus on trading out-of-the-money options.

14. ***Spreading:*** A trader spreads options in order to dilute (enhance) his or her flat-price, volatility, or time decay risk (profit). Accordingly, spreading allows the trader to subtract or add one degree of conviction to his or her strategy without adjusting the contract month or strike price.

15. In every risk/reward analysis, the goal is to focus on the appropriate risk for each strategy under consideration. Each risk is then weighed against potential profit to make it comparable to other strategies. The strategy that offers the lowest risk relative to profit is the optimal, although the trader can adjust this according to his or her knowledge of future events (for example, government reports, announcements, and so on).

16. Calendar spreads involve option positions taken in two separate contract months where the nearby call (put) is sold and the deferred call (put) option is bought. When the spread involves positions taken at the same strike price, the strategy is called a horizontal spread. When the spread involves different strike prices, the strategy is called a diagonal spread.

17. A trader would use the horizontal spread with the conviction that implied volatility will rise but the underlying futures will trade in a range. If volatility remains flat, profits are much lower and breakeven ranges are narrower. If volatility collapses, losses result at every flat-price level.

18. Traders must take into consideration spread relationships between the underlying futures prices when they implement calender spreads. If the futures spread widens so that the deferred futures gain on the nearby, more profit or less loss will result; otherwise, if the spread narrows so that the nearby futures gain on the deferred, less profit or more loss will result.

19. Like the horizontal spread, the diagonal spread also profits as volatility rises; however, unlike the horizontal spread, there is a definite flat-price (delta) bias. In agricultural markets, it is more logical to assume that flat-price rallies or collapses occur concurrently with rising volatility.

20. Synthetic futures and options serve two basic purposes. First, they are the ingredients of arbitrage strategies. Second, they allow a trader to understand hedging applications and the prices at which these hedges are implemented. The most pragmatic application of synthetics lies in their use in hedging strategies, for example, turning a long futures or cash position into a synthetic call, and so on.

21. After a strategy is formulated and implemented, the trader must monitor each segment of the risk—delta, gamma, vega, and theta—on a daily basis. If the trader has several strategies in place, each strategy should be collapsed into one option position (or option book) in order to quantify overall risk.

Chapter 5

Hedging Applications of Options

From the previous chapters, it is evident that options are complex instruments. Consistently successful options trading requires a solid conceptual base of knowledge in addition to an understanding of the underlying futures and cash-related markets. It is difficult to come up the learning curve in options, and for this reason options are often not utilized to the extent they could be in hedging applications.

The objective here is to identify the basic option hedging strategies available to producers and consumers of commodities. Emphasis is given to matching strategy variations to different market expectations and to the hedger's risk preferences; this underscores the innovative power and flexibility of option hedges. Hedge management strategies are also discussed at length, as they are often the most important aspect of successful options hedging.

The reader is forewarned that numerous equations and formulas are given in this chapter and in its accompanying appendix (Appendix B). They are not meant to confuse; rather, they accomplish two goals. First, they provide a way to quantify information about a hedge that allows one to compare strategies and to anticipate the impact of hedge management decisions. This makes the decision structure for hedge implementation and management rigorous and objective. Second, the astute reader will find in the numerous equations and formulas given in this chapter a rich set of tools that are easily integrated into a computer spreadsheet for quick analysis.

Note that only a basic explanation of cash and futures hedging will be presented here. Readers who are already familiar with these principles should continue with the following section, Creating Minimum and Maximum Prices. Those who need even more information should refer to the bibliography.

Preliminaries: Cash and Futures Hedging Basics

Producers or consumers hedge in order to lock in a price that gives them a favorable profit margin. They do this by taking an offsetting—equal, but opposite—position in the cash or futures market. Any variation from this is called **speculating** or **position-taking.**

Producer Example

*A soybean producer who has soybeans either in the field or in storage on a farm is **long** soybeans.* Assuming a local basis of 25 cents under the nearby futures (local cash price per bushel = futures price per bushel − basis), the producer is subject to the price schedule given by the dashed line in Figure 5–1: As long as the futures price increases and the basis is static, the producer gets a higher per bushel cash price; otherwise, the producer gets a lower per bushel cash price. To that extent, the producer is no different from a long speculator.

But if the futures price reaches a level where the producer believes he or she is earning an adequate margin, the producer can lock it in by selling the soybeans in the local cash market. In a perfect hedge, the number of bushels that the producer sells in the cash market is equivalent to the number of bushels in the producer's field or in storage. Obviously, the number of bushels in the field is only

FIGURE 5–1

Unhedged and Hedged Price Relationships for a Soybean Producer

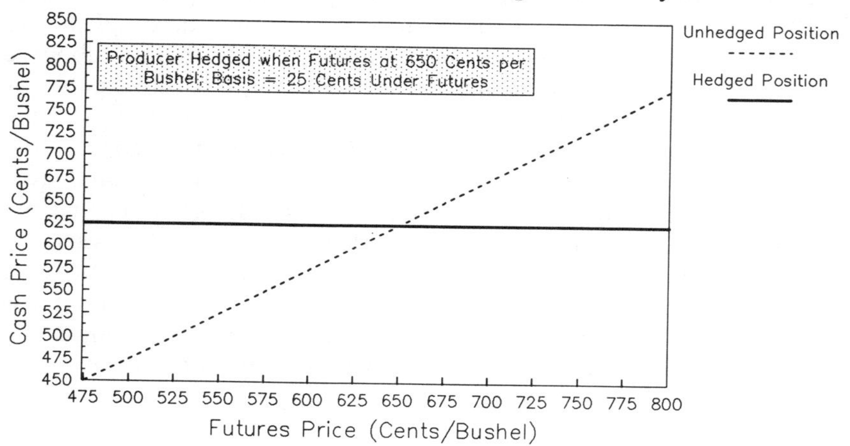

an estimate due to the fact that the final yield varies according to weather and the effectiveness of the technology applied. In short, there is quantity risk associated with the over- or under-estimation of yield. That problem will be left aside for the moment and explored later.

Assuming the farmer decides to market the crop when the futures price is at 650 cents per bushel, he or she calls the local elevator and sells at a cash price of 625 cents per bushel (625 = 650 − 25). The producer's sale (or short) in the cash market is the offsetting trade against his or her long in the physical commodity; hence, the soybean producer receives 625 cents per bushel, regardless of any subsequent change in the futures or basis. This is shown by the solid line in Figure 5–1.

A second method of creating an offsetting trade is to use the futures market. In the previous example, this would entail selling futures contracts so that any unfavorable (favorable) move in cash prices is offset by profit (loss) in the futures market. To illustrate, assume the producer sells November futures at 650 cents per bushel in August. In October the producer unwinds the hedge by buying back the short futures and selling his or her soybeans in the local cash market. As shown in Table 5–1, the producer has locked in a 625 cent per bushel price regardless of where the futures are trading in October (again, assuming a static basis relationship of 25 cents under).

Note that the cash hedge and futures hedge are equivalent in that they lock in the same price. The difference is the basis risk

TABLE 5–1 Using Futures to Hedge a Cash Long; Futures Sold in August at 650 Cents per Bushel

(A) If Futures Are at:	(B) Basis at:	(C) = (A) + (B) Cash at:	(D) = 650 − (A) Profit/Loss on Short Futures:	(E) = (C) + (D) Final Price Is:
580	−25	555	70	625
600	−25	575	50	625
620	−25	595	30	625
640	−25	615	10	625
660	−25	635	−10	625
680	−25	655	−30	625
700	−25	675	−50	625
720	−25	695	−70	625
740	−25	715	−90	625
760	−25	735	−110	625
780	−25	755	−130	625

inherent to the futures hedge.[1] When a producer uses futures to hedge his or her crop, the producer stops speculating on the flat-price and begins speculating on the basis relationship.

In the previous example, the soybean producer is long the basis, that is, long cash soybeans and short the futures. If the cash market strengthens relative to the futures markets (the basis strengthens), the producer will receive a better price than that implied in the initial hedge. If the basis weakens, however, the producer will receive a lower price than that implied by the initial hedge (see Table 5–2).

The same holds for the person who is short the basis (short cash and long futures). Unless a hedger wants to speculate on basis movement, he or she is probably better off buying or selling flat-price cash as the final price is known with certainty.

Consumer Example

Consumers who have not covered their processing or manufacturing needs are **short** *commodities*. For example, a Japanese soybean importer needs to buy soybeans for food use or for soyoil and soymeal production. The importer has three options: (1) Take no action and thus speculate that the price of soybeans will decline, (2) Buy soybeans in the cash market of any one of the three major export origins (Argentina, Brazil, United States), or (3) Buy soybean futures in Chicago and speculate on the basis relationship.

The dashed line in Figure 5–2 shows the importer's unhedged cash price schedule for U.S. origin soybeans at various futures levels. The basis used is 73.5 cents per bushel over futures: f.o.b. U.S. soybeans at New Orleans of 15 cents over and freight Gulf/Japan of 58.5 cents per bushel. The solid line in Figure 5–2 shows the price the importer can lock in either through an outright cash purchase or by buying futures at 650 cents per bushel as shown in Table 5–3 (options 2 and 3 in the previous paragraph).

In the futures hedge, it is assumed that f.o.b. levels and freight

TABLE 5–2 Impact of a Stronger or Weaker Basis on the Producer's Final Hedge Price

Basis	Final Hedge Price
Stronger	Higher
Weaker	Lower

1. Another difference is that the futures hedge requires margin funds; however, margin funds can be deposited as Treasury Bills and thus earn interest.

FIGURE 5–2

Unhedged and Hedged Price Relationships for a Soybean Consumer

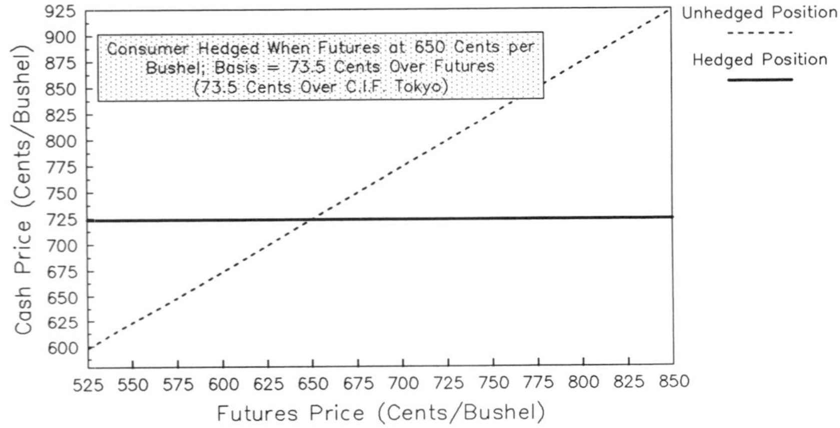

rates remain static over time. That is a big assumption; hence, the basis risks outlined in Table 5–2 apply. The importer pays a lower price if at the time he or she unwinds the hedge the basis has weakened, or a higher price if it has strengthened.

Quantity Risk

In the first example, producers cannot perfectly forecast crop yield; thus, the quantity they hedge in cash or futures may be larger

TABLE 5–3 Using Futures to Hedge a Cash Short; Futures Bought in August at 650 Cents per Bushel

(A) If Futures Are at:	(B) Basis at:	(C) = (A) + (B) Cash at:	(D) = (A) − 650 Profit/Loss on Long Futures:	(E) = (C) − (D) Final Price Is:
580	73.5	653.5	−70	723.5
600	73.5	673.5	−50	723.5
620	73.5	693.5	−30	723.5
640	73.5	713.5	−10	723.5
660	73.5	733.5	10	723.5
680	73.5	753.5	30	723.5
700	73.5	773.5	50	723.5
720	73.5	793.5	70	723.5
740	73.5	813.5	90	723.5
760	73.5	833.5	110	723.5
780	73.5	853.5	130	723.5

or smaller than the ultimate quantity in their fields or storage bins. It will be larger if crop yield is low, or smaller if yield is high. Assuming a static basis relationship, this will result in either a profit or a loss depending on the direction of prices after the hedge was placed.

For example, assume a soybean producer has a 600-acre farm and expects a yield of 33.3 bushels per acre and thus a total crop of 20,000 bushels. To hedge the crop, the producer sells four soybean futures (5,000 bushel contract). Figure 5–3 shows the results. The producer is subject to losses in the area below the solid line, that is, when the producer's yield is lower than expected and the futures price rises, or when yield is higher than expected and the futures price falls.

Weather and its subsequent effect on crop yield is the predominant cause of quantity risk for the producer: Adverse weather causes lower yields, and if the effect is pervasive, prices rise in general. The producer over-hedged because a larger quantitiy of commodity than possessed was sold forward, and thus the producer suffers losses. In the opposite case, beneficial weather produces a bumper crop, and if the effect is pervasive, prices fall in general. The producer under-hedged and loses money since less commodity than possessed was sold forward.

Figure 5–3 is important; it will be referenced to analyze how an

FIGURE 5–3

Effect of Quantity Risk on the Hedge of a Soybean Producer
Futures Sold @ 650; Basis @ −25; 600-Acre Farm

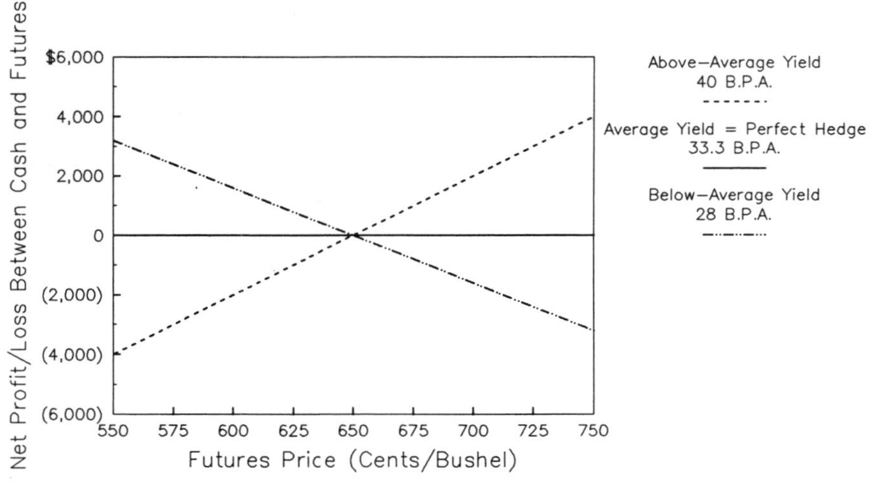

options hedge may alter the losses or gains due to quantity risk. Note that consumers are also exposed to quantity risk if they cannot buy in the cash market because either the physical commodity is not there or there are delays in bringing it to market.[2] The Japanese soybean importer may find little or no cash soybeans to buy when unwinding the hedge, since there could be a strike or work slowdown at the export origin (common in Brazil and Argentina) or an embargo such as that imposed by the United States in 1973.

Finally, it should be mentioned that producers and consumers rarely hedge one hundred percent of their exposure. Farmers normally hedge only a part of their crop, while consumers cover only a percentage of their needs. They do this in order to benefit from favorable price moves that full hedging would lock out; in turn, they leave themselves exposed to unfavorable price moves. This is a quandary, but one that has a solution in the use of options.

Options Hedging I: Creating Minimum and Maximum Prices

Futures and cash markets allow producers and consumers to lock in a fixed price, but as demonstrated previously, they lock out the ability to get a better price. Thus, a producer cannot benefit from a price rally and a consumer cannot benefit from a price collapse. With the use of options, however, a producer can buy a put to create a minimum selling price, and can leave open the opportunity to sell at higher price if the market rises. Conversely, a consumer can buy a call to create a maximum buying price and can leave open the opportunity to buy a lower price if the market falls.

The reason for this is clear given the concept of delta. The option—put or call—acts like a future if it is in-the-money and close to expiration, that is, when the market is below or above the strike price where the hedger bought protection. Therefore, any change in the value of a producer's cash commodity is offset by the in-the-money option just as in a standard futures hedge. Otherwise, the option is out-of-the-money and does not move one-to-one with futures. As such, the hedger has no futures obligation and can thus lock in a better price—less the cost of the premium—when the market moves in the producer's favor.

2. Granted, these situations are rarer than the producer's quantity risk. Usually, the commodity can be obtained from somewhere; the only question is at what price.

Minimum Prices

A minimum price is created by buying a put option. The minimum price is equal to the strike price of the put option, less the value of the premium, plus the basis[3]:

$$\text{Minimum Price} = [\text{Put\_Strike} - \text{Put\_Premium} + \text{Basis}]$$

Consider a soybean producer. In early March, new crop (November) soybean futures are trading at 743.25 cents per bushel and the local basis is 30 cents under futures. The producer fears that the government's March 31st planting intentions report will show a substantial increase in soybean acreage and thus cause new crop prices to tumble. On the other hand, the weather outlook in the coming months is uncertain. Precipitation has been sparse and sub-soil moisture is low. If the weather pattern continues, prices will be above current levels despite acreage increases, and the producer wants the ability to sell at higher levels.

Instead of locking in a flat-price by selling cash or futures, the producer creates a minimum selling price by purchasing out-of-the-money November 700 put options at a premium of 35 cents per bushel. The minimum price created is

Put Strike:	700.00	
Put Premium:	−35.00	
Basis:	−30.00	
Minimum Price:	635.00	Cents/Bushel

The outcome at expiration over different November futures prices is shown in Table 5–4.

Figure 5–4 compares the minimum price hedge with the standard futures or cash hedge and the unhedged position; it serves to illustrate some crucial points. First, if a producer were decidedly bearish, he or she should use the standard cash or futures hedge. As opposed to the minimum price hedge, this gives the producer a better cash price at every futures level below 778.25 cents per bushel (the method for calculating this point is elaborated later). Second, it follows that if the producer is outright bullish he or she should do nothing, as the unhedged position outperforms the minimum price hedge and the standard futures hedge at every futures price above 743.25 cents per bushel.

3. The basis can be positive ("over") or negative ("under"). As a standard, when one adds the basis in any of the equations in this chapter, one is adding either a positive or negative number.

TABLE 5–4 Using the 700 November Put to Hedge a Cash Long; Puts Bought at 35 Cents per Bushel; Futures at 743.25 Cents per Bushel

(A) If Futures Are at:	(B) Basis at:	(C) = (A) + (B) Cash at:	(D) Profit/Loss on Long 700 Puts	(E) = (C) + (D) Final Price Is:
625	−30	595	40	635
650	−30	620	15	635
675	−30	645	−10	635
700	−30	670	−35	635
725	−30	695	−35	660
750	−30	720	−35	685
775	−30	745	−35	710
800	−30	770	−35	735
825	−30	795	−35	760
850	−30	820	−35	785
875	−30	845	−35	810

In short, the put hedge is attractive only to the extent that it allows the producer to participate in price rallies while it guarantees a minimum price. It is the best alternative in the event of an unexpected and prolonged price rally. A weather scare is one event that would spark such a rally. In a drought scenario, the producer does not want to be short futures because the margin calls will be substan-

FIGURE 5–4

Comparison of Minimum Price Put Option Hedge with Futures Hedge and Unhedged Positions

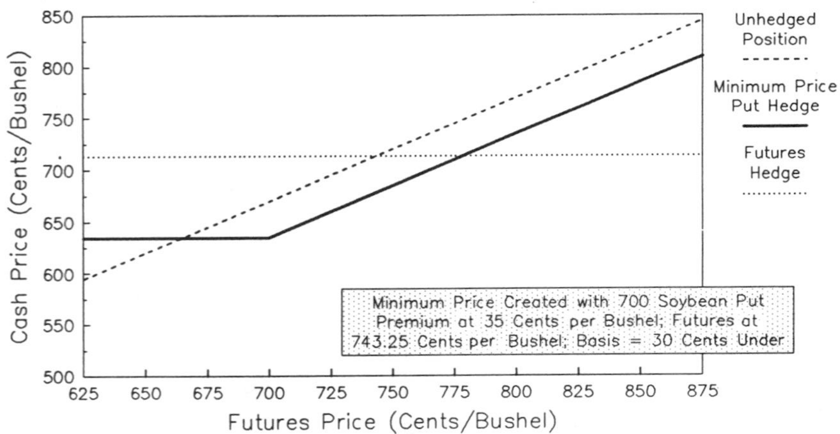

tial (long options positions require no margin funds)[4]; the producer is also susceptible to quantity risk. To be outright long the physical commodity is desirable as well, but then no minimum price is guaranteed if prices suddenly collapse.

The negative aspect of this particular minimum price hedge is that despite the use of an out-of-the-money put, the premium is expensive. Since the November 700 put was bought in March with eight months to expiration, the time value brings down the minimum price. High implied volatility has a similar effect.

The producer has two ways to circumvent this problem. First, the producer can buy a put with a higher strike price; the higher delta provides more downside protection. Observe in Figure 5–5 that as the strike of the put increases from 675 to 725, the minimum price increases from 620 cents per bushel to 653 cents per bushel. *Nevertheless, there is a trade-off: higher-struck puts are more expensive, and this reduces the producer's ability to participate in price rallies.*

The second alternative is to buy a put with less time value. For instance, the producer can buy a July, August, or September put. This is viable only if the futures' spread relationships remain static, but if the nearby contracts strengthen relative to the November contract, the producer incurs losses. In addition, each time a nearby option expires, the producer must roll forward the hedge, that is,

FIGURE 5–5

Comparison of Put Option Hedges: 675, 700, and 725 Strike Puts
Futures at 743.25 Cents per Bushel

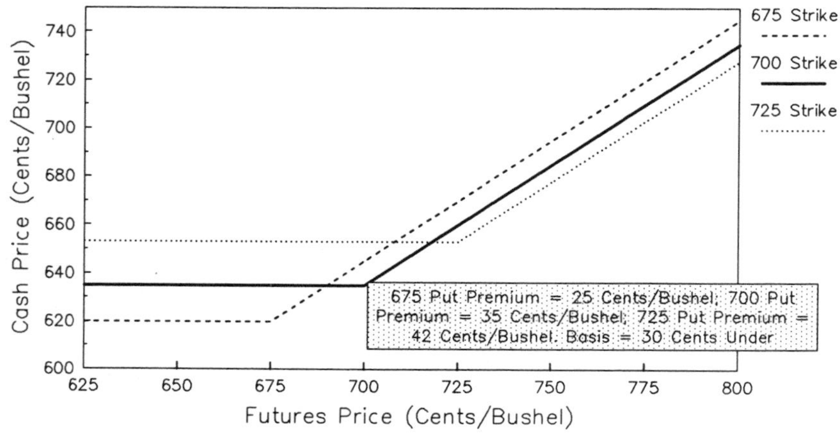

4. Nonetheless, option purchases must be paid for up-front, which represents an out-flow of cash and an opportunity cost.

when the July expires the producer rolls forward into the August and so on. This is costly as commissions must be paid each time the position is rolled forward. Since this solution adds to spread risk and entails higher transaction costs, it is suboptimal to adjusting the strike price.

It makes more sense to use cheap nearby puts (with 30 to 40 days to expire) to hedge inventory that is already in store and soon to be marketed. As an example, a farmer may have unhedged soybeans in storage from the previous crop year. If the farmer plans to sell in the next 20 to 40 days and believes prices could move sharply up or down, the farmer can create a minimum price by buying a cheap nearby put option. Depending on the strike price, and assuming implied volatility is not high, a cheap premium gives the producer a high minimum selling price and the ability to quickly participate in price rallies.

Equivalent Hedge Price

At some futures price at expiration, the minimum price hedge is equivalent to the standard futures hedge that can be placed at the outset; that is, at some point they both render the same fixed cash price. In Figure 5–4, this is where the solid line (minimum price hedge) crosses the dotted line (standard futures hedge). This is defined here as the **equivalent hedge price** (hereafter referred to as the **EHP**).

The EHP is significant because it represents an indifference point. Above it the minimum price hedge is optimal; below it the standard futures hedge is best. *Accordingly, the EHP serves as a reference point for the hedger's market outlook.* Any rational hedger who believes prices will surpass the EHP prefers the minimum price hedge; otherwise, the hedger sells futures or flat-price cash.

The simplest method of calculating the EHP is to take the current futures price that can be sold in the standard hedge and add the put premium:

$$\text{Equivalent\_Hedge\_Price} = [\text{Futures\_Price} + \text{Put\_Premium}]$$

In the previous example, the producer can implement a standard hedge by selling futures at 743.25 cents per bushel and lock in a cash price of 713.25 cents per bushel (given a static basis of 30 under). The problem is to find the futures price which gives the same fixed cash price (713.25 cents per bushel) when the producer uses the minimum price hedge. As the EHP equation shows, this is simply a matter of adding the cost of the 700 put:

Futures Price:	743.25	
700 Put Premium:	+35.00	
EHP:	778.25	Cents/Bushel

To review: if the producer uses the minimum price hedge and futures rise to 778.25 at expiration, the producer has done no better than the standard futures or cash hedge. If the producer views the probability of the market going to 778.25 as low, he or she should use the standard futures hedge, sell flat-price, or look for an alternative options strategy (more on alternatives later).

The EHP calculation will be given for each option hedge outlined here. It provides a benchmark against the standard futures or cash hedge. Furthermore, it allows the hedger to compare two or more option hedges in order to decide which best fits the market outlook. It is also an easy way for the hedger to indirectly gauge the impact of time value and implied volatility on the cost and feasibility of the hedge.[5]

Maximum Prices

A maximum price is created by buying a call option. The maximum price is equal to the strike of the call purchased, plus the call premium, plus the basis:

$$\text{Maximum Price} = [\text{Call\_Strike} + \text{Call\_Premium} + \text{Basis}]$$

For example, assume that in May Japanese soybean importers are contemplating whether to cover their July import requirements. The importers' research department warns them not to buy soybeans now, because a record South American harvest will weigh on prices during the coming months. (Brazil and Argentina harvest their soybean crop between the end of March and the beginning of May, and a large percentage of their crop is normally sold immediately thereafter.)

On the surface, the researchers make sense; however, the importers know from experience that several factors can delay the South Americans from selling their crop. One is an undervalued exchange rate or high inflation that gives South American farmers no incentive to sell; another is strikes or work stoppages that prevent the commodity from getting to or leaving port. Or perhaps South American farmers believe world prices will increase and hence they hold back

5. A more rigorous proof of the EHP is obtained by using option synthetics. This is given in Appendix B, Section I.

their crop from the market. Such aberrations in the flow of supply will certainly cause prices to rise as other importers scramble to cover their needs. What do the importers do?

The market scenario just described is not straightforward. It is an either/or situation where the maximum price hedge is particularly appropriate. With August soybean futures trading at 727.50 cents per bushel, the importers can create a maximum price for July imports by purchasing an August 775 soybean call for 17.5 cents per bushel. Assuming a basis of 73.5 cents over futures (f.o.b. U.S. soybeans at New Orleans of 15 over and freight Gulf/Japan of 58.5 cents per bushel), the maximum price is,

Call Strike:	775.00	
Call Premium:	+17.50	
Basis:	+73.50	
Maximum Price:	866.00	Cents/Bushel

The range of outcomes at expiration given different August futures levels is shown in Table 5–5.

Figure 5–6 compares the maximum price hedge with the standard futures hedge and the unhedged short position. From Figure 5–6, it is evident that prices need only fall slightly in order for the importer to begin buying a lower price than that offered by the stand-

TABLE 5–5 Using the 775 August Soybean Call to Hedge a Cash Short; Calls Bought at 17.5 Cents/Bushel; Futures at 727.50 Cents/Bushel

(A) If Futures Are at:	(B) Basis at:	(C) = (A) + (B) Cash at:	(D) Profit/Loss on Long 775 Call:	(E) = (C) − (D) Final Price Is:
675	73.5	748.5	−17.5	766.0
700	73.5	773.5	−17.5	791.0
725	73.5	798.5	−17.5	816.0
750	73.5	823.5	−17.5	841.0
775	73.5	848.5	−17.5	866.0
800	73.5	873.5	7.5	866.0
825	73.5	898.5	32.5	866.0
850	73.5	923.5	57.5	866.0
875	73.5	948.5	82.5	866.0
900	73.5	973.5	107.5	866.0
925	73.5	998.5	132.5	866.0

Note: In Table 5–5, losses increase the final price, while profits decrease the final price.

FIGURE 5–6

Comparison of Maximum Price Call Option Hedge with Futures Hedge and Unhedged Positions

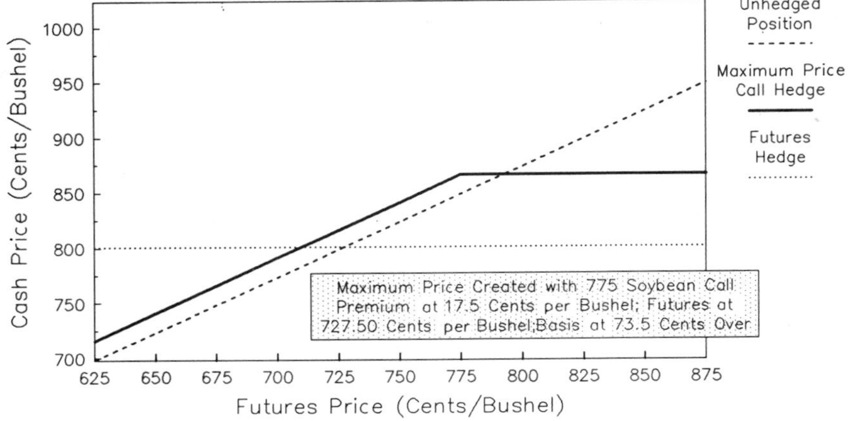

ard futures hedge. But exactly how much is slightly? Again, one can apply the equivalent hedge price concept to find the futures price at which the importer is indifferent between the maximum price hedge and the standard hedge. For the maximum price hedge, the EHP is,

$$\text{Equivalent Hedge Price} = [\text{Futures\_Price} - \text{Call\_Premium}]$$

Just as in the case of the minimum price hedge, the EHP for the maximum price hedge is simply a function of the option premium, which is another way of evaluating the cost of time value and implied volatility. From the prices given previously, the EHP of the call hedge is,

Futures Price:	727.50	
775 Call Premium:	−17.50	
EHP:	710.00	Cents/Bushel

The soybean importer should find this strategy attractive: If the expected selling pressure materializes out of South America and August futures fall to 675 cents per bushel, the importer can price at 766 cents per bushel and is at a significant advantage over competitors who panicked and priced at 801 cents per bushel. Conversely, if futures rally to 825 cents per bushel, the importer is pricing at 866 versus 898.50 for unhedged competitors.

FIGURE 5–7

Comparison of Call Option Hedges: 750, 775, and 800 Strike Calls
Futures at 727.50 Cents per Bushel

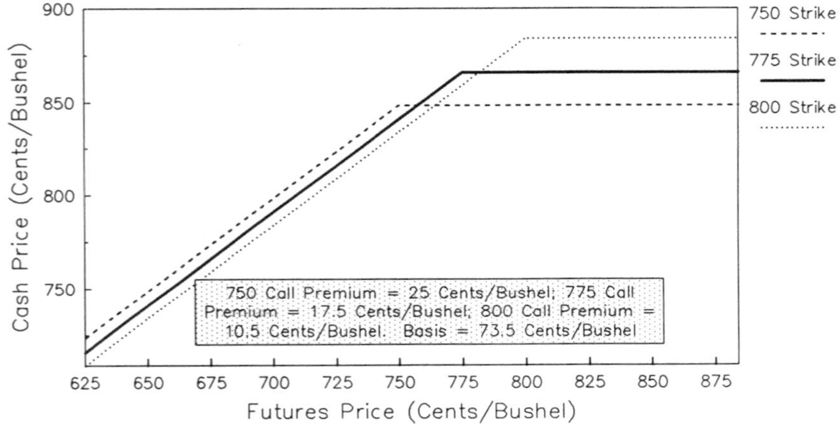

Of course, the importer may require a lower maximum price and can accomplish this by simply buying a call with a lower strike. Figure 5–7 demonstrates how the maximum price decreases as the strike of the call decreases from 800 to 750. Again, this is a function of delta. The lower-struck call has a higher delta and allows greater participation in price rallies. Nonetheless, the higher premium detracts from the ability to take advantage of lower prices. The hedger must calculate the EHP for several strikes and select the strike that gives a reasonable tradeoff between upside protection and downside pricing flexibility.[6]

Synthetic Equivalents of Minimum/Maximum Price Hedges

The equivalent hedge price calculation (EHP) was presented in order to facilitate calculations. It is easier to remember and quicker to use than formulas for synthetic options. Nonetheless, it is important to understand what the synthetic calculations imply about the hedge (see Appendix B).

In the minimum price example, the soybean producer essentially bought a synthetic 700 call for 78.25 cents. That is, the producer bought an in-the-money call that allows him or her greater participa-

6. See Appendix B, Section II, for synthetic option calculations of the maximum price and EHP.

tion in upside price movement since an in-the-money call has a higher delta. But it also entails the risk of losing a large premium; thus, the producer's minimum price (635 cents per bushel) is low given that he or she could realize a loss on the entire 78.25 cent premium (see Appendix B, Section I).

The same rationale applies to the soybean importer. The importer purchases an in-the-money put; as such, he or she can quickly take advantage of lower prices due to the large delta. Conversely, the importer will lose a large premium if prices increase, and this makes his or her maximum price high.

Quite different results hold if the hedgers used out-of-the-money synthetics. For the producer, the purchase of an out-of-the-money synthetic call allows less potential to participate in price rallies, but it gives a higher minimum price. For the consumer, the purchase of an out-of-the-money synthetic put provides less opportunity to price at lower levels, but it locks in a lower maximum price. Table 5–6 summarizes the synthetic equivalents of minimum and maximum price hedges as well as the effect of in-the-money and out-of-the-money synthetics on the minimum/maximum price and the equivalent hedge price.

Quantity and Basis Risk and Minimum and Maximum Price Contracts

If the option used to create the minimum or maximum price contract is out-of-the-money by expiration, the hedger will not exer-

TABLE 5–6 Synthetic Equivalents of Minimum/Maximum Price Hedges

Type of Hedge	Synthetic Position between Physical Commodity and Option	Effect on Minimum/Maximum Price and EHP
Minimum price	Long synthetic call	In-the-money: Low minimum price Low EHP Out-of-the-money: High minimum price High EHP
Maximum price	Long synthetic put	In-the-money: High maximum price High EHP Out-of-the-money: Low maximum price Low EHP

FIGURE 5–8

Quantity Risk of Soybean Minimum Price Hedge.

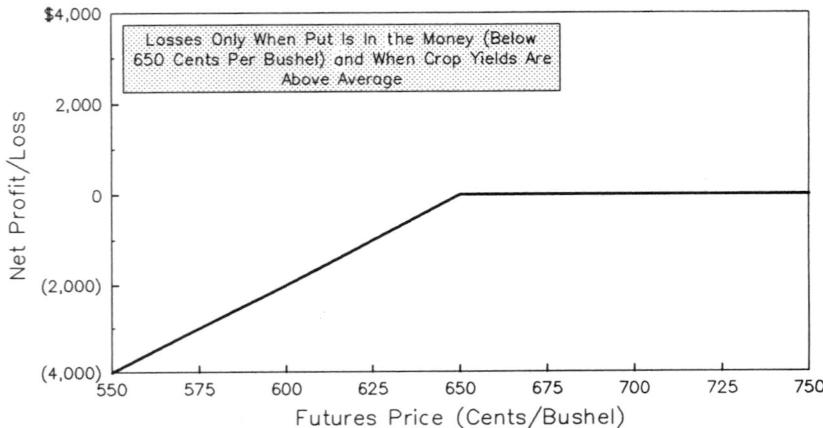

cise the option. Either the option is allowed to expire worthless or the hedger sells it before expiration to recoup part of the premium cost when he or she unwinds the hedge. In that circumstance, the hedger has no quantity risk since he or she has no futures position against the physical commodity. The hedger has no basis risk either, because there is no offsetting sale or purchase in futures. The hedger simply unwinds the hedge and sells or buys one final flat-price.

This is not the case if the option expires in-the-money. At that point the hedger exercises the option, receives a futures position, and is subject to quantity and basis risk.

Figure 5–8 demonstrates the quantity risk associated with a minimum price contract. It is simply a modification of Figure 5–3 in that losses are only possible if the futures price at expiration is less than the strike price of the option, that is, when the put option is in-the-money and crop yields are above expectations.

Managing the Minimum Price Hedge: Rolling-Down the Strike

Thus far, the minimum and maximum price hedges have been analyzed on an expiration basis; that is, the hedge was put in place and unwound at expiration. Although this facilitates the explanation of the hedge, it is unacceptable in reality. *Option hedges call for dynamic management since the hedger can take advantage of volatile price swings to improve either the minimum/maximum price or the equivalent hedge price.*

Consider a corn producer whose long-term outlook is bearish but who anticipates weather-related price rallies in July when corn reaches the crucial pollination stage. The producer would like to sell the crop now (in March) with new crop (December) futures trading at 272.50 cents per bushel and the local basis at 20 under; however, the producer also wants the ability to sell at a higher price if adverse weather develops. He or she decides to use a minimum price hedge by purchasing a December 260 corn put for 17.25 cents per bushel.

From the previous formulas, both the minimum price and the equivalent hedge price are as follows:

Strike Price:	260.00	
Put Premium:	−17.25	
Basis:	−20.00	
Minimum Price:	222.75	Cents/Bushel
Futures Price:	272.50	
Put Premium:	+17.25	
EHP:	289.75	Cents/Bushel

The minimum price of 222.75 cents per bushel is certainly less attractive than the 252.50 cents per bushel the producer can receive in the standard hedge, but if a weather problem occurs, corn futures will easily trade above the EHP of 289.75 cents per bushel.

Unfortunately, it happens that the producer's forecast was premature because plentiful rains in May caused December futures to plummet to 235 cents per bushel by the end of the month; the 260 December put is now valued at 32.50 cents per bushel. If the producer does nothing, the minimum price and the EHP still hold, that is, 222.75 and 289.75 cents per bushel, respectively. But with December futures at 235, the odds of the market rallying to the EHP appear low. *Therefore, in order to lower the EHP to a more attractive level without affecting the minimum price to a great extent, the best alternative is to roll-down the hedge to a put with a lower strike.*

The producer decides to sell the 260 put for 32.50 cents per bushel and roll-down to the 240 put which is trading at 18 cents per bushel. Assuming the basis is unchanged at 20 under, the steps to calculating the new minimum price and EHP are as follows:

Profit on Long 260 Put: [32.50 − 17.25] = 15.25

Strike Price:	240.00	
Put Premium:	−18.00	} = Net Cost of 240 Put = 2.75 Cents/Bushel
Profit on 260 Put:	+15.25	

Basis:	−20.00	
New Minimum Price:	217.25	Cents/Bushel
Futures Price:	235.00	
Put Premium:	+18.00	
Profit on 260 Put:	−15.25	
New EHP:	237.75	Cents/Bushel

Although the new minimum price is 5.50 cents below the former minimum price, it still outperforms the current standard cash or futures hedge of 215 cents per bushel. More important, the producer has lowered his or her EHP to a very attractive level (see Figure 5–9).

Assume at this point that the producer is vindicated in mid-July, and December futures rally to 300 cents per bushel. The 240 December put is now worth 1.5 cents per bushel. The producer decides to price the crop. He or she calls the local elevator and sells at a flat-price of 280 cents per bushel (300 December futures less 20 cent basis). But what should the producer do with the put? There are two choices: (1) Sell it for 1.5 cents per bushel in order to partially recoup the original cost of 2.75 cents per bushel (18.00 − 15.25), or (2) Keep the put and speculate on the flat-price.

The first alternative gives the producer a final cash price of

FIGURE 5–9

Rolling–Down a Put in a Minimum Price Hedge Roll–Down from a 260 Put to a 240 Put

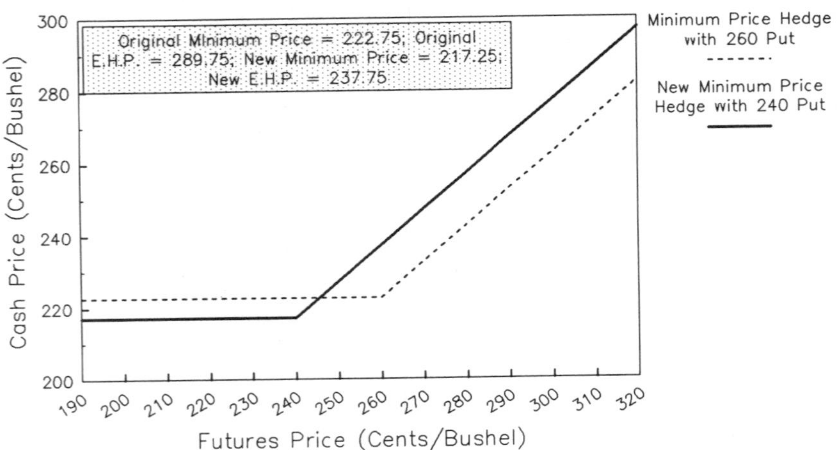

278.75 cents per bushel; the second renders 277.25 if the 240 put expires worthless.

Alternative 1: Sell 240 Put, Sell Cash

December Futures:	300.00	
Basis:	−20.00	
Profit on 260 Put:	+15.25	
Cost of 240 Put:	−18.00	
Sell 240 Put At Market:	+1.50	
Final Cash Price:	278.75	vs. 252.50 Standard Hedge

Alternative 2: Keep 240 Put, Sell Cash

December Futures:	300.00	
Basis:	−20.00	
Profit on 260 Put:	+15.25	
Cost of 240 Put:	−18.00	
Final(?) Cash Price:	277.25	vs. 252.50 Standard Hedge
Profit of 240 Put:	??.??	
Final Cash Price:	??.??	

In the second alternative, the final price will not be known until expiration; although it will be no lower than 277.25. With four months to expire, almost anything could happen. For instance, if good rains develop and a bumper crop results, prices may collapse to 200 to 220 cents per bushel. This would result in a windfall profit for the farmer. Since there is only a 1.5 cent difference between the up-front prices of the two alternatives, why not keep the 240 put?

Rolling-Up the Strike

Assume that the corn farmer's neighbor was unhedged going into May as corn prices plunged from 272.50 cents per bushel to 235 cents per bushel. The farmer reminds his or her neighbor that it is only May and summer weather could still be detrimental to the crop. The farmer recommends that his or her neighbor create a minimum price at current levels, and they construct a hedge using a 220 December put valued at 8 cents per bushel with December futures at 235 cents per bushel. The familiar calculations are as follows:

Strike Price:	220.00	
Put Premium:	−8.00	
Basis:	−20.00	
Minimum Price:	192.00	Cents/Bushel

Futures Price:	235.00	
Put Premium:	+8.00	
EHP:	243.00	Cents/Bushel

In late June and early July, futures steadily rise as forecasts portend hot and dry weather. With futures at 271.50 cents per bushel and the 220 put trading at 1.75 cents per bushel, the farmer recommends that his or her neighbor roll-up the hedge to the 260 strike put that is trading at 14.5 cents per bushel. Hence, the neighbor sells the 220 put and buys the 260 put. This changes the neighbor's minimum price and EHP as follows:

Loss on 220 December put: [1.75 − 8] = −6.25

Strike Price:	260.00	
Put Premium:	−14.50	
Loss on 220 Put:	−6.25	
Basis:	−20.00	
New Minimum Price:	219.25	Cents/Bushel
Futures Price:	271.50	
Put Premium:	+14.50	
Loss on 200 Put:	+6.25	
New EHP:	292.25	Cents/Bushel

By rolling-up the hedge, the neighbor increased the minimum price by 27.25 cents (219.25 versus 192), although the EHP is higher due to the loss realized on the 220 put (see Figure 5–10). But assume the neighbor also sells when futures reach 300 cents per bushel and that the 260 put is now worth 5 cents per bushel. If the neighbor sells the put, a 9.5 cent loss in addition to the loss of 6.25 cents on the 220 put is realized, for a total loss of 15.75 cents per bushel. Thus, the neighbor's final cash price is as follows:

Loss on 260 December Put: [5 − 14.50] = −9.50

December Futures:	300.00	
Basis:	−20.00	
Loss on 220 Put:	−6.25	
Loss on 260 Put:	−9.50	
Final Cash Price:	264.25	vs 215 Standard Hedge

FIGURE 5–10

Rolling–Up a Put in a Minimum Price Hedge Roll–Up from a 220 Put to a 260 Put

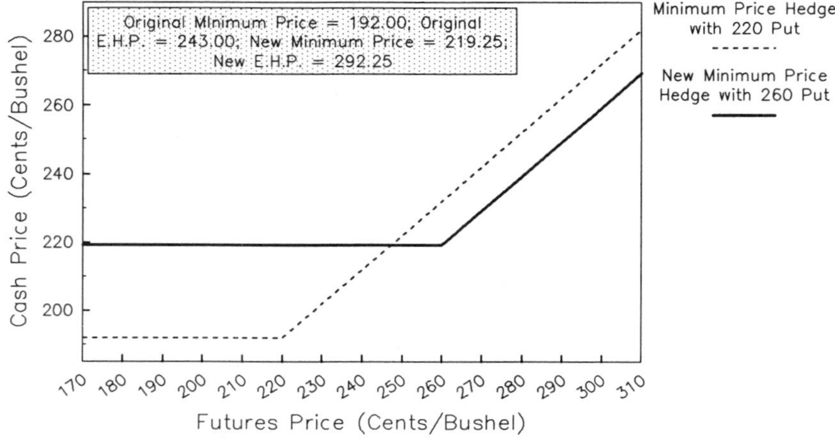

This is well above the 215 price the farmer would have received had he or she panicked and hedged with futures at 235 cents per bushel.

Managing the Maximum Price Hedge

The same general principles in managing the minimum price hedge hold for the maximum price hedge. *If the market rallies, the hedger should sell his or her call and buy a higher strike; if the market falls, the hedger should sell his or her call and buy a lower strike.*

Return to the Japanese soybean importer and examine a situation where the importer rolls-down his or her hedge. In May, the importer bought an August 775 call for 17.5 cents per bushel with futures trading at 727.50 cents per bushel; the basis was 73.5 over. The maximum price and EHP were 866 and 710 cents per bushel, respectively. In June, August futures collapse to 662.50 cents per bushel and the 775 call is valued at 1.50 cents. The importer decides to sell the 775 call and roll down to the 725 call, which is worth 5 cents. The new minimum price and EHP are as follows:

Loss on 775 call = [1.50 − 17.5] = −16

Call Strike Price:	725.00	
Call Premium:	+5.00	
Loss on 775 Call:	+16.00	
Basis:	+73.50	
New Maximum Price:	819.50	Cents/Bushel

Futures Price:	662.50	
Call Premium:	−5.00	
Loss on 775 Call:	−16.00	
New EHP:	641.50	Cents/Bushel

This results in a more attractive maximum price, albeit a lower EHP. In early July, August soybeans make a resounding recovery to 744.50 cents per bushel as a June 31st stocks report indicates a much lower carry-over supply than previously thought. Furthermore, Brazilian farmers are not selling and ports there are congested; nearby export executions are difficult. The importer decides to price his or her requirements now rather than waiting until the end of the month when prices may be higher.

Since futures have rallied substantially, the 725 call is now valued at 39 cents per bushel; the importer books his or her cash at 73.5 over and sells the call for a profit of 34 cents. The final cash price paid for the soybeans is 800 cents per bushel:

August futures:	744.50	
Basis:	+73.50	
Loss on Long 775 Call:	+16.00	
Gain on Long 725 Call:	−34.00	
Final Cash Price:	800.00	vs. 801 Standard Hedge

In hindsight, the importer should have priced when futures were at 662.50 cents per bushel; however, the 800 price is just as good as the standard hedge price of 801 when futures were at 727.50 cents per bushel. It is also better than the 818 price that his or her unhedged competitors pay at 744.5 cents per bushel.

Quantifying the Roll-Up and Roll-Down Decision

In the previous examples, there was no reason given for rolling-up or rolling-down to one particular strike or another. Indeed, it is reasonable to ask whether the hedge should be rolled at all. A hedger must have some rationale for rolling the hedge and for choosing the new strike. After all, the outcome must suit risk preference and market outlook.

Specifically, the hedger must have tools that quantify the impact of rolling-up or rolling-down on minimum or maximum price and equivalent hedge price. Given a range of possible new strike prices and corresponding premiums, these tools will allow the hedger to perform a "what if" analysis in order to find what strike—if any—best suits his or her needs and market outlook.

This can be accomplished by examining the changes in the minimum or maximum price equations and in the EHP equation:

$$\Delta\text{Minimum\_Price} = [\Delta\text{Put\_Strike} - \Delta\text{Put\_Premium}]$$
$$\Delta\text{Maximum\_Price} = [\Delta\text{Call\_Strike} + \Delta\text{Call\_Premium}]$$

Note that the basis is assumed to be static. If that were not the case, another term would have to be added to the above equations to adjust for basis changes. This is not done here in order to simplify the examples. The changes in the minimum and maximum price EHP equations are as follows:

$$\Delta\text{Min\_Price\_EHP} = [\Delta\text{Futures\_Price} + \Delta\text{Put\_Premium}]$$
$$\Delta\text{Max\_Price\_EHP} = [\Delta\text{Futures\_Price} - \Delta\text{Call\_Premium}]$$

The change in the strike price and futures price is self-explanatory. The change in the put and call premium, respectively, follows:

$$\Delta\text{Put\_Premium} = [\text{Put\_Premium}_2 - \text{Put\_Premium}_1]$$
$$\Delta\text{Call\_Premium} = [\text{Call\_Premium}_2 - \text{Call\_Premium}_1], \text{ where}$$
$$\text{Premium}_1 = \text{Current value of the original option}$$
$$\text{Premium}_2 = \text{Current value of the new strike under consideration}$$

Note that option premiums are evaluated at the same point in time; that is, they are the premiums of the respective strikes at the time of the roll-up or roll-down. Some examples will help.

The corn producer from the previous example originally bought a 260 put with a premium of 17.25 cents. At that point, the minimum price was 222.75 cents per bushel and the EHP was 289.75 cents per bushel. Afterward, the futures price fell from 272.50 cents per bushel to 235 cents per bushel; the 260 put was then worth 32.5 cents. The producer rolled-down to a 240 put worth 18 cents. The change in put premium as defined above is

Put_Premium_2:	18.00
Put_Premium_1:	−32.50
$\Delta\text{Put\_Premium}$:	−14.50

The change in the strike price was −20 cents (240 − 260); thus, the change in the minimum price is,

ΔPut_Strike:	−20.00
ΔPut_Premium:	−(−14.50)
ΔMinimum_Price:	−5.50

The change in futures price was −37.50 (235 − 272.50), thus the change in EHP is,

ΔFutures_Price:	−37.50
ΔPut_Premium:	+(−14.50)
ΔMin_Price_EHP:	−52.00

Therefore, the new minimum price and the new EHP can be calculated as follows:

Old Minimum Price:	222.75	
ΔMinimum_Price:	−5.50	
New Minimum Price:	217.25	Cents/Bushel
Old EHP:	289.75	
ΔMin_Price_EHP:	−52.00	
New EHP:	237.75	Cents/Bushel

These are exactly the same numbers arrived at in the former example.

By utilizing the above equations, the corn producer can construct a table of different put strikes in order to choose the best roll-down alternative. For example, assume the producer wants to analyze the impact of the minimum price and the EHP for a roll-down to the 210, 220, 230, 240, and 250 put. Table 5–7 shows the relevant statistics.

The 240 put was chosen as the strike to roll-down to because it gave the producer an EHP just above the market (237.75 versus 235 cents per bushel), and this allowed the producer to quickly participate in price rallies. That was the original objective. Furthermore, it did not adversely affect the minimum price. Had the producer wanted to preserve the original minimum price, he or she should have used the 250 put; however, this did not give the producer an adequate EHP.

In short, the previous simple equations allow the hedger to anticipate the bottom-line impact of rolling-up or -down on the minimum or maximum price and the EHP. This allows the hedger to optimally adjust the hedge according to preferences and objectives.

TABLE 5–7 Effect of Rolling-Down from a 260 Put Valued at 32.5 Cents after Futures Collapse of 37.5 Cents; Original Minimum Price = 222.75; Original EHP = 289.75

Effect on Minimum Price:

Put	Premium	ΔPut_Strike	ΔPut_Prem	ΔMinimum_Price	New Minimum_ Price
210	3.00	−50	−29.50	−20.50	202.25
220	7.75	−40	−24.75	−15.25	207.50
230	12.00	−30	−20.50	−9.50	213.25
240	18.00	−20	−14.50	−5.50	217.25
250	23.50	−10	−9.00	−1.00	221.75

Effect on EHP:

Put	ΔFutures	ΔPut_Premium	ΔEHP	New EHP
210	−37.50	−29.50	−67.00	222.75
220	−37.50	−24.75	−62.25	227.50
230	−37.50	−20.50	−58.00	231.75
240	−37.50	−14.50	−52.00	237.75
250	−37.50	−9.00	−46.50	243.25

Options Hedging II: Combining the Standard Futures or Cash Hedge with Options to Create Minimum and Maximum Prices

If a producer or consumer has already locked in a fixed or flat-price through either a cash or futures hedge, he or she can still create a minimum or maximum price. This entails the purchase of a call in the producer's case, and the purchase of a put in the consumer's case.

Producer Example

In late May, November soybean futures have collapsed to 618 cents per bushel, and respected analysts are calling for a continued slide in prices to 550 to 580 cents per bushel. Faced with those prospects, a soybean producer decides (reluctantly) to sell the new crop soybeans to the local elevator. With the local basis at 30 under November futures, the producer receives a flat-price of 588 cents per bushel.

Two weeks later, November futures are trading at 633.50 cents per bushel, and the analysts have turned bullish because of a hot and dry weather forecast. They see the potential for a rally to 800. The producer wants a better price but cannot withdraw from the contractual agreement with the local elevator. What can the producer do?

The alternative here is to buy a call option, and the minimum price created is equal to the flat-price received in the cash sale less the maximum potential loss on the call, that is, the premium paid. Specifically, the formula for this type of minimum price hedge is as follows:

Minimum Price = [Futures_Price_Sold − Call_Prem + Basis]

In the example, the farmer sold flat-price cash, which was equivalent to selling November futures at 618 cents per bushel. Assume the farmer decides to buy a November 700 call for 16.5 cents. The minimum price created is as follows:

Futures Sold at:	618.00	
Call Premium:	−16.50	
Basis:	−30.00	
Minimum Price:	571.50	Cents/Bushel

This price is less than the farmer's original flat-price sale of 588; however, the farmer now has the potential to add to this price should the expected rally take place. Table 5–8 and Figure 5–11 show the possible outcomes at expiration.

The equivalent hedge price for this trade is the break-even point

TABLE 5–8 Buying a November 700 Soybean Call against a Flat-price Sale to Create a Minimum Price; Calls Bought at 16.5 Cents/Bushel; Cash Sold at 588 Cents/Bushel

(A) If Futures Are at:	(B) Profit/Loss Long 700 Calls:	(C) Cash Sold at:	(D) = (B) + (C) Final Price Is:
575	−16.5	588	571.5
600	−16.5	588	571.5
625	−16.5	588	571.5
650	−16.5	588	571.5
675	−16.5	588	571.5
700	−16.5	588	571.5
725	8.5	588	596.5
750	33.5	588	621.5
775	58.5	588	646.5
800	83.5	588	671.5
825	108.5	588	696.5

FIGURE 5–11

Buying Calls against a Flat–Price Sale to Create a Minimum Price

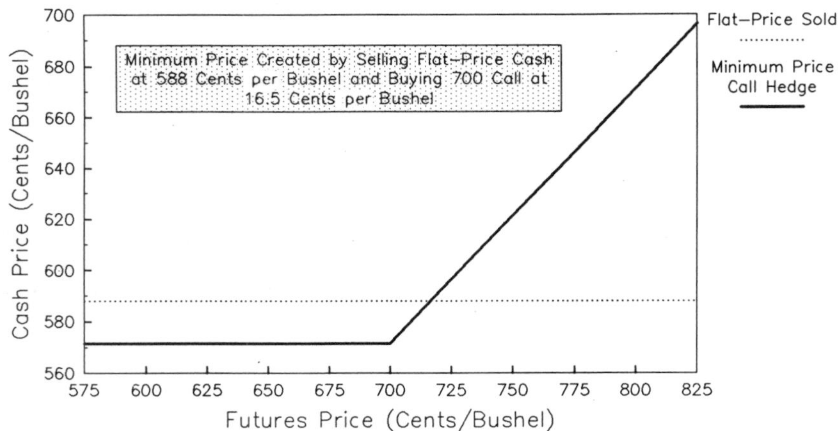

for the long 700 call, or 716.50 cents per bushel. At that price, the producer recoups the initial cost of the call and receives the standard hedge price of 588 cents per bushel. Therefore, the EHP calculation is as follows:

$$\text{EHP} = [\text{Call\_Breakeven}]$$

If the farmer wants to participate more actively in any rally, he or she should buy a lower-struck call. Of course, such a call is more expensive, and this will lower the minimum price. Conversely, if the farmer wants to maintain a reasonable minimum price, he or she should buy a higher-struck call as the premium is normally cheap.

Consumer Example

Assume the soybean importer from past examples bought at a flat-price of 801 cents per bushel (futures at 727.50 cents per bushel and a basis of 73.5 over). If prices fall after the hedge is placed, the importer is locked in and cannot price at a lower level. Nevertheless, if upon buying the soybeans the importer also purchased a put, he or she creates a maximum price equal to the flat-price plus the cost of the put:

$$\text{Maximum Price} = [\text{Futures\_Price\_Bought} + \text{Put\_Prem} + \text{Basis}]$$

In turn, the EHP is equal to the breakeven point on the put, or:

EHP = [Put_Breakeven]

The calculations for the maximum price and EHP are as follows:

Futures Bought at:	727.50	
Put Premium:	+31.00	
Basis:	+73.50	
Maximum Price:	832.00	Cents/Bushel
Put Strike:	725.00	
Put Premium:	−31.00	
EHP:	694.00	Cents/Bushel

Table 5–9 and Figure 5–12 show the possible outcomes at expiration if the importer buys a 725 put for 31 cents per bushel. As an aside, compare this maximum price hedge with the call maximum price in Options Hedging I: Creating Minimum and Maximum Prices: The maximum price is lower (832 versus 866), although the EHP is not as attractive.

Note that the near-the-money put offers more opportunity to benefit from lower prices since futures need only fall to 694 before a lower price is obtained. This is in contrast to the producer example, where purchasing low value gives low potential. The drawback for the importer is the higher premium that raises the maximum price[7].

TABLE 5–9 Buying August 725 Soybean Puts against a Cash Purchase to Create a Maximum Price; Puts Bought at 31 Cents/Bushel; Cash Bought at 801 Cents/Bushel

(A) If Futures Are at:	(B) Profit/Loss Long 725 Puts:	(C) Cash Sold at:	(D) = (B) − (C) Final Price Is:
525	169	801	632
550	144	801	657
575	119	801	682
600	94	801	707
625	69	801	732
650	44	801	757
675	19	801	782
700	−6	801	807
725	−31	801	832
750	−31	801	832
775	−31	801	832

7. See Appendix B, Section III, for the appropriate hedge management equations.

FIGURE 5–12

Buying Puts against a Flat–Price Purchase to Create a Maximum Price

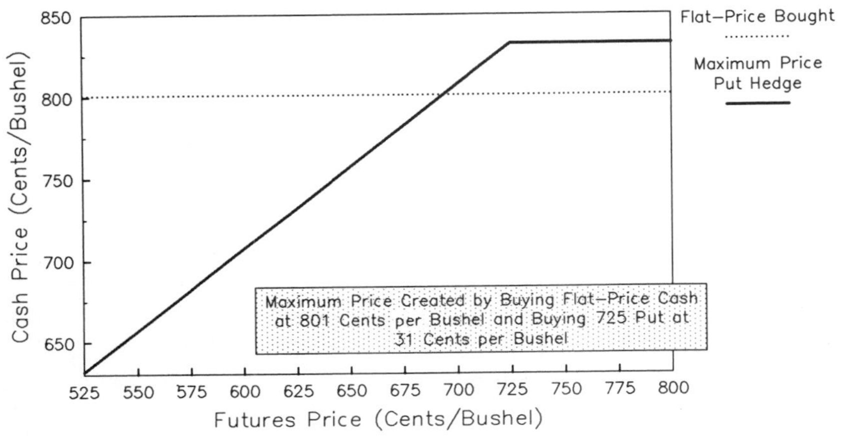

Options Hedging III: Writing Calls to Create Price Caps and Writing Puts to Create Price Floors

The option hedging strategies presented up to this point are appropriate when a hedger anticipates large and volatile price moves. Indeed, most of the examples given were within the context of some critical point in the crop cycle, for example, during the growing season or harvest period. But clearly there are market situations where these strategies are not appropriate. Specifically, if the hedger expects sideways price activity and low volatility, he or she should consider option writing strategies. For the producer or holder of physical commodities, this entails writing calls; for the consumer of commodities it entails writing puts.

In the producer's case, the call writing strategy creates a price cap. If prices are above the call strike the producer can be assigned a short futures position against a long position in the physical commodity. Therefore, above the call strike, the producer is locked into one price as in the standard futures hedge in Figure 5–1. But if the market is below the strike price, the producer keeps all the writing income, and this augments the final price. However, by definition, the value of the writing income is the maximum increment to the final price.

For the consumer, a put writing strategy creates a price floor. If prices are below the put strike price, the consumer can be assigned a long futures position against the short in the physical commodity. To that extent, the consumer is no different from the hedger in Figure 5–2 who buys futures against the cash short. Above the put strike, the consumer keeps all the writing income and this lowers the final price. But as prices continue to rise, the only cushion is the writing income.

It is important to understand that these tactics are not hedges in the traditional sense, and they offer neither the protection of the standard futures hedge nor the open-ended benefits of the minimum and maximum price option hedges. This is evident in that the producer is still vunerable to a large downside move in prices and the consumer is exposed to price rallies, while their maximum benefit is always capped or floored. Nonetheless, if these strategies are viewed within the context of stable markets, they are usually superior to other option hedges.

The Price Cap

A price cap is created by selling a call option. The cap is equal to the strike price of the call, plus the premium, plus the basis:

$$\text{Price\_Cap} = [\text{Call\_Strike} + \text{Call\_Premium} + \text{Basis}]$$

To illustrate, suppose a soybean processor needs to hedge the November soymeal production. The processor expects soymeal prices to trade in a band between 210 to 230 dollars per short ton. The processor believes there is good buying interest at 210 dollars per ton and good selling interest at 230 dollars per ton. In September, the processor decides to sell a December 220 call for 11.10 dollars with December futures trading at 221.90 dollars per ton. Assuming a basis of 5 over, the price cap created is as follows:

Strike Price:	220.00	
Call Premium:	+11.10	
Basis:	+5.00	
Price Cap:	236.10	Dollars/Ton

Table 5–10 shows the possible outcomes at expiration. Figure 5–13 compares the price cap strategy with the standard futures hedge and unhedged positions[8].

8. See Appendix B, Section IV, for the synthetic option calculation of the price cap.

TABLE 5–10 Writing December Soymeal 220 Calls against Cash Inventory; Calls Sold at 11.10 Dollars/Ton; Futures at 221.90 Dollars/Ton

(A) If Futures Are at:	(B) Basis at:	(C) + (A) + (B) Cash at:	(D) Profit/Loss on Short 220 Calls:	(E) = (C) + (D) Final Price Is:
190	5	195	11.10	206.10
195	5	200	11.10	211.10
200	5	205	11.10	216.10
205	5	210	11.10	221.10
210	5	215	11.10	226.10
215	5	220	11.10	231.10
220	5	225	11.10	236.10
225	5	230	6.10	236.10
230	5	235	1.10	236.10
235	5	240	−3.90	236.10
240	5	245	−8.90	236.10

FIGURE 5–13

Creating a Price Cap by Selling Calls against Cash Inventory
Price Cap = 236.10 Dollars per Short Ton

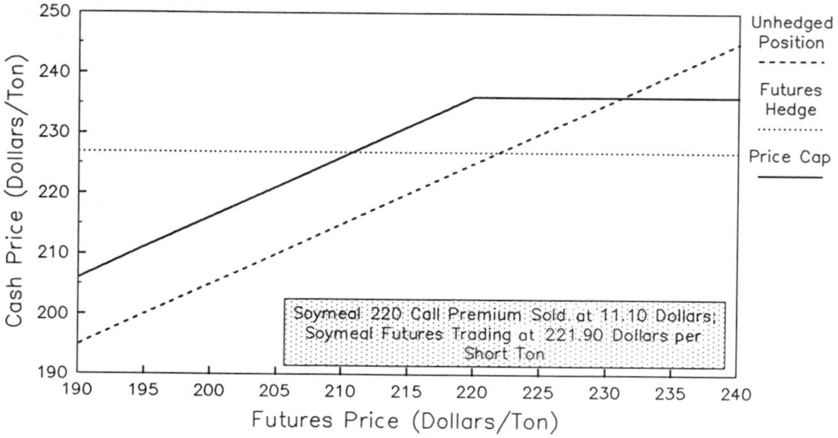

From Figure 5–13, the price cap strategy clearly outperforms the standard futures hedge and the unhedged position between the futures price ranges predicted by the processor (that is, 210 and 230). The equivalent hedge price—the futures price at which the processor has done no better than selling futures at the current level of 221.90—can be calculated with the following formula:

EHP = [Futures_Price − Call_Premium]

Futures Price:	221.90	
Call Premium:	−11.10	
EHP:	210.80	Dollars/Ton

In the price cap strategy, the EHP provides a check against the processor's downside price target of 210 dollars per ton. The upside selling target of 230 dollars per ton is more than satisfied by the price cap at 236.10.

Notice that the processor sold an at-the-money call. A more aggressive strategy would be to write an out-of-the-money call, while the least aggressive approach is to write an in-the-money call. Figure 5–14 shows the effect on the synthetic put EHP's and the price cap as the strategy changes from writing an in-the-money to an out-of-the-money call. The more aggressive the strategy, the higher the price cap and the higher the EHP.

FIGURE 5–14

Comparison of Price Cap Strategies Using 210, 220, and 230 Calls
Futures at 221.90 Dollars per Ton

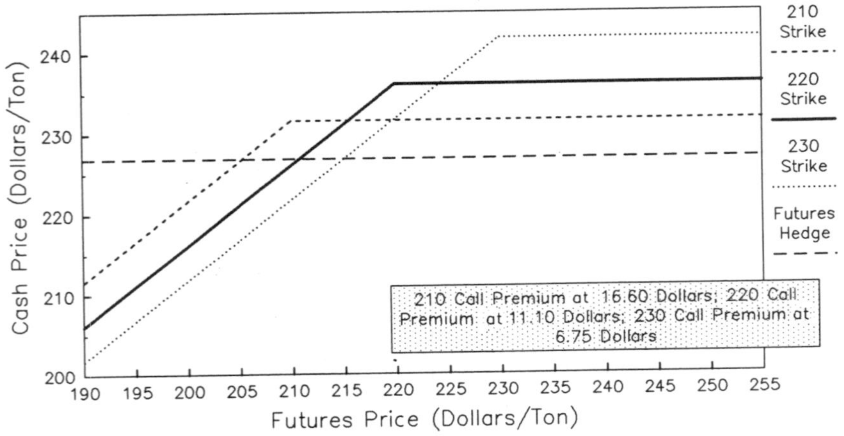

The Price Floor

A price floor is created by selling a put option. The floor is equal to the strike price of the put, less the premium, plus the basis:

Price_Floor = [Put_Strike − Put_Premium + Basis]

Consider a food processor who needs to buy soybean oil to meet June ingredient requirements. In the beginning of May, July soyoil futures are trading at 23.70 cents per pound, and the processor believes that soyoil is fairly priced, given all known fundamental information in the market. At most, the processor believes prices will fluctuate by +/− .50 cents (between 23.20 and 24.20), but he or she has no bias either way. With the basis at .10 cents under futures, the processor decides to sell a 23-cent put valued at .50 cents. The price floor created is

Put Strike:	23.00	
Put Premium:	−00.50	
Basis:	−00.10	
Price Floor:	22.40	Cents/Pound

The processor's equivalent hedge price is equal to the futures price he or she can buy now plus the income from the put premium:

EHP = [Futures_Price + Put_Premium]

Futures Price:	23.70	
Put Premium:	+00.50	
EHP:	24.20	Cents/Pound

Thus, at 24.20 the processor has done no better than the standard futures hedge. Table 5–11 and Figure 5–15 show the results of the price floor at expiration.

As in previous examples, one can view the price floor as a synthetic strategy. Selling puts against a short in the physical commodity is equivalent to a synthetic short call.[9] Again, this is useful in order to understand how the price floor of 22.40 cents per pound and the EHP of 24.20 are formulated; it also gives an indication of how aggressive the strategy is.

For example, the above strategy is aggressive in the sense that the processor is essentially writing an in-the-money synthetic call. As

9. See Appendix B, Section V, for the synthetic option calculation of the price floor.

TABLE 5–11 Writing July Soyoil 23 Puts against Cash Inventory; Puts Sold at .50 Cents/Pound; Futures at 23.70 Cents/Pound

(A) If Futures Are at	(B) Basis at:	(C) = (A) + (B) Cash at:	(D) Profit/Loss on Short 23 Puts:	(E) = (C) − (D) Final Price Is:
20.00	−0.10	19.90	−2.50	22.40
20.50	−0.10	20.40	−2.00	22.40
21.00	−0.10	20.90	−1.50	22.40
21.50	−0.10	21.40	−1.00	22.40
22.00	−0.10	21.90	−0.50	22.40
22.50	−0.10	22.40	0.00	22.40
23.00	−0.10	22.90	0.50	22.40
23.50	−0.10	23.40	0.50	22.90
24.00	−0.10	23.90	0.50	23.40
24.50	−0.10	24.40	0.50	23.90
25.00	−0.10	24.90	0.50	24.40

FIGURE 5–15

Creating a Price Floor by Selling Puts against Cash Requirements
Price Floor = 22.40 Cents per Pound

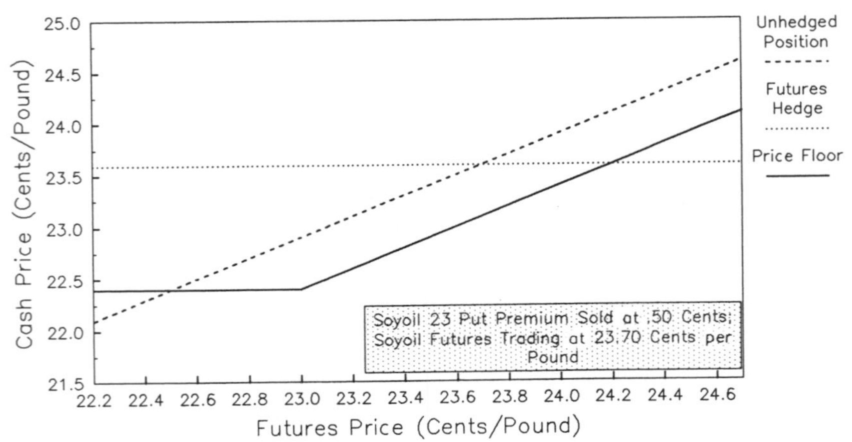

such, it gives the processor more of a buffer on the downside than the original price projections called for, although the EHP exactly meets the upside price expectations. If the processor's market assessment proves correct, the price floor will be superior to the standard futures hedge and the unhedged position.

Figure 5–16 shows the effect of changing the strike price on the floor strategy. If uncomfortable with the upside break-even (the EHP), the processor could sell an in-the-money put. As the short put is moved from out-of-the-money to in-the-money, the EHP increases. In turn, the drawback is that the price floor also increases.[10]

Quantity and Basis Risk in Price Caps and Price Floors

In the price cap and price floor strategy, quantity and basis risk are present only when the futures price is above the strike price of the call or below the strike price of the put, since that is where the hedger runs the risk of being assigned a futures position. As a corollary, margin calls will be a problem if the market moves against the hedger. Contrast this with the long option hedger who pays only for the initial premium.

In the most common example, a farmer is subject to quantity risk when selling the crop before a sharp weather-related price rally. In the extreme, detrimental weather will cause a total loss of the

FIGURE 5–16

Comparison of Price Floor Strategies Using 22, 23, and 24 Puts
Futures at 23.70 Cents per Pound

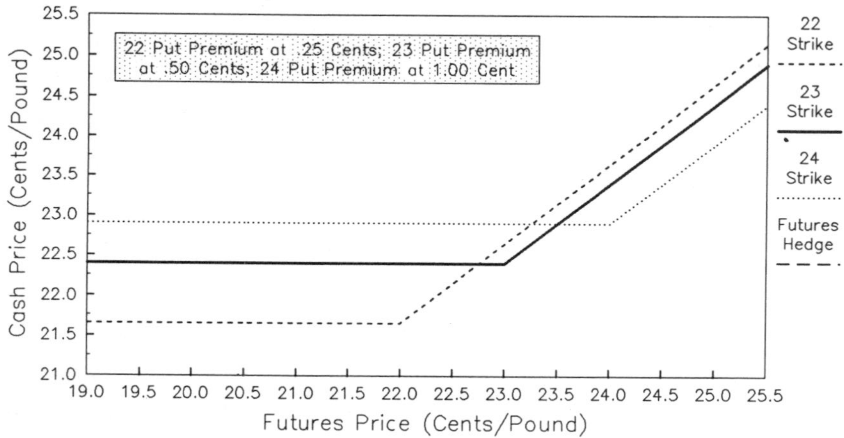

10. Readers interested in the hedge management aspects of the price cap and floor are referred to Appendix B, Section VI.

crop. Therefore, it is obvious that under those circumstances, the minimum price hedge is superior to the price cap.

Options Hedging IV: Buying and Selling Options to Create Price Fences and Price Windows

The problem with the minimum and maximum price hedging strategies is the high cost of the option premium. Two solutions were introduced: (1) Buy a different strike, or (2) Buy an option with less time value. The first solution always generates a corresponding negative outcome; for example, in the producer's case a higher-struck put raises the minimum price but increases the EHP. The second alternative provides only a narrow time horizon; accordingly, it forces the hedger to continually roll forward the hedge, which incurs higher transactions costs and increases the possibility of futures spread risk.

But there is a third alternative. In order to finance the purchase of an option, the hedger can sell an option. For example, if the hedger buys a put he or she can sell a call and vice versa. The option sold is usually in the same class (same expiration date) as the option bought.

These hedges are really combinations of minimum price hedges and price caps, or maximum price hedges and price floors. The former is referred to here as a **fence**, while the latter is called a **window**. As such, a producer long the cash commodity can create a fence by buying a put and selling a call at a higher strike; a consumer short the cash commodity creates a window by buying a call and selling a put at a lower strike.

In these strategies, a minimum or maximum price is guaranteed without locking out a better price, but only up to a certain point. That point is the strike price of the option sold; beyond that point a cap or floor is created. The fence or window is especially powerful when the hedger wants to subtract one degree of conviction from the market outlook. The hedger may be bullish or bearish but only up to a certain price level. Thus, at that level the hedger sells an option with the closest strike, while maintaining a minimum or maximum price. The simultaneous purchase and sale will result in either a debit or credit depending, of course, on the premiums and the strikes used.

The Option Fence

The fence is created by buying a put and selling an upper strike call. The result is a combination of a minimum price and a price cap:

Minimum Price = [Put_Strike + (Credit or Debit) + Basis]
Price Cap = [Call_Strike + (Credit or Debit) + Basis]

Again, between the minimum price and the price cap, the producer's price schedule is similar to that of an unhedged position. To illustrate, consider the soybean producer. Originally, the producer created a minimum price by buying a November 700 put for 35 cents, which gave a minimum price of 635 cents per bushel given a basis of 30 cents under futures. Now the added assumption is made that the producer believes that November soybeans will not surpass the 800 cent per bushel level; hence, the producer sells a November 800 call for 36 cents per bushel in order to reduce the cost of the 700 put. The minimum price and price cap created are as follows:

Sell 800 Call:	+36.00	
Buy 700 Put:	−35.00	
Net Credit:	+1.00	
Put Strike Price:	700.00	
Credit:	+1.00	
Basis:	−30.00	
Minimum Price:	671.00	Cents/Bushel
Call Strike:	800.00	
Credit:	+1.00	
Basis:	−30.00	
Price Cap:	771.00	Cents/Bushel

Again, the result is to increase the minimum price from 635 to 671 via a reduction in the put cost; however, upside benefits are now capped at 771.00. Table 5–12 and Figure 5–17 compare the option fence with the standard futures hedge and the unhedged position at expiration over different futures prices.

Figure 5–17 and Table 5–12 show that the option fence allows the producer to participate in futures price rallies between 700 cents per bushel and 800 cents per bushel; to that extent, the fence is identical to the unhedged position except for the 1 cent credit. But since futures are at 743.25 when the fence is initiated, the only profitable participation is between 742.25 and 800 cents per bushel. Below 742.25, the hedger has done no better than the standard futures hedge. Accordingly, the EHP of the fence is as follows:

TABLE 5–12 Creating a November 700/800 Fence to Hedge a Cash Long; Put Bought at 35 Cents/Bushel; Call Sold at 36 Cents/Bushel; Futures at 743.25 Cents/Bushel

(A) If Futures Are at:	(B) Basis at:	(C) = (A) + (B) Cash at:	(D) Profit/Loss Long 700 Put	(E) Profit/Loss Short 800 Call	(F) = (C) + (D) + (E) Final Price
625	−30	595	40	36	671
650	−30	620	15	36	671
675	−30	645	−10	36	671
700	−30	670	−35	36	671
725	−30	695	−35	36	696
750	−30	720	−35	36	721
775	−30	745	−35	36	746
800	−30	770	−35	36	771
825	−30	795	−35	11	771
850	−30	820	−35	−14	771
875	−30	845	−35	−39	771

FIGURE 5–17

Comparison of Option Fence Strategy with Futures Hedge and Unhedged Positions

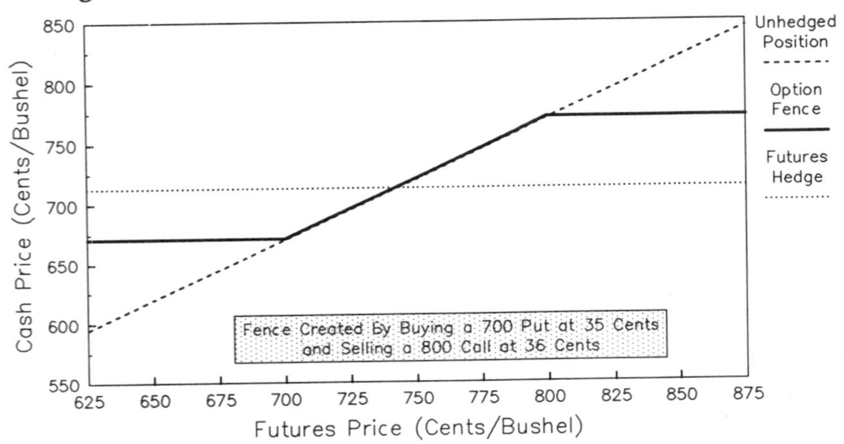

Fence EHP = [Futures_Price − (Credit or Debit)]

Futures Price:	743.25	
Credit:	−1.00	
EHP:	742.25	Cents/Bushel

Below the EHP the option fence is inferior to the standard futures hedge. Again, if the producer is decidedly bearish he or she should not bother with any option hedge but should sell cash or futures. The fence is only useful within the context of the producer's market outlook, that is, bullish from 742.25 to 800 cents per bushel. Above 800, the unhedged position is superior.

Figure 5–18 compares the fence with the regular minimum price and price cap strategies. The graph shows that the fence provides a more attractive minimum price albeit a lower cap; this is appropriate for a slightly bullish outlook. The minimum price hedge is the most bullish option strategy since prices must rise substantially before the hedge outperforms the fence or cap. The price cap takes a neutral to slightly bullish stance; this strategy is optimal only if the producer foresees no major price collapse. To summarize, the option fence allows the producer to subtract one degree of conviction from a bullish outlook by raising the minimum price while maintaining some potential upside participation.

FIGURE 5–18

Comparison of Option Fence Strategy with Minimum Price Hedge and Price Cap

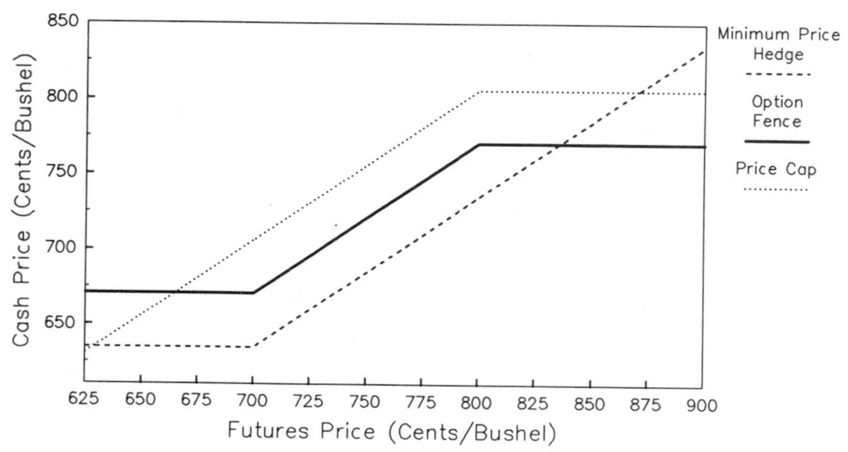

The Option Window

The window is created by buying a call and selling a put with a lower strike. The result is a maximum price and a price floor:

Maximum Price = [Call_Strike − (Credit or Debit) + Basis]
Price Floor = [Put_strike − (Credit or Debit) + Basis]

The option window serves two purposes: (1) A maximum price is set, and the consumer defrays the cost of the call option via a put sale, (2) It lets the consumer participate in any price break up to the price floor; the price floor is chosen according to the consumer's market expectations.

The Japanese soybean importer provides a good illustration. In the original example, the importer bought an out-of-the-money 775 call for 17.5 cents with futures at 727.50 cents per bushel. The maximum price and EHP were 866 and 710 cents per bushel, respectively. The relatively cheap out-of-the-money call allowed the importer to quickly take advantage of price breaks; however, if the importer expected strong market support at 650 cents per bushel, he or she could simultaneously sell a 650 put priced at 8 cents. The result is as follows:

Sell 650 Put:	+8.00	
Buy 775 Call:	−17.50	
Net Debit:	−9.50	
Call Strike:	775.00	
Debit:	−(−9.50)	
Basis:	+73.50	
Maximum Price:	858.00	Cents/Bushel
Put Strike:	650.00	
Debit:	−(−9.50)	
Basis:	+73.50	
Price Floor:	733.00	Cents/Bushel

Table 5–13 and Figure 5–19 compare the option window with the standard futures hedge and the unhedged position at expiration over different futures prices.

Similar to the fence strategy, the option window behaves like the unhedged position between the strikes of the options used; the only difference is the debit of 9.5 cents. Nevertheless, the only meaningful range for the consumer is between 650 cents per bushel and

TABLE 5–13 Creating an August 650/775 Window to Hedge a Cash Short; Call Bought at 17.5 Cents/Bushel; Put Sold at 8 Cents/Bushel; Futures at 727.50 Cents/Bushel

(A) If Futures Are at:	(B) Basis at:	(C) = (A) + (B) Cash at:	(D) Profit/Loss Long 775 Call	(E) Profit/Loss Short 650 Put	(F) (C) + (D) + (E) Final Price
600	73.5	673.5	−17.5	−42	733
625	73.5	698.5	−17.5	−17	733
650	73.5	723.5	−17.5	8	733
675	73.5	748.5	−17.5	8	758
700	73.5	773.5	−17.5	8	783
725	73.5	798.5	−17.5	8	808
750	73.5	823.5	−17.5	8	833
775	73.5	848.5	−17.5	8	858
800	73.5	873.5	7.5	8	858
825	73.5	898.5	32.5	8	858
850	73.5	923.5	57.5	8	858

718 cents per bushel since that is where the consumer can receive a lower price vis-à-vis the standard futures hedge. Accordingly, the EHP of the option window is as follows:

FIGURE 5–19

Comparison of Option Window Strategy with Futures Hedge and Unhedged Positions

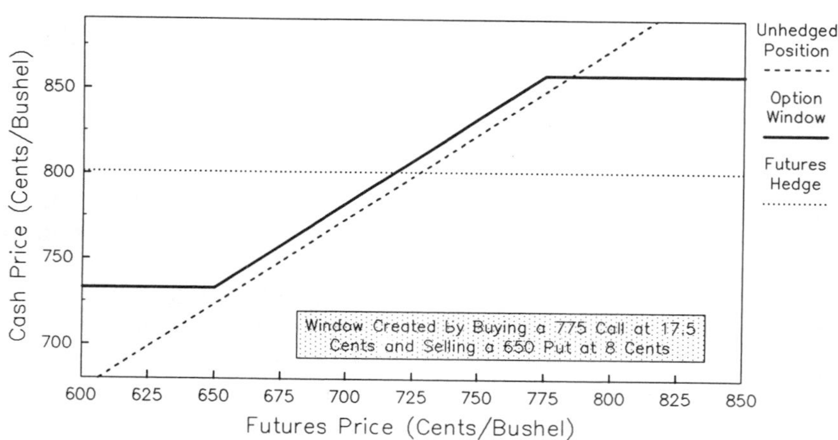

FIGURE 5–20

Comparison of Option Window Strategy with Maximum Price Hedge and Price Floor

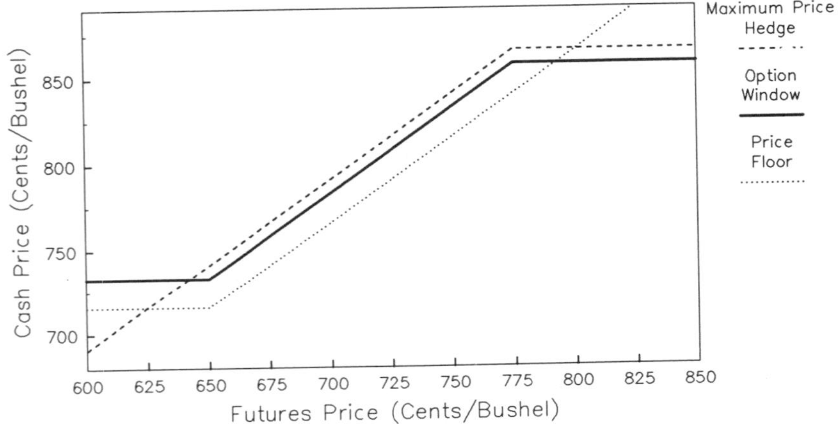

Window EHP = [Futures_Price + (Credit or Debit)]

Futures Price:	727.50	
Debit:	−9.50	
EHP:	718.00	Cents/Bushel

Below 718 cents per bushel, the window is superior to the standard futures hedge but inferior to the unhedged position (see Figure 5–19). This is due to the 9.5 cent debit. The debit is the price the importer pays for the right to receive a maximum price if futures rise or a lower price if futures fall. Above 718 cents per bushel, the unhedged position is superior to the window. However, both the window and the unhedged position are inferior to the standard futures hedge above 727.50.

Figure 5–20 compares the three consumer option strategies: the maximum price, the price floor, and the window. The maximum price hedge is the most bearish strategy since prices must fall substantially before the hedge is superior to the window or floor. The price floor is neutral to bearish; it offers the lowest price within the expected price range but no upside buffer. Again, the benefit of the window is that it reduces the cost of the maximum price hedge and puts a definite ceiling on prices if the importer proves wrong in his or her bearish outlook, but it allows some participation in falling prices should the importer prove correct.[11]

11. Readers interested in the hedge management aspects of price fences and windows are referred to Appendix B, Section VII.

Comparing Different Option Hedge Strategies

Given a set of price objectives and risk preferences, a hedger must decide which option strategy best suits the marketing plan and risk profile. The tools for that analysis have already been presented; it only remains to summarize the proceedure with a final example.

The soybean importer was faced with a fundamentally bearish market, but with the outside possibility that supply aberrations could lead to a substantial rally. The importer's bearishness was limited, however, to the 650 cents per bushel level (the current market is at 727.50 cents per bushel). On the other hand, the importer has no idea what the upside price potential is; he or she only wants to be protected in the event of a major price surge.

Hence, with a slight bear bias, the importer decides to take a less aggressive stance in selecting the call and put. For the analysis, the importer choses the out-of-the-money 775 call and the out-of-the-money 650 put. The prices of the 775 call and 650 put are 17.50 cents per bushel and 8 cents per bushel, respectively. The results of integrating the options into the different hedge strategies are presented in Table 5–14. Along the top of Table 5–14 are the possible futures prices at expiration. Below each futures price is the corresponding cash price resulting from the hedge strategy employed in the first column. The second column lists the EHP of the hedge.

The table suggests that the option window best suits the importer's objectives and risk profile. It gives the greatest ability to buy at a lower price up to the downside limit of 650, and the quick potential to do so with an EHP of 718. It also provides a maximum price of 858 if prices explode.

Granted, the price floor is superior at the lower range (625–700), and it has an excellent EHP, but it provides no upside insurance. The maximum price strategy with calls is attractive but expensive; it is only superior at much lower levels that are outside the range of predicted possibilities. Finally, the maximum price with puts is suboptimal because no benefit is obtained until the 650 put is in-the-money; again, that only occurs outside the predicted lower range of prices. A higher-struck put could have been purchased, but there is a trade-off due to the higher cost of the premium and a higher maximum price. There is also a greater cash outlay for the put purchase. The window provides the same protection as buying a higher-struck put with the added benefit of a smaller cash outlay.

Table 5–15 is a quick reference to the individual hedge strategies; it can also be used to roughly compare among strategies. Precise comparisons are best obtained by creating a spreadsheet template that integrates all the relevant formulas.

TABLE 5–14 Finding the Optimal Hedge for a Soybean Importer

Hedge Strategy	Futures Equivalent	Futures Prices at Expiration:	600	625	650	675	700	(*) 725	750	775	800	825	850
1) Futures/cash	728	CASH	801	801	801	801	801	801	801	801	801	801	801
2) Maximum price with Calls	710		691	716	741	766	791	816	841	866	866	866	866
3) Maximum price with Puts	642	PRICE	759	784	809	809	809	809	809	809	809	809	809
4) Price floors	736		716	716	716	741	766	791	816	841	866	891	916
5) Window	718		733	733	733	758	783	808	833	858	858	858	858

(*) = Level at Time of Decision/Implementation

Parameters	Strike	Premium
Call	775	17.50
Put	650	8.00
Futures		727.50
Basis		73.50
Flat-Price Cash		801

TABLE 5–15*

Creating Minimum and Maximum Prices

Cash Position	Strategy	Min/Max Price	Equivalent Hedge Price	Final Price	Advantage	Disadvantage	Follow-up
Long	Buy Put	Min_Price = Strike Strike – Prem + Basis Min_Price @ < = Put_Stk	Equivalent_ Hedge_ Price = Futures_ Price + Prem	Final_Price = Futs_Price + Basis + Put Profit or – Put Loss Max loss on Put = premium Max profit on Put = max [Stk-Futs – Prem,0]	Guarantees minimum; does not lock-out higher prices No margin funds required	Premium cost high if expiration far and volatility high	Market higher: Sell Put, roll-up strike, or sell futures and keep put Market lower: Sell Put, roll-down strike
Short	Buy Call	Max_price = Strike + Prem + Basis	Equivalent_ Hedge_ Price = Standard_ Hedge_ Price – Prem	Final Price = Futs_ Price + Basis – Call Profit or + Call loss Max loss on Call =	Guarantees Maximum; does not lock-out lower prices No margin funds required	Premium cost high if expiration far and volatility high	Market higher: Sell Call, roll-up strike Market lower: Sell Call, roll-down strike, or

		Max_Price @ > = Call_Stk		premium Max profit on Call = max [Futs-Stk − Prem,0]			buy futures and keep call

Combining Futures or Forward Contracting with Options to Create Min/Max Prices

Cash Position	Strategy	Min/Max Price	Equivalent Hedge Price	Final Price	Advantage	Disadvantage	Follow-up
Long	Sell Futures or Cash & Buy Calls	Min_Price = Futures_ Price_ Sold − Prem + Basis Min_Price @ < = Call_Stk	Equivalent_ Hedge_ Price = Stk + Prem	Final_Price = Futs_Price_ Sold + Basis + + Call Profit or − Call Loss Max loss on Call = premium Max profit on Call = max [Futs-Stk − Prem,0]	Higher min price than put strategy Reduced margin cost Guarantees minimum; does not lock-out higher prices	Premium cost offers less upside price potential than with Put strategy	Market higher: Sell Call, roll-up strike Market lower: Sell Call, roll-down strike

(*continued*)

TABLE 5–15* *(continued)*

Cash Position	Strategy	Min/Max Price	Equivalent Hedge Price	Final Price	Advantage	Disadvantage	Follow-up
Combining Futures or Forward Contracting with Options to Create Min/Max Prices							
Short	Buy Futures or Cash and Buy Puts	Max_Price = Futures_Price_Bought + Prem + Basis Max_Price @ > – Put_Stk	Equivalent_Hedge_Price = Stk – Prem	Final_Price = Futs_Price_Bought + Basis – Put Profit, or + Put Loss Max loss on Put = premium Max profit on Put = max [Futs-Stk – Prem,0]	Lower max price than call strategy Reduced margin cost Guarantees maximum; does not lock-out lower prices	Premium cost offers less downside price potential than with call strategy	Market higher: Sell Put roll-up strike Market lower: Sell Put roll-down strike
Creating Price Caps and Floors by Selling Options							
Cash Position	**Strategy**	**Min/Max Price**	**Equivalent Hedge Price**	**Final Price**	**Advantage**	**Disadvantage**	**Follow-up**
Long	Sell calls against cash inventory	Price_Cap = Call_Strike + Prem + Basis	Equivalent_Hedge_Price Futures_Price –	Final_Price = Futs_Price + Basis	Earn time decay in a steady to lower market	Places a price cap on upside potential Margin	Market higher: Buy-Back Call, Roll-Up

		Price_Cap @ > = Call_ Strike	Prem	+ Call Profit or − Call Loss Max loss on Call = max [Futs-Stk − Prem,0] Max profit on Call = prem	Possibility of being assigned short futures position	requirement on short Calls If prices decline only buffer is Call premium	Market lower: Buy-Back Call, Roll-Down
Short	Sell Puts against cash needs	Price_Floor = Put_Strike − Prem + Basis Price_Floor @ < = Put_ Strike	Equivalent_ Hedge_ Price = Futures_ Price + Prem	Final_Price = Futs_Price + Basis − Put Profit, or + Put Loss Max profit on Put = prem Max loss on Put = max [Stk-Futs − Prem,0]	Earn time decay in a steady to higher market Possibility of being assigned long futures position	Places a price floor on downside potential Margin requirement on short Puts If prices rise only buffer is Put premium	Market higher: Buy-Back Put, Roll-Up Market lower: Buy-Back Put, Roll-Down

(*continued*)

TABLE 5–15 *(continued)*

Creating Price Windows and Fences							
Cash Position	**Strategy**	**Min/Max Price**	**Equivalent Hedge Price**	**Final Price**	**Advantage**	**Disadvantage**	**Follow-up**
Long	Fence Buy Put and Sell Call at Higher Strike	Min_Price = Put_ Strike + Credit, or Debit + Basis Price_Cap = Call_ Strike + Credit, or Debit + Basis Min_Price @ < = Put_ Strike Max_Price @ > = Call_ Strike	Equivalent_ Hedge_ Price = Futures_ Price − Credit, or Debit	Final Price = Futs_Price + Basis + Credit, or Debit (Between Min and Max Prices)	Reduces cost of Put Higher Min_Price than with naked long Put	Places price cap on upside potential Margin requirement on short calls Possibility of being assigned short futures position	Market higher: Sell Put, roll-up strike Buy-back Call, Roll-up strike Market lower: Sell Put, Roll-down strike Buy-back Call, roll-down

Short	Window Buy Call and Sell Put at Lower Strike	Max_Price = Call_ Strike − Credit, or Debit + Basis Price_Floor = Put_ Strike − Credit, or Debit + Basis Max_Price @ > = Call_ Strike Min_Price @ < = Put_ Strike	Equivalent_ Hedge_ Price = Futures_ Price + Credit, or Debit	Final Price = Futs_Price + Basis + Credit, or Debit (Between Min and Max Prices)	Reduces cost of Call Lower Max_ Price than with naked long Call	Places price floor on downside potential Margin requirement on short Puts Possibility of being assigned long futures position	Market higher: Sell Call, roll-up strike Buy-back Put roll-up strike Market lower: Buy-back Put, roll-down Sell Call, roll-down strike

Chapter 6

Case Studies of Option Trades

The following case studies demonstrate the major factors in trading agricultural options, that is, price, time, and volatility; however, volatility is emphasized in particular. Volatility risk is a recurring theme in options trading simply because it is unique to options. Time decay risk is also unique to options, but this is more of a known risk as time only moves in one direction. There is one exception to the preponderance of volatility: gamma. Gamma is a flat price risk that futures traders do not have to deal with because the gamma of a futures contract is always zero. Therefore, aspects of gamma risk will also be shown where appropriate.

Note that the purpose of each case study is to analyze how the profit/loss of each trade unfolded under the market conditions present at the time. By no means are these case studies meant to be detailed outlines of trades for future replication. Rather, they should be used as analogies from which traders may gain some insight into current or future trading situations.

Four cases are analyzed: (a) covered call writing for income, (b) vertical call ratio spread, (c) writing puts for income, and (d) long call strategies. Note that the cases involve very rudimentary strategies. This is because simple strategies convey option risk and reward more fully, and complicated strategies are generally variations of the simple ones.

CASE I: *Writing Covered Calls for Income*

March Call Writing Program: Position initiated on January 4th, 1988, and held to expiration on February 19th, 1988.

Background

With 46 calendar days to expiration and March 88 soybean futures trading at 625 cents per bushel, March 88 soybean calls were written at the following strikes: 575, 600, 650, and 675 for premiums of 55, 35, 12.5, and 7.5 cents, respectively. At each of these strikes, 100 calls were sold, except for the 650s and 675s where the short was increased to 200 and 175 contracts, respectively. The reader can calculate that the extrinsic or time values of the above premiums were 5, 10, 12.5, and 7.5 cents, for a total value of $265,625.

A long futures position was maintained against the short calls as a hedge; for example, the futures were adjusted daily in order to maintain an approximate delta neutral position. The details of the futures trading are not important. It suffices to say that the trader bought and sold futures near the close of each session to keep the position more or less delta neutral. The real purpose here is to focus on the accumulated profit/loss of the options position.

Market Environment

Figure 6–1 shows that the intra-day fluctuations of the March 88 futures were great. Nevertheless, on a close-only basis, March 88 futures traded in a forty-cent range over the course of two months. For soybeans, this cannot be considered a terribly volatile market.

This conclusion is reinforced by Figure 6–2, which plots both historical and implied volatility. Historical volatility peaked in mid-January at 20 percent and trended downward to a low of 15 percent. Conversely, the implied volatility of the position bottomed in mid-January at 18 percent and trended higher to 26 percent. (Implied volatility of the position was calculated by taking the average implied volatility of each call option weighted by the number of contracts at each strike. The rise in volatility towards the end of expiration is exaggerated due to the out-of-the-money options that tend to be valued at a much higher volatility as expiration approaches.)

Two points can be drawn from Figure 6–2: (a) Implied volatility

FIGURE 6–1

Case Study I: March 88 Soybeans

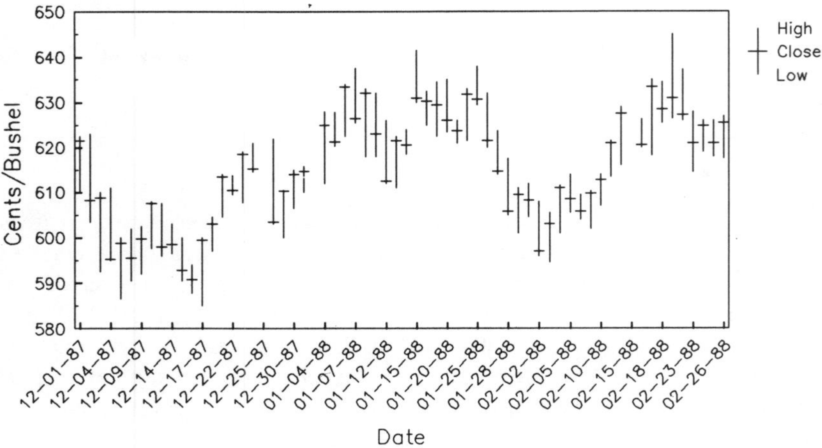

FIGURE 6–2

Case Study I: Implied Volatility of Position versus Historical Volatility

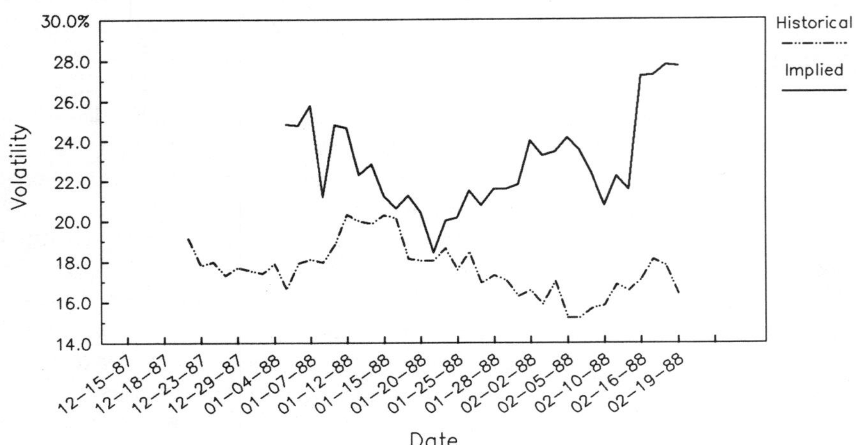

FIGURE 6–3

Case Study I: Accumulated Profit/Loss of Position versus Futures Price

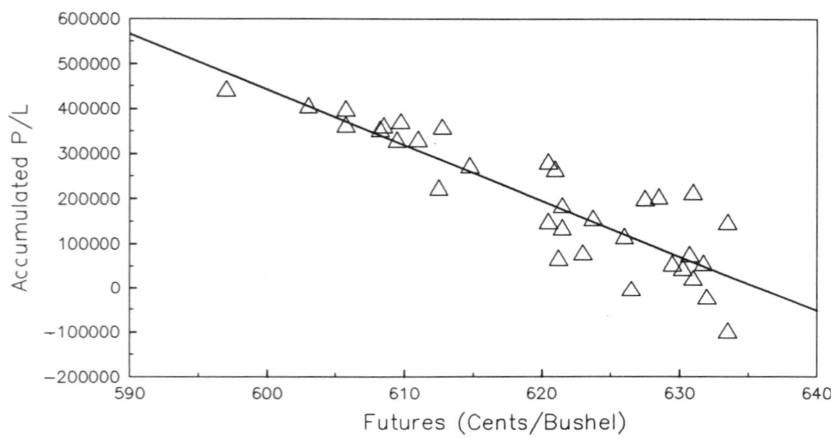

traded in a relatively narrow band, and (b) There was a clear divergence between the behavior of implied and historical volatility.

Figure 6–3 shows that there was clearly a relationship between flat price and profit. Since short calls have negative deltas the position makes money as the market moves lower. Surely, on a delta basis, more profit would have been earned if the futures had moved even lower over the course of the trade (as Figure 6–3 clearly demonstrates); conversely, a loss would have been sustained if the market had moved sharply higher.

Nonetheless, this does not mean the position profited only when the futures market moved lower; in fact, the market actually closed 6 cents higher than the entry point of the trade and a profit of $209,844 was still earned at expiration. The entire $265,625 of time value was not earned due to the futures price rise of 6 cents. The long futures position held against the short calls was able to make up for $4,900 of the difference. However, $50,881 of time value was lost due to slippage, that is, imperfect hedging. (This will be discussed further below with regard to gamma).

Conclusions

It can be concluded from Figures 6–1 through 6–3 that a relatively flat futures market was translated into low and stable historical volatility. But call option implied volatility was bid up by the market with the expectation that futures would rise and become more volatile. When that did not materialize the option premiums were ipso facto over-valued, and the trader short the premiums earned a good portion of the time (extrinsic) value of the option.

This is further emphasized in Figure 6–4. For the most part, implied volatility moved in narrow band from 20 to 26 percent; that is, on a day-to-day basis, decreases in implied volatility netted-out increases so that volatility fluctuations did not impinge on accumulated profit per se. For example, from the graph there is no clear statistical correlation between the range of implied volatility and accumulated profit. In turn, this allowed time value to accrue as a profit by expiration as shown in Figure 6–5.

There is also a statistical way to explain the success of this trade. The average implied volatility over the period in question was approximately 22 percent. Volatility of 22 percent over 256 trading days calculates to 9 percent volatility over 46 trading days, or, $(22\%)/\sqrt{(256/46)}$. If futures were at 625 cents per bushel when the trade was initiated, the implied 46-day trading range was 625 ± 58 cents (625 • .09 = 58), or between 567 to 683 cents per bushel. The actual market range, however, was 590 to 640. In effect, the same conclusion has been reached. The trader correctly anticipated the future market range vis-à-vis other market participants; the reward received was $209,844 of writing income.

Finally, Figure 6–6 conveys the relation between the delta equiv-

FIGURE 6–4

Case Study I: Accumulated Profit/Loss of Position versus Implied Volatility

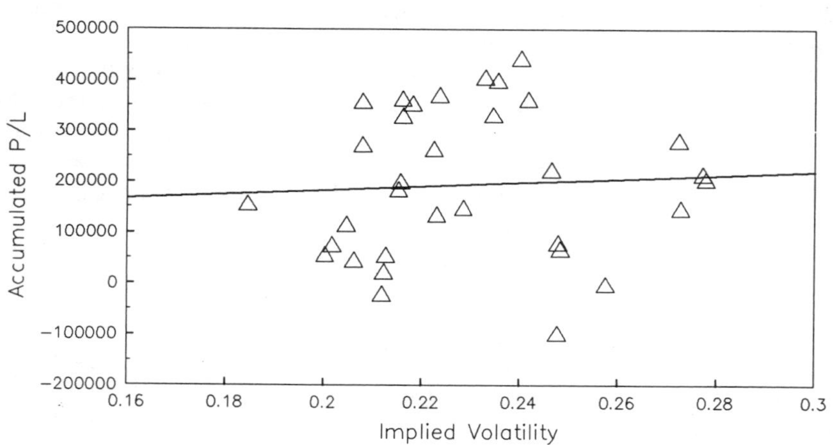

FIGURE 6–5

Case Study I: Accumulated Profit/Loss of Position versus Days to Expiration

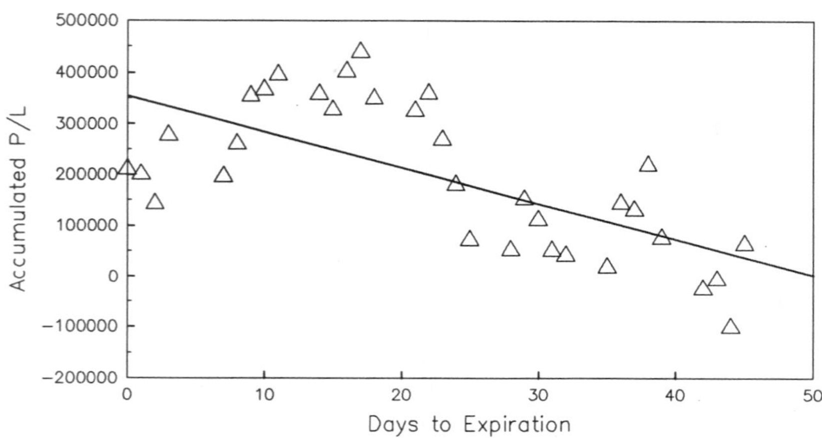

FIGURE 6–6

Case Study I: Relationship between Delta Equivalent of Position and March Futures Price

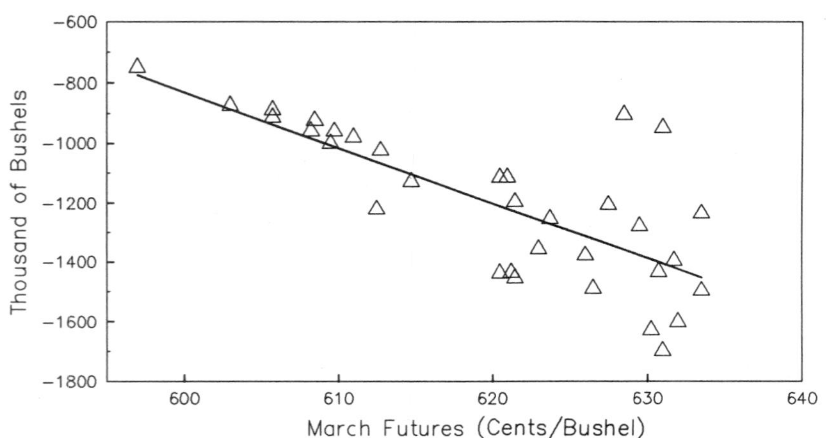

alent of the position in bushels and the futures price, that is, gamma. As discussed in the section on option pricing, short calls are assigned negative gammas. Therefore, as Figure 6–6 shows the position became shorter as futures moved higher and less short (longer) as futures moved lower. Over the course of the trade, the position fluctuated between roughly 800 thousand bushels short and 1.6 million bushels short. Therefore, adjustments to the long futures hedge amounted to 800 thousand bushels.

Given the large number of option contracts written and the non-volatile nature of the market, the magnitude of adjustments (800 thousand bushels over the life of the trade) cannot be considered burdensome. Albeit slippage occurred due to gamma, the market is always one step ahead of the trader, since as futures moved down the long futures hedge was too large. As it moved up, it was too small. The trader was constantly playing a catch-up game at the end of each trading session. This is why the full amount of extrinsic value is never earned completely in covered call strategies.

The alternative is to adjust during the trading session, but the risk of getting whipsawed in a volatile intra-day market is greater than the gamma (slippage) risk.

CASE II: *Vertical Call Ratio Spread*

July Vertical Call Ratio Spread: Position initiated on April 13th, 1988, and held to expiration on June 17th, 1988.

Background

The July 88 vertical call ratio spread position was begun with 64 days to expiration; July 88 futures were trading at 684.5 cents per bushel. The market was seasonally vulnerable to an upward movement in both prices and volatility as spring planting progressed and the summer growing season approached. Thus, out-of-the-money 725 call options were purchased against the sale of 750 and 775 calls. Twenty-five days into the trade, and after futures had rallied 83 cents, 800 calls were also sold. 245 contracts of the 725 call were purchased for 18.75; 200 contracts each of the 750 and 775 were sold for 13.5 and 9.75, respectively; 100 contracts of the 800 call were sold for 16.25. Given the previous ratio, this led to a net credit of $84,062.

Note that although the purchase of the 725 call covers some of the volatility risk, the trader was still net short volatility. Finally, futures were used opportunistically to adjust the position close to delta neutral.

Market Environment

Figure 6–7 coveys the extent of price movement in the July 88 soybean futures from April to June 1988. Although obviously a powerful and volatile bull market, there were some drastic contrasts between the early and later stage of the market that an options trader should note. First, the market traded between 675 and 725 cents per bushel from April to mid-May, that is, in a 50-cent range (much the same way March 88 futures had traded). Second, Figure 6–8 demonstrates that this initial tight trading range was translated into a contra-seasonal move in volatility. From mid-April to mid-May implied volatility moved from a high of 32 percent to a low of 22 percent; historical volatility traded down to a low of 15 percent at one point.

This contra-seasonal move in volatility was deceptive. It left many traders wondering why they were long volatility; however, the fact that implied volatility was trading above historical volatility suggests traders still expected a radical move in prices and volatility.

FIGURE 6–7

Case Study II: July 88 Soybeans

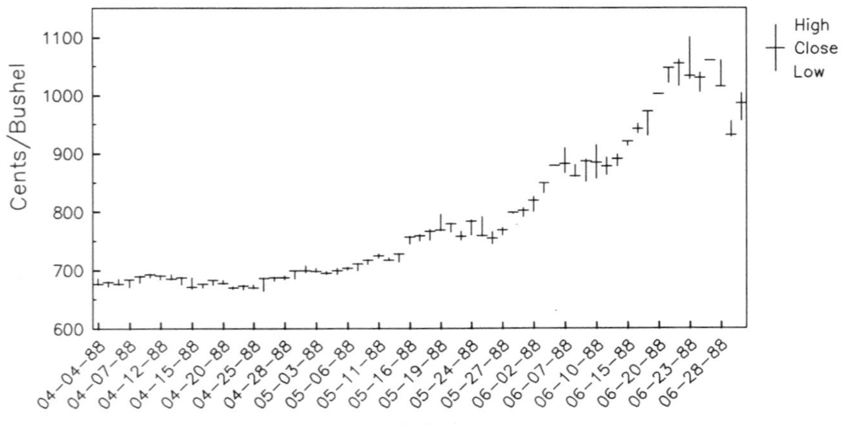

FIGURE 6–8

Case Study II: Implied Volatility of Position versus Historical Volatility

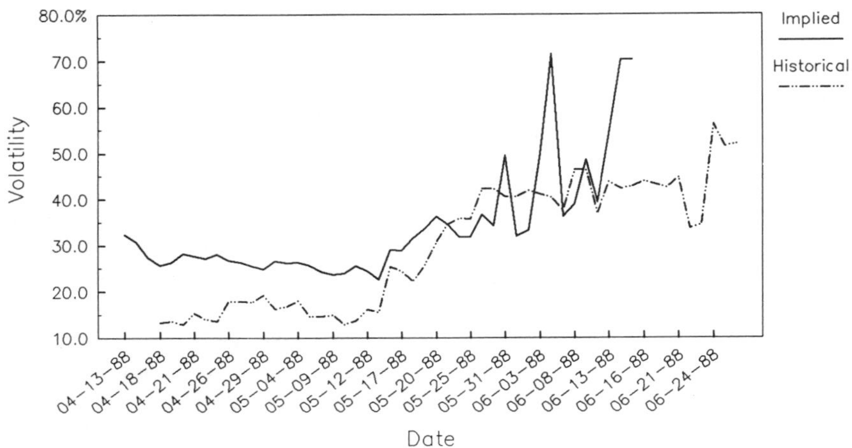

Therefore, they assigned higher premiums to the out-of-the-money options (vis-à-vis premiums valued at historical volatility).

The anticipated move in futures price and volatility finally occurred in mid-May: The key indicator was historical volatility, since it rose more sharply than implied volatility. But the most convincing evidence was a volatility breakout above 35 percent, because this was a move outside historical boundaries (refer to Chapter 3). Nonetheless, the fact that this move was expected from a seasonal standpoint (that is, it was not an anomaly) should have made all volatility shorts re-analyze their strategies.

From mid-May onward, the market was characterized by high volatility and pronounced fluctuations. Volatility was volatile! These radical shifts were due to limit-up (or limit-down) moves in futures that caused futures shorts (or longs) to use options to cover their positions. The cost to do this was inflated volatility.

It is obvious from Figure 6–9 that this trade was in trouble as soon as futures moved above 800 to 825 cents per bushel. Coincidentally, this is more or less the breakeven area for the trade at expiration. (If one considers the options position alone, a maximum profit of $446,563 would have occurred at 775 cents per bushel at expiration; the reader should calculate these profit, loss, and breakeven points as an exercise).

The level of flat-price was not the only factor to undermine the profitability of this trade as Figure 6–10 demonstrates. Once implied

FIGURE 6–9

Case Study II: Accumulated Profit/Loss of Position versus Futures Price

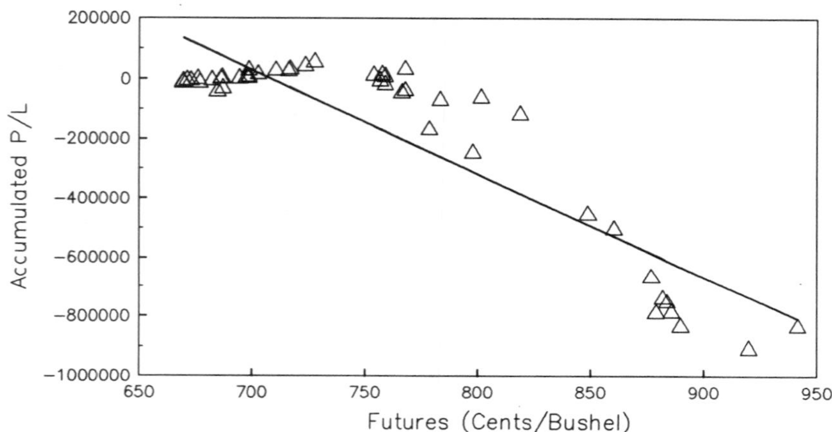

FIGURE 6–10

Case Study II: Accumulated Profit/Loss of Position versus Implied Volatility

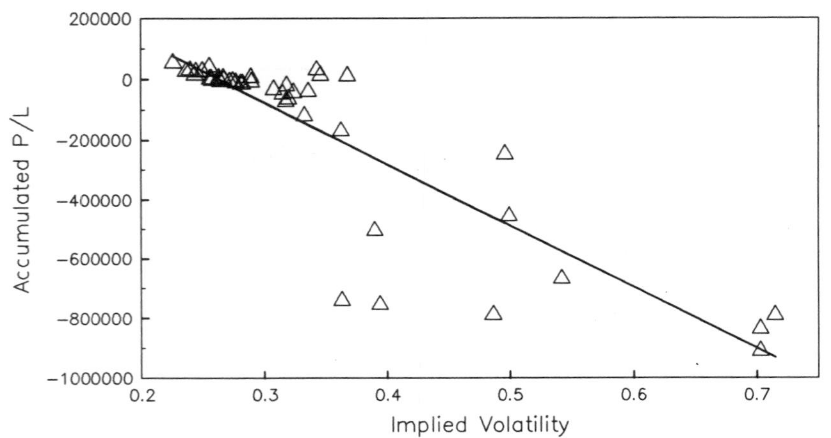

FIGURE 6–11

Case Study II: Accumulated Profit/Loss of Position versus Days to Expiration

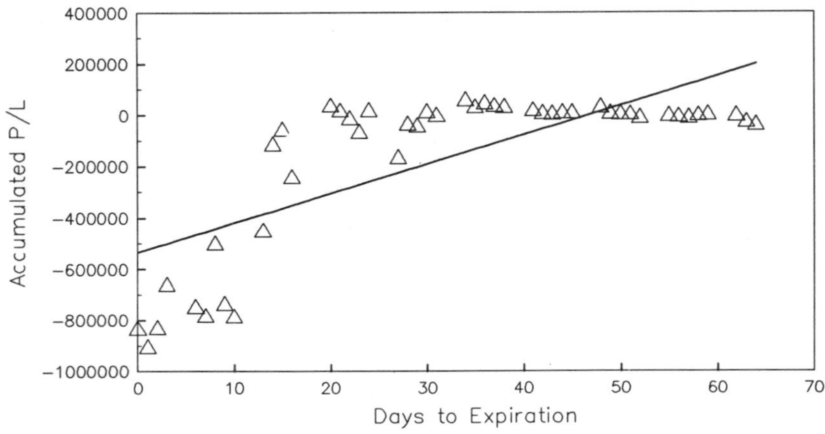

volatility moved over 35 percent, profitability collapsed, since the trader took daily losses due to surging volatility. With all the options deep in-the-money and volatility high, time value disappears and does not accrue as a profit as shown in Figure 6–11.

The net result of this trade was a $838,019 loss on the options position and a $902,198 gain on the futures position for a net profit of $64,179. The options loss was reduced by adjusting the position (that is, buying back some of the short calls) during the latter stages of the bull market. If the options position were held to expiration as implemented, a loss of over $1.5 million would have occurred.

Conclusions

The main conclusion can be phrased very simply. The position was not worth holding onto once volatility broke out of its historical boundary, that is, 30 to 35 percent. At that point the trade should have been adjusted to a 1:1 ratio, for example, long 245 contracts of the 725 call, short 245 contracts of the 750 call. Alternatively, the short could have been placed in either the 775 or 800 call.

Likewise, the reward of $446,563 was worth the risk involved until the market began assaulting the position's breakeven area. At that point, severe losses accrued on a daily basis, due to either: (a) volatility losses out-pacing any gains in the long futures position, or (b) the trader's inability to adjust with futures due to exchange limits, since one cannot increase (decrease) a futures long when the market is limit-up (limit-down); this increased slippage costs. Indeed, futures adjustments were nightmarish as the position went from a delta long of 100 thousand bushels to a delta short of 1.1 million bushels at expiration (see Figure 6–12). This is yet another example of the importance of understanding the concept of gamma.

Here is the statistical method for explaining the failure of this trade. Upon initiating the trade, implied volatility was at 30 percent with futures trading at 685 cents per bushel. This suggested an annual trading range of 685 ± 206 or 479 on the downside and 891 on the upside. Over the course of 64 days, however, the implied trading range was 685 ± 103 (582 on the downside and 788 on the upside). Obviously, the upside range was violated, as futures surpassed 788 by the end of May and settled at 941 at expiration.

In the final analysis, the flat-price violation of 800 to 825 cents per bushel (which was slightly above the area of maximum profit) and a volatility breakout above 35 percent were strong signals to adjust or exit the trade. Incidentally, these two warning signals were received simultaneously at the beginning of June 1988 (see Figures 6–7 and 6–8).

FIGURE 6–12

Case Study II: Relationship between Delta Equivalent of Position and July Futures Price

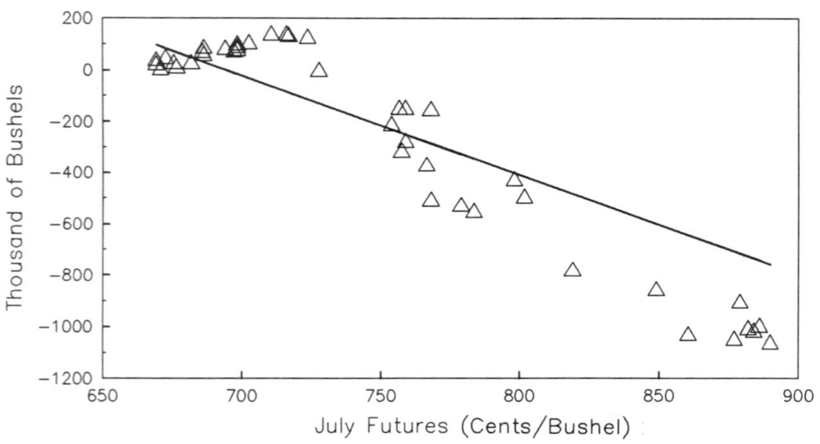

CASE III: *Writing Puts*

July Put Writing Program: Position initiated on May 16th, 1988, and held to expiration on June 16th, 1988.

Background

With 32 calendar days to expiration, 120 July 725 soybean puts were sold uncovered for 9.25 cents per bushel with July futures trading at 756.75. The implied volatility of the July options was approximately 24–26 percent.

The premise of the trade was to sell volatility with the price trend, that is, sell puts in a market that is trending higher. Contrary to prevailing wisdom, volatility can be sold against its seasonal trend. At any other time of the year, volatility is sold with the idea that risk can be offset through covered writing (as in Case I). But this is not feasible during the late spring/early summer due to higher slippage costs (as in Case II). Therefore, selling volatility during this period requires a greater flat-price conviction, vis-à-vis a pure volatility conviction.

Market Environment

The reader can use Figure 6–7 as a guide to the market environment. July futures had rallied to 750 cents per bushel and then traded in a volatile range between 750 and 800 cents per bushel. The trade was put on at that stage with the idea that the market was poised for another rally.

The high conviction needed to place such a trade should be appreciated from the following factors: (1) The daily bar chart became extremely volatile in the latter half of May (see Figure 6–7); (2) The market could just as well have collapsed as rallied; and (3) The short put was placed only one strike away from where the market was trading.

In addition, to make any amount of money from this trade it was almost a prerequisite that the puts be sold uncovered, since hedging delta neutral would have been a logistical nightmare. This takes daring given that the risk of a short option is unlimited. Option spreads could have been used, but buying a put against the low initial premium (9.25 cents) would have reduced total income from $55,500 to $33,000 (the 700 put was trading at 3.75 cents per bushel).

Nonetheless, there were two factors that favored this trade from the outset. First, there were 32 days to expiration; that is, the period of rapid time decay and decreasing sensitivity to volatility was about to take place. Second, although it is true that the market could have collapsed, there were strong technical and fundamental indications that the market would at least trade at this level for a period of time until the damage to the crop could be assessed (the initial stages of the 1988 drought were underway).

Conclusion: The Purpose and Power of Position Monitoring

Given the high level of risk built into this trade, the problem is reduced to one of monitoring its progress to assure that it is a "healthy" trade. From the knowledge of option prices and risk, a short volatility trade is progressing smoothly (is "healthy") when theta is rising (time decay profits are accruing) and vega is decreasing (volatility risk is decreasing).

This is true for any short volatility trade from uncovered short options to straddles, strangles, and income spreads. A neat statistic to use as an index of progression is the absolute value of the daily theta dollar profit of the position divided by the one percent vega dollar risk of the position. The resulting ratio should be increasing steadily in the last 30 to 40 days of the life of an option; if not, the

FIGURE 6–13

Case Study III: Short July 725 Put, Daily Profit/Loss

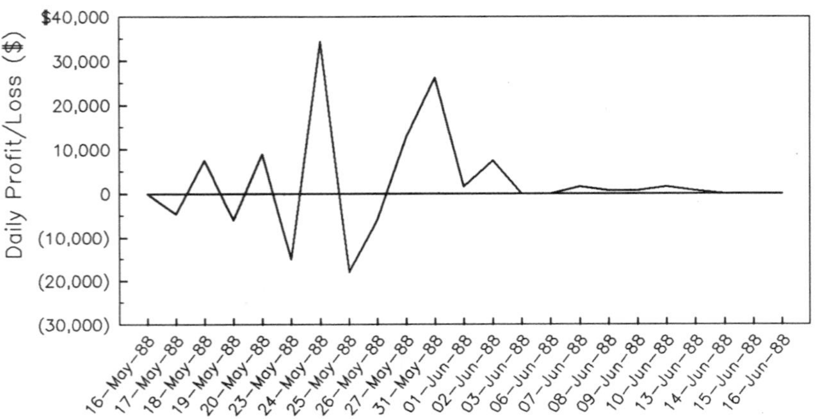

trade is not progressing normally and the trader who initiated the position is probably not sleeping well at night.

Of course, one could use daily or accumulated profit as an indice of the trade's progress. This is a valid argument; however, Figure 6–13 demonstrates that for the first eight trading days, daily profit was a poor statistic for monitoring the progress of the trade. Accumulated profit (Figure 6–14) was only $1,500 by the eighth day; certainly, this is not an encouraging amount in light of the sharp daily fluctuations.

The theta/vega ratio is shown in Figure 6–15. Note that during the life of the trade, the ratio was in a steady uptrend. Compare this with the initial volatility of the position's daily profit/loss in Figure 6–13. The leverage that this ratio gives to a trader's conviction should not be underestimated. It is important to keep in mind that short volatility strategies are bets on price over time, with the underlying assumption that time will ultimately win over price and the options will expire worthless.

Finally, the implied volatility of the 725 put is shown in Figure 6–16. Despite the steady increase in the option's implied volatility, the overall position was still profitable (Figure 6–14). Again, volatility can be sold against its seasonal direction as long as the trader realizes that more weight is placed on his or her flat-price conviction.

FIGURE 6–14

Case Study III: Short July 725 Put, Accumulated Profit/Loss

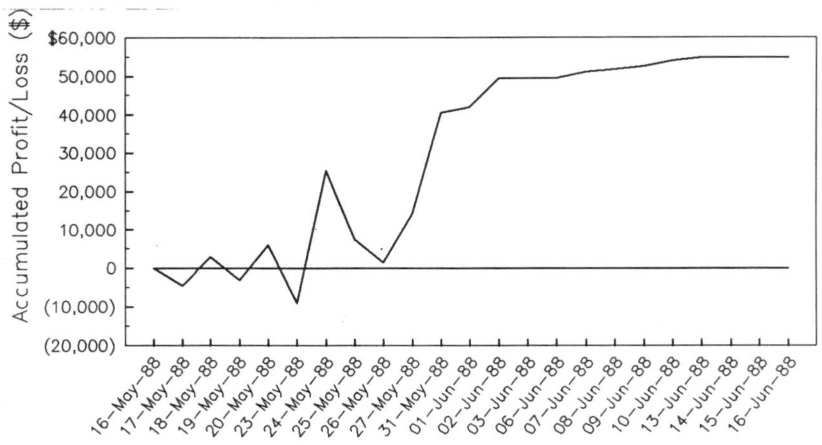

FIGURE 6–15

Case Study III: Theta/Vega Ratio
Daily Theta Dollar Profit Divided by One Percent Vega Dollar Risk

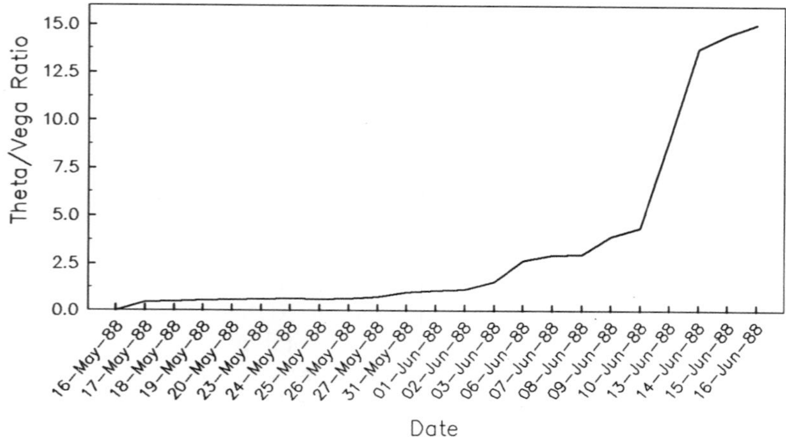

FIGURE 6–16

Case Study III: July 725 Put Implied Volatility

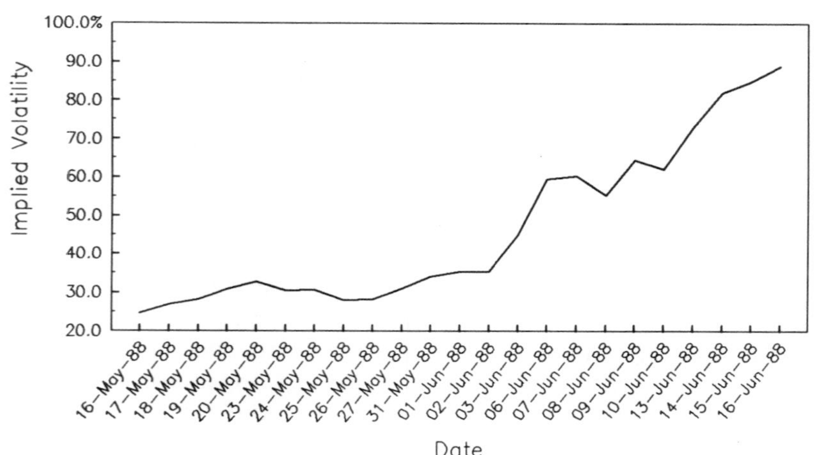

CASE IV: *Buying Calls*

November Call Buying Program: Position initiated on July 25th, 1988, and held to August llth, 1988 (17 calender days).

Background/Market Environment

In midsummer of 1988, the soybean market experienced a severe price collapse after rains entered the Midwest in late July. Nonetheless, the effect of the precipitation was unclear, and there was doubt that any benefit was forthcoming after months of drought. With November soybeans at 801 cents per bushel, 50 November 875 soybean calls were purchased for 31 cents for a total outlay of $77,500. The trade was equivalent to making a side bet that rains would remain erractic or would shut off completely, and the drought would resume.

The volatility purchased was around 37 to 38 percent, and in light of the volatilities seen earlier in the summer of 70 to 80 percent, the premiums were considered cheap. Two risks are obvious from our knowledge of options in general and agricultural options in particular: (1) time decay, and (2) The implied volatility of soybean options tends to peak out in late July and early August. The risks were mitigated, however, by holding the position for a short period of time (14 trading days or 17 calender days).

Conclusion: The Importance of Trading the Position

After the position was initiated, November futures immediately plummeted 45 cents to 756 cents per bushel (see Figure 6–17). Nonetheless, the trader's conviction and foresight slowly paid off as soybeans rallied from that level to a high of 889 cents per bushel by August 5th. The behavior of implied volatility is more interesting (see also Figure 6–17). It peaked before the flat-price on August 1st.

This demonstrates one of the most common attributes of long volatility positions. As the market moves favorably, the trade often makes money at a rate higher than what the bushel equivalent (delta) of the position would imply. The difference lies in the volatility profits that accrue as volatility shorts exit the market and bid-up premiums. Once they exit, however, a vacuum remains, and this is further accentuated if the futures trend is simultaneously stalling.

FIGURE 6–17

Case Study IV: November 88 Futures versus 875 November Call Volatility

July 25th to August 11th

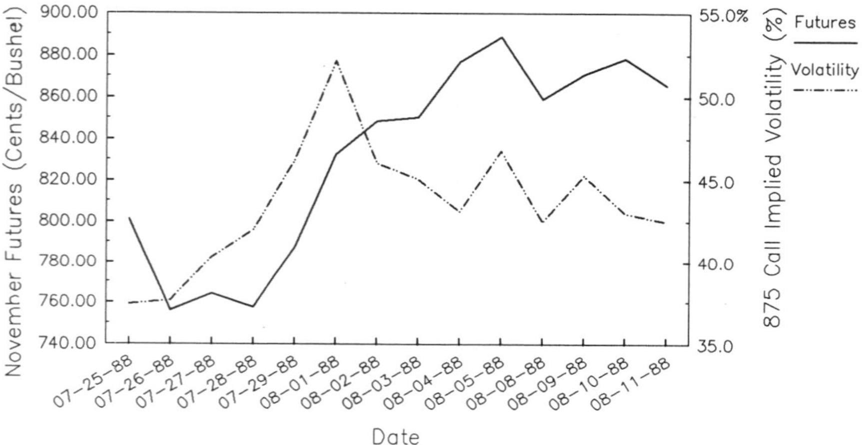

Figure 6–18 demonstrates this phenomenon for the long 875 soybean call position. The graph is constructed by comparing the accumulated profit/loss of the long call position with that of a theoretical futures position that is equal in bushel equivalents. In effect, the distance between the two lines measures the extent of volatility losses or gains. Initially, the option position gains on the equivalent futures position but then falters as the flat-price stalls out between 865 to 880 cents per bushel. The pivot point is August 1st: precisely the day in which implied volatility peaked. After that day, the equivalent futures position is superior in profit.

If the key to success for short volatility positions is patience (in order for time decay to take its toll), the key to long volatility positions is to lock in any profit by trading the position; especially when a windfall profit occurs due to favorable volatility movements. It is important to keep in mind that the 875 call went from out-of-the-money to near-the-money, and futures spent only three days above the call's strike price. Why not lock in all or some of the accrued profit, since at expiration, this call is still virtually worthless? Indeed, the 6 percent spike in volatility on August 1st was a clue to the trader either to take some of his or her profit or to sell calls at a higher strike price, for example, 900 or 925 calls.

To illustrate, the trader can sell 900 strike calls on August 1st for 56 cents per bushel. By the time the position was liquidated on

FIGURE 6–18

Case Study IV: Profit/Loss of Long 875 Call Position versus Profit/ Loss of Equivalent Futures Position

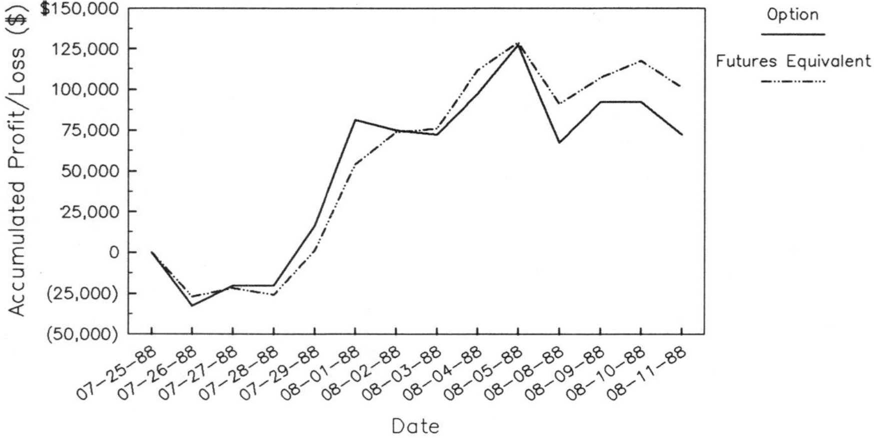

August 11th, the 900 call was worth 52.5 cents (−3.5 cents) and the 875 call was worth 60 cents versus 63.5 cents on August 1st. Hence, the sale of the 900 call exactly offset volatility losses in the long 875 call and made the position as attractive as the equivalent futures trade in Figure 6–18.

At the very least, the short 900 call maneuver locks in a profit of 25 cents if futures were to collapse by expiration (56 cents from the sale of the 900 call less 31 cents for the initial payment of the 875 call). Conversely, the trader can earn a maximum of 50 additional cents per contract if futures are above 925 by expiration; that is, the trader effectively legs into a 1:1 bull call spread for a *credit* of 25 cents.

Appendix **A**

The Black Option Pricing Model and Derivative Equations

The following outlines the Black formula for calculating the theoretical price of puts and calls as well as the derivative formulas for *delta, gamma, vega,* and *theta*. An example for puts and calls is given at the end of the appendix so that traders may work through the calculations.

Note: The following mathematical notation is used in this manual:

$+$ = Addition
$-$ = Subtraction
$\cdot$ = Multiplication
$/$ = Division

I. The Black Theoretical Price of Calls and Puts

$$C = e^{(-r \cdot t)} \cdot [U \cdot N(x1) - E \cdot N(x2)]$$
$$P = -e^{(-r \cdot t)} \cdot [U \cdot N(-x1) - E \cdot N(-x2)]$$

Where:

$$x1 = [Ln(U/E) + (v^2 \cdot t)/2]/(v \cdot t^{.5})$$
$$x2 = [Ln(U/E) - (v^2 \cdot t)/2]/(v \cdot t^{.5})$$

And:

C = Call Premium
P = Put Premium

U = Underlying Futures Price
E = Strike Price of Option
v = Volatility in Decimal Format
t = Time Expressed as # Days to Expiration Divided by 365
r = Interest Rate in Decimal Format
$N(x1)$ = Normal Cumulative Probability of the Term $x1$
$N(x2)$ = Normal Cumulative Probability of the Term $x2$

(See Table 1–A at end of this section)

e = 2.7183
Ln = Natural Log

II. Equation for Delta

$$\text{Call Delta} = N(x1)$$
$$\text{Put Delta} = N(-x1)$$

III. Equation for Gamma

$$\text{Gamma} = [1/(U \cdot v \cdot t^{.5})] \cdot [N'(x1)]$$

Where:

$$N'(x1) = [1/(2 \cdot PI)^{.5} \cdot e^{-x1^2/2}]$$
$$PI = 3.1416$$

IV. Equation for Vega

$$\text{Vega} = [U \cdot t^{.5}] \cdot [N'(x1)]$$

V. Equation for Theta

For CALLS:

$$\text{Theta} = [[U \cdot N'(x1) \cdot Q - E \cdot N'(x2) \cdot Z] - r \cdot [U \cdot N(x1) - E \cdot N(x2)]]$$

Where:

$$Q = [.25 \cdot v \cdot t^{-.5}] + [.5 \cdot \text{Ln}(U/E) \cdot (1/v) \cdot t^{-1.5}]$$
$$Z = [-.25 \cdot v \cdot t^{-.5}] + [.5 \cdot \text{Ln}(U/E) \cdot (1/v) \cdot t^{-1.5}]$$

For Puts:

$$\text{Theta} = -1 \cdot [[\text{U} \cdot \text{N}'(x1) \cdot \text{Z} - \text{E} \cdot \text{N}'(x2) \cdot \text{Q}] + r \cdot [\text{U} \cdot \text{N}(-x1) - \text{E} \cdot \text{N}(-x2)]]$$

VI. Calculating the Appropriate Interest Rate

Assume you need to calculate the appropriate interest rate to use for a March 89 soybean option. The March 89 contract expires on February 17th. From the Wall Street Journal, we can find the bid/ask of a T-Bill maturing on February 16th:

US TREASURY BILL

MATURITY DATE	BID	ASK	YIELD
1989: 2/16	8.01	7.97	8.24

On November 22nd, the number of calender days to maturity is 86 days. The current price of the T-Bill is as follows:

$$\text{Current Price} = \$10{,}000 \cdot [1 - .01 \cdot [(\text{B} + \text{A})/2] \cdot (n/360)]$$

$$\text{Current Price} = \$10{,}000 \cdot [1 - .01 \cdot [(8.01 + 7.97)/2] \cdot (86/360)]$$

Current Price = $9,809.12, and

$$r = 1 - (9809.12/10000)^{-1/t} \qquad t = 86/360 = .2389$$

$$r = 1 - (9809.12/10000)^{-1/.2389}$$

$$r = .084 \text{ or } 8.4\%$$

VII. Examples with Puts

Assume the following:

750 January Soybean Put
Volatility = 22.74%
Days to Expiration = 28
Interest Rate = 7%
Futures Trading At: 731

From the above information, calculate:

1. **a.** Theoretical price of the put option
   b. Delta
   c. Gamma

d. Vega
e. Theta

2. For a trader short 150 of these puts, calculate:
a. Flat Price Exposure
b. Increase/Decrease in Flat Price Exposure per Point Increase in Soybean Futures
c. Gain/Loss per 1% increase in Volatility
d. Gain/Loss per day of Time Decay

ANSWERS:
1. a. Theoretical Price of 750 Put Option:

$$U = 731$$
$$E = 750$$
$$v = .2274$$
$$t = (28/365) = .0767$$
$$r = .07$$

$$-x1 = -1 \cdot [\text{Ln}(731/750) + (.2274^2 \cdot .0767)/2]/(.2274 \cdot .0767^{.5})$$
$$-x1 = -1 \cdot [-.0257 + .002]/(.063)$$
$$-x1 = -1 \cdot [-.0237]/(.063)$$
$$-x1 = .3762 \text{ or } .38$$
$$-x2 = -1 \cdot [\text{Ln}(731/750) - (.2274^2 \cdot .0767)/2]/(.2274 \cdot .0767^{.5})$$
$$-x2 = -1 \cdot [-.0257 - .002]/(.063)$$
$$-x2 = -1 \cdot [-.0277]/(.063)$$
$$-x2 = .4397 \text{ or } .44$$

On page 222, from the Normal Cumulative Probability Table, we have the following:

$$N(.38) = .648$$
$$N(.44) = .670$$

Therefore:

$$P = -2.7183^{-.07 \cdot .0767} \cdot [(731) \cdot (.648) - (750)(.670)]$$
$$P = -.9946 \cdot [473.7 - 502.5]$$
$$P = -.9946 \cdot [-28.8]$$
$$P = 28.64 \text{ or Approximately } 28.75 \text{ Cents}$$

b. Delta: From the above, we already see that Delta is .648 or approximately .65 since N(.38) = .648.

c. Gamma:

$$N'(x1) = [1/(2 \cdot 3.1416)^{.5} \cdot e^{-.38^2/2}]$$
$$N'(x1) = [1/(2.506) \cdot e^{-.0722}]$$
$$N'(x1) = [(.3990) \cdot (.9303)]$$
$$N'(x1) = .3712$$
$$\text{GAMMA} = [1/(731 \cdot .2274 \cdot .0767^{.5})] \cdot [N'(x1)]$$
$$\text{GAMMA} = [1/(46.03)] \cdot [.3712]$$
$$\text{GAMMA} = [.0217] \cdot [.3712]$$
$$\text{GAMMA} = .0081$$

d. Vega:

$$\text{VEGA} = [731 \cdot .0767^{.5} \cdot [N'(x1)]$$
$$\text{VEGA} = [202.44] \cdot [.3712]$$
$$\text{VEGA} = 75.1$$

e. Theta:

$$Q = [.25 \cdot .2274 \cdot .0767^{-.5}] + [.5 \cdot \text{Ln}(731/750) \cdot (1/.2274) \cdot .0767^{-1.5}]$$
$$Q = [.2053] + [.5 \cdot (-.0257) \cdot (4.397) \cdot 47.076]$$
$$Q = [.2053] + [-2.6599]$$
$$Q = -2.4546$$
$$Z = [-.25 \cdot .2274 \cdot .0767^{-.5}] + [.5 \cdot \text{Ln}(731/750) \cdot (1/.2274) \cdot .0767^{-1.5}]$$
$$Z = [-.2053] + [-2.6561]$$
$$Z = -2.8614$$
$$N'(x2) = [1/(2 \cdot 3.1416)^{.5} \cdot e^{-.44^2/2}]$$
$$N'(x2) = [1/(2.506) \cdot e^{-(.0968)}]$$
$$N'(x2) = [.3990 \cdot .9077]$$
$$N'(x2) = .3622$$
$$\text{Theta} = -1 \cdot [731 \cdot .3712 \cdot -2.86 - 750 \cdot .3622 \cdot -2.45] + .07[731 \cdot .65 - 750 \cdot .67]$$
$$\text{Theta} = -1 \cdot [-776.7 - -665.5] + .07\,[472.2 - 502.5]$$
$$\text{Theta} = -1 \cdot [-111.2] + -1.91$$
$$\text{Theta} = 111.2 + -1.91$$
$$\text{Theta} = 109.3$$

2. From the first part of the example, we can sum-up for a short put position:

Theoretical	Premium:	28.75
Delta:	+.6500	
Gamma:	−0.0081	
Vega:	−75.1	
Theta:	+109.3	

a. Flat Price Exposure for trader short 150 of these Puts:

Flat Px Exposure = (Delta) · (5000) · (#Contracts)
= (.6500) · (5000) · (150)
= +487,500 Bushels, or
Long Approx 490,000 Bushels.

b. Increase/Decrease in Flat Price Exposure per Point Increase in Soybean Futures Price:
From Formula in Section 3:

Gamma = (Change in Delta)/(Change in Futures)
= $(\Delta D/\Delta F)$

From Above:

Gamma = −.0081
$\Delta F = 1$
$-.0081 = \Delta D/1,\ \Delta D = -.0081$
$(-.0081)(5000)(150) = -6{,}075$ Bushels

In other words, with each penny increase (decrease) in futures, the position gets shorter (longer) by 6,075 bushels.

c. Gain/Loss per 1% Increase in Volatility:
From Formula in Section 3:

Vega = (Change in Option Premium)/(Change in Volatility)
Vega = $(\Delta P/\Delta V)$
Where: Vega = −75.1 and $\Delta V = .01$
$\Delta P = (-75.1) \cdot (.01) = -.7510$ points or −.00751 dollars
Loss on Entire Position with 1% Volatility Increase:
$(-.00751) \cdot (5000) \cdot (150) = -\$5{,}632.5$

d. Gain/Loss per Day of Time Decay:
From Formula in Section 3:

Theta = (Change in Option Premium)/(Change in Time)

Theta = $(\Delta P/\Delta T)$

Where: Theta = +109.1 and ΔT = (1/365) = .0027

ΔP = (109.3) · (.0027) = .2951 points or +.0030 dollars

Gain on Entire Position with 1 Day's Time Decay:

(.0030) · (5000) · (150) = +2,213.32

Comment: There is no doubt that the above equations are laborious when done on a calculator. Traders are encouraged to obtain software that does the calculations rapidly or to input the formulas into a spreadsheet.

VIII. Example with Calls:

Assume the Following:

850 January Soybean Call
Volatility = 31.05%
Days to Expiration = 28
Interest Rate = 7%
Futures Trading At: 746.25

From the above information, calculate:

1. **a.** Theoretical price of the call option
b. Delta
c. Gamma
d. Vega
e. Theta

2. For a trader short 100 of these calls, calculate:
a. Flat Price Exposure
b. Increase/Decrease in Flat Price Exposure per Point Increase in Soybean Futures
c. Gain/Loss per 1% increase in Volatility
d. Gain/Loss per day of Time Decay

ANSWERS:

1. a. Theoretical Price of 850 Call Option:

$$U = 746.25$$
$$E = 850$$
$$v = .3105$$
$$t = (28/365) = .0767$$
$$r = .07$$

$$x1 = [\text{Ln}(746.25/850) + (.3105^2 \cdot .0767)/2]/(.3105 \cdot .0767^{.5})$$
$$x1 = [-.1302 + .0037]/(.086)$$
$$x1 = [-.1265]/(.086)$$
$$x1 = -1.47$$
$$x2 = [\text{Ln}(746.25/850) - (.3105^2 \cdot .0767)/2]/(.3105 \cdot .0767^{.5})$$
$$x2 = [-.1302 - .0037]/(.086)$$
$$x2 = [-.1339]/(.086)$$
$$x2 = -1.56$$

From the Normal Cumulative Probability Table we have the following:

$$N(-1.47) = .0708$$
$$N(-1.56) = .0594$$

Therefore:

$$C = 2.7183^{(-.07 \cdot .0767)} \cdot [(746.25) \cdot (.0708) - (850)(.0594)]$$
$$C = .9946 \cdot [52.83 - 50.49]$$
$$C = .9946 \cdot [2.34]$$
$$C = 2.32 \text{ or Approx } 2.25 \text{ Cents}$$

b. Delta: From the above, we already see that Delta is .0708 or approximately .07 since $N(x1) = .07$.

c. Gamma:

$$N'(x1) = [1/(2 \cdot 3.1416)^{.5} \cdot e^{-1.47^2/2}]$$
$$N'(x1) = [1/(2.506) \cdot e^{-1.0805}]$$
$$N'(x1) = [(.3990) \cdot (.3394)]$$
$$N'(x1) = .1354$$
$$\text{Gamma} = [1/(746.25 \cdot .3105 \cdot .0767^{.5})] \cdot [N'(x1)]$$
$$\text{Gamma} = [1/(64.17)] \cdot [.1354]$$
$$\text{Gamma} = [.0156] \cdot [.1354]$$
$$\text{Gamma} = .0021$$

d. Vega:

$$\text{Vega} = [746.25 \cdot .0767^{.5}] \cdot [\text{N}'(x1)]$$
$$\text{Vega} = [206.67] \cdot [.1354]$$
$$\text{Vega} = 27.9$$

e. Theta:

$$\text{Q} = [.25 \cdot .3105 \cdot .0767^{-.5}] + [.5 \cdot \text{Ln}(746.25/850) \cdot (1/.3105) \cdot .0767^{-1.5}]$$
$$\text{Q} = [.2803] + [.5 \cdot (-.1302) \cdot (3.2206) \cdot 47.07]$$
$$\text{Q} = [.2803] + [-9.8687]$$
$$\text{Q} = -9.5884$$
$$\text{Q} = [-.25 \cdot .3105 \cdot .0767^{-.5}] + [.5 \cdot \text{Ln}(746.25/850) \cdot (1/.3105) \cdot .0767^{-1.5}]$$
$$\text{Z} = [-.2803] + [-9.8687]$$
$$\text{Z} = -10.149$$
$$\text{N}'(x2) = [1/(2 \cdot 3.1416)^{.5} \cdot e^{-1.56^2/2}]$$
$$\text{N}'(x2) = [1/(2.506) \cdot \text{e}^{-1.2168}]$$
$$\text{N}'(x2) = [.3990 \cdot .2962]$$
$$\text{N}'(x2) = .1182$$
$$\text{Theta} = [746.25 \cdot .1354 \cdot -9.59 - 850 \cdot .1182 \cdot -10.15] + .07[746.25 \cdot .07 - 850 \cdot .059]$$
$$\text{Theta} = [-968.99 - -1019.77] + .07[52.23 - 50.15]$$
$$\text{Theta} = [50.78] + .1456$$
$$\text{Theta} = 50.9$$

2. From the first part of the example, we can sum-up for a short put position:

Theoretical	Premium:	2.25
Delta:	−0.0700	
Gamma:	−0.0021	
Vega:	−27.9	
Theta:	+50.9	

a. Flat Price Exposure for trader short 100 of these Puts:

Flat Px Exposure = (Delta) · (5000) · (#Contracts)

$$= (-.0700) \cdot (5000) \cdot (100)$$
$$= -35{,}000 \text{ Bushels}$$

b. Increase/Decrease in Flat Price Exposure per Point Increase in Soybean Futures Price:

From Formula in Section 3:

$$\text{Gamma} = (\text{Change in Delta})/(\text{Change in Futures})$$
$$= (\Delta D/\Delta F)$$

From Above:

$$\text{Gamma} = -.0021$$
$$\Delta F = 1$$
$$-.0021 = \Delta D/1, \ \Delta D = -.0021$$
$$(-.0021)(5000)(100) = -1{,}050 \text{ Bushels}$$

In other words, with each penny increase (decrease) in futures, the position gets shorter (longer) by 1,050 bushels.

c. Gain/Loss per 1% Increase in Volatility:

From Formula in Section 3:

$$\text{Vega} = (\text{Change in Option Premium})/(\text{Change in Volatility})$$
$$\text{Vega} = (\Delta P/\Delta V)$$

Where: Vega $= -27.9$ and $\Delta V = .01$

$\Delta P = (-27.9) \cdot (.01) = -.2790$ points or $-.00279$ dollars

Loss on Entire Position with 1% Volatility Increase:

$$(-.00279) \cdot (5000) \cdot (100) = -\$1{,}395.00$$

d. Gain/Loss per Day of Time Decay:

From Formula in Section 3:

$$\text{Theta} = (\text{Change in Option Premium})/(\text{Change in Time})$$
$$\text{Theta} = (\Delta P/\Delta T)$$

Where: Theta $= +50.9$ and $\Delta T = (1/365) = .0027$

$\Delta P = (50.9) \cdot (.0027) = .1374$ points or $+.001374$ dollars

Gain on Entire Position with 1 Day's Time Decay:

$$(.002989) \cdot (5000) \cdot (100) = +687.15$$

Statistical Review

Option traders should have an intuitive grasp of the statistical concept of mean and standard deviation. The mean is simply the average of a series of numbers—in this case a series of daily percentage changes in prices.

Standard deviation measures the distribution of percentage changes around the mean. By definition, the standard deviation of the average *annual* percentage change in price is what is referred to as volatility. We will see that a random normal distribution assumes that the average annual percentage change is effectively 0 percent, so that volatility is just a measure of the number of percentage points above and below 0 percent.

The series of price ratios in Table 2–9 gives us the percentage change from one trading day to the next; for example, from October 25th to October 26th the price of soybean meal increased 1.2 percent. Disregarding the transformation to a log-normal distribution for the moment, the average of all the price ratios is .9999 (effectively 1.0), or 0 percent. To find the distribution around the mean of 1.0, we take each ratio and subtract 1.0 (the mean); the result is then squared in order to obtain a non-negative number.

By taking the "average" of all the daily deviations from the mean [.0038/(20 − 1)] and then taking the square root of the result, we get the standard deviation above and below the mean of 1.0. In Table 2–9, this is approximately +/− 1.4 percent. Assuming the normal bell curve, +/− 1.4 percent takes into account 68 percent of all daily percentage changes:

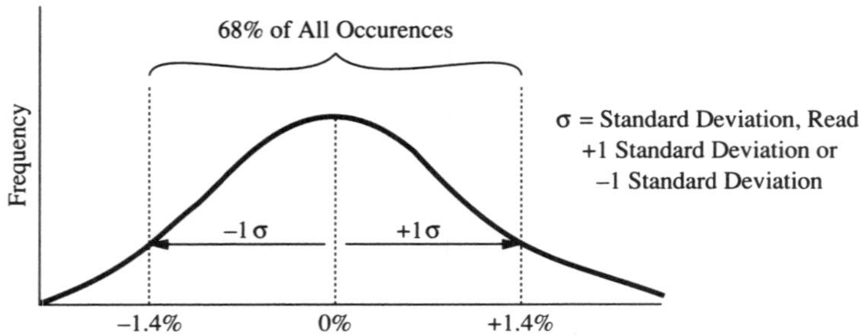

The square root is taken since we squared the data to obtain non-negative numbers; thus, to bring the data back to its original units, we simply perform the reverse operation of taking the square root.

Note that we have been discussing *daily* deviations from the

TABLE A-1 Normal Cumulative Probability Table

	0.00	0.01	0.02	0.03	0.04	0.05	0.06	0.07	0.08	0.09
0.00	0.5000	0.5040	0.5080	0.5120	0.5160	0.5199	0.5239	0.5279	0.5319	0.5359
0.10	0.5398	0.5438	0.5478	0.5517	0.5557	0.5596	0.5636	0.5675	0.5714	0.5753
0.20	0.5793	0.5832	0.5871	0.5910	0.5948	0.5987	0.6026	0.6064	0.6103	0.6141
0.30	0.6179	0.6217	0.6255	0.6293	0.6331	0.6368	0.6406	0.6443	0.6480	0.6517
0.40	0.6554	0.6591	0.6628	0.6664	0.6700	0.6736	0.6772	0.6808	0.6844	0.6879
0.50	0.6915	0.6950	0.6985	0.7019	0.7054	0.7088	0.7123	0.7157	0.7190	0.7224
0.60	0.7257	0.7291	0.7324	0.7357	0.7389	0.7422	0.7454	0.7486	0.7517	0.7549
0.70	0.7580	0.7611	0.7642	0.7673	0.7704	0.7734	0.7794	0.7794	0.7823	0.7852
0.80	0.7881	0.7910	0.7939	0.7967	0.7995	0.8023	0.8051	0.8079	0.8106	0.8133
0.90	0.8159	0.8186	0.8212	0.8238	0.8264	0.8289	0.8315	0.8340	0.8365	0.8389
1.00	0.8413	0.8438	0.8461	0.8485	0.8508	0.8531	0.8554	0.8577	0.8599	0.8621
1.10	0.8643	0.8665	0.8686	0.8708	0.8729	0.8749	0.8770	0.8790	0.8810	0.8830
1.20	0.8849	0.8869	0.8888	0.8907	0.8925	0.8944	0.8962	0.8980	0.8997	0.9015
1.30	0.9032	0.9049	0.9066	0.9082	0.9099	0.9115	0.9131	0.9147	0.9162	0.9177
1.40	0.9192	0.9207	0.9222	0.9236	0.9251	0.9265	0.9279	0.9292	0.9306	0.9319
1.50	0.9332	0.9345	0.9357	0.9370	0.9382	0.9394	0.9406	0.9418	0.9429	0.9441
1.60	0.9452	0.9463	0.9474	0.9484	0.9495	0.9505	0.9515	0.9525	0.9535	0.9545
1.70	0.9554	0.9564	0.9573	0.9582	0.9591	0.9599	0.9608	0.9616	0.9625	0.9633
1.80	0.9641	0.9649	0.9656	0.9664	0.9671	0.9678	0.9686	0.9693	0.9699	0.9706
1.90	0.9713	0.9719	0.9726	0.9732	0.9738	0.9744	0.9750	0.9756	0.9761	0.9767
2.00	0.9773	0.9778	0.9783	0.9788	0.9793	0.9798	0.9803	0.9808	0.9812	0.9817

2.10	0.9821	0.9826	0.9830	0.9834	0.9838	0.9842	0.9846	0.9850	0.9854	0.9857
2.20	0.9861	0.9864	0.9868	0.9871	0.9875	0.9878	0.9881	0.9884	0.9887	0.9890
2.30	0.9893	0.9896	0.9898	0.9901	0.9904	0.9906	0.9909	0.9911	0.9913	0.9916
2.40	0.9918	0.9920	0.9922	0.9925	0.9927	0.9929	0.9931	0.9932	0.9934	0.9936
2.50	0.9938	0.9940	0.9941	0.9943	0.9945	0.9946	0.9948	0.9949	0.9951	0.9952
2.60	0.9953	0.9955	0.9956	0.9957	0.9959	0.9960	0.9961	0.9962	0.9963	0.9964
2.70	0.9965	0.9966	0.9967	0.9968	0.9969	0.9970	0.9971	0.9972	0.9973	0.9974
2.80	0.9974	0.9975	0.9976	0.9977	0.9977	0.9978	0.9979	0.9979	0.9980	0.9981
2.90	0.9981	0.9982	0.9982	0.9983	0.9984	0.9984	0.9985	0.9985	0.9986	0.9986
3.00	0.9987	0.9987	0.9987	0.9988	0.9988	0.9989	0.9989	0.9989	0.9990	0.9990
3.10	0.9990	0.9991	0.9991	0.9991	0.9992	0.9992	0.9992	0.9992	0.9993	0.9993
3.20	0.9993	0.9993	0.9994	0.9994	0.9994	0.9994	0.9994	0.9995	0.9995	0.9995
3.30	0.9995	0.9995	0.9995	0.9996	0.9996	0.9996	0.9996	0.9996	0.9996	0.9997
3.40	0.9997	0.9997	0.9997	0.9997	0.9997	0.9997	0.9997	0.9997	0.9997	0.9998
3.50	0.9998	0.9998	0.9998	0.9998	0.9998	0.9998	0.9998	0.9998	0.9998	0.9998

(*continued*)

TABLE A-1 Normal Cumulative Probability Table *(continued)*

	0.00	0.01	0.02	0.03	0.04	0.05	0.06	0.07	0.08	0.09
0.00	0.5000	0.4960	0.4920	0.4880	0.4840	0.4801	0.4761	0.4721	0.4681	0.4641
−0.10	0.4602	0.4562	0.4522	0.4483	0.4443	0.4404	0.4364	0.4325	0.4286	0.4247
−0.20	0.4207	0.4168	0.4129	0.4090	0.4052	0.4013	0.3974	0.3936	0.3897	0.3859
−0.30	0.3821	0.3783	0.3745	0.3707	0.3669	0.3632	0.3594	0.3557	0.3520	0.3483
−0.40	0.3446	0.3409	0.3372	0.3336	0.3300	0.3264	0.3228	0.3192	0.3156	0.3121
−0.50	0.3085	0.3050	0.3015	0.2981	0.2946	0.2912	0.2877	0.2843	0.2810	0.2776
−0.60	0.2743	0.2709	0.2676	0.2643	0.2611	0.2578	0.2546	0.2514	0.2483	0.2451
−0.70	0.2420	0.2389	0.2358	0.2327	0.2296	0.2266	0.2236	0.2206	0.2177	0.2148
−0.80	0.2119	0.2090	0.2061	0.2033	0.2005	0.1977	0.1949	0.1921	0.1894	0.1867
−0.90	0.1841	0.1814	0.1788	0.1762	0.1736	0.1711	0.1685	0.1660	0.1635	0.1611
−1.00	0.1587	0.1562	0.1539	0.1515	0.1492	0.1469	0.1446	0.1423	0.1401	0.1379
−1.10	0.1357	0.1335	0.1314	0.1292	0.1271	0.1251	0.1230	0.1210	0.1190	0.1170
−1.20	0.1151	0.1131	0.1112	0.1093	0.1075	0.1056	0.1038	0.1020	0.1003	0.0985
−1.30	0.0968	0.0951	0.0934	0.0918	0.0901	0.0885	0.0869	0.0853	0.0838	0.0823
−1.40	0.0808	0.0793	0.0778	0.0764	0.0749	0.0735	0.0721	0.0708	0.0694	0.0681
−1.50	0.0668	0.0655	0.0643	0.0630	0.0618	0.0606	0.0594	0.0582	0.0571	0.0559
−1.60	0.0548	0.0537	0.0526	0.0516	0.0505	0.0495	0.0485	0.0475	0.0465	0.0455
−1.70	0.0446	0.0436	0.0427	0.0418	0.0409	0.0401	0.0392	0.0384	0.0375	0.0367
−1.80	0.0359	0.0351	0.0344	0.0336	0.0329	0.0322	0.0314	0.0307	0.0301	0.0294
−1.90	0.0287	0.0281	0.0274	0.0268	0.0262	0.0256	0.0250	0.0244	0.0239	0.0233
−2.00	0.0227	0.0222	0.0217	0.0212	0.0207	0.0202	0.0197	0.0192	0.0188	0.0183

−2.10	0.0179	0.0174	0.0170	0.0166	0.0162	0.0158	0.0154	0.0150	0.0146	0.0143
−2.20	0.0139	0.0136	0.0132	0.0129	0.0125	0.0122	0.0119	0.0116	0.0113	0.0110
−2.30	0.0107	0.0104	0.0102	0.0099	0.0096	0.0094	0.0091	0.0089	0.0087	0.0084
−2.40	0.0082	0.0080	0.0078	0.0075	0.0073	0.0071	0.0069	0.0068	0.0066	0.0064
−2.50	0.0062	0.0060	0.0059	0.0057	0.0055	0.0054	0.0052	0.0051	0.0049	0.0048
−2.60	0.0047	0.0045	0.0044	0.0043	0.0041	0.0040	0.0039	0.0038	0.0037	0.0036
−2.70	0.0035	0.0034	0.0033	0.0032	0.0031	0.0030	0.0029	0.0028	0.0027	0.0026
−2.80	0.0026	0.0025	0.0024	0.0023	0.0023	0.0022	0.0021	0.0021	0.0020	0.0019
−2.90	0.0019	0.0018	0.0018	0.0017	0.0016	0.0016	0.0015	0.0015	0.0014	0.0014
−3.00	0.0013	0.0013	0.0013	0.0012	0.0012	0.0011	0.0011	0.0011	0.0010	0.0010
−3.10	0.0010	0.0009	0.0009	0.0009	0.0008	0.0008	0.0008	0.0008	0.0007	0.0007
−3.20	0.0007	0.0007	0.0006	0.0006	0.0006	0.0006	0.0006	0.0005	0.0005	0.0005
−3.30	0.0005	0.0005	0.0005	0.0004	0.0004	0.0004	0.0004	0.0004	0.0004	0.0003
−3.40	0.0003	0.0003	0.0003	0.0003	0.0003	0.0003	0.0003	0.0003	0.0003	0.0002
−3.50	0.0002	0.0002	0.0002	0.0002	0.0002	0.0002	0.0002	0.0002	0.0002	0.0002

mean. Since volatility is a measurement of the annual fluctuation of prices, a further transformation is made by multiplying the average daily deviation by 256 trading days to give an annual deviation. The result from Table 2–9 is 22.6 percent:

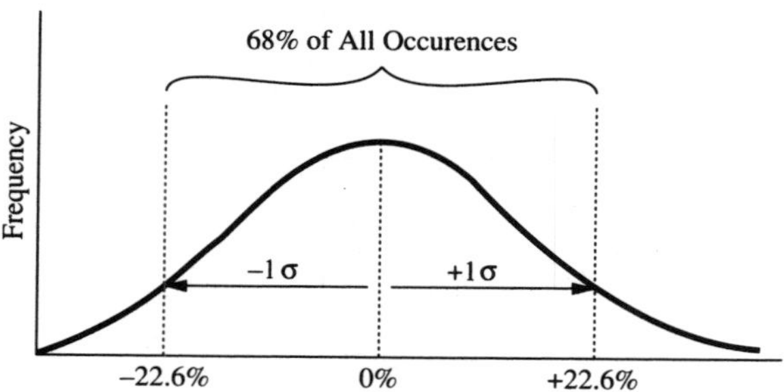

Finally, the log-normal distribution was used in Table 2–9 because we assumed prices could not be less than zero. This is simply a transformation, and the reader should not let this prevent him or her from grasping the concept of standard deviation (volatility). The reader should refer to the bibliography if a more detailed explanation of these statistical terms is required.

Appendix **B**

Additions and Elaborations on Options Hedging

I. Synthetic of a Minimum Price Contract

The second method of calculating the EHP is to treat the purchase of the put against the cash long as a synthetic long call; the only difference is the basis. From Chapter 4, Synthetic Futures and Options, the formula for a synthetic long call is as follows:

$$
\begin{aligned}
C_p &= [P_p + F - S], \text{ where} \\
C_p &= \text{Call Premium} \\
P_p &= \text{Put Premium} \\
F &= \text{Futures Price} \\
S &= \text{Strike}
\end{aligned}
$$

Thus, when the 700 put Premium is at 35 cents per bushel, the 700 synthetic call is priced as follows:

$$
\begin{aligned}
C_p &= [35 + 743.25 - 700] \\
C_p &= 78.25 \text{ Cents/Bushel}
\end{aligned}
$$

It can now be shown that being long the cash commodity with futures at 743.25 cents per bushel and buying a 700 put at 35 cents is equivalent to selling futures at 743.25 and buying the actual 700 call. First, consider the break-even of the 700 call:

$$
\begin{aligned}
\text{Synthetic Call Break-even} &= 700 + 78.25 \\
&= 778.25 \text{ Cents/Bushel}
\end{aligned}
$$

This is the EHP because the market must move beyond the 778.25 level for the producer to make money on the call and thus increase his final cash price of 713.25 cents per bushel. Secondly, at 700 cents per bushel, the call expires worthless: The producer loses 78.25 cents but makes 43.25 cents from the drop in futures prices. His final cash price is

Futures at:	700.00
Loss on Long 700 Call:	−78.25
Gain on Short Futures:	+43.25
Basis:	−30.00
Final Price:	635.00 Cents/Bushel

This, of course, is the minimum price. The reader can check that it is the price he or she will receive at every futures level below 700 cents per bushel.

II. Synthetic of a Maximum Price Contract

Alternatively, consider the maximum price hedge as a synthetic long put where a call is purchased against a cash short. From the formulas in Chapter 4, Synthetic Futures and Options, a synthetic long put premium is formulated as follows:

$$
\begin{aligned}
P_p &= [C_p + (-F) + S], \text{ where} \\
P_p &= \text{Put Premium} \\
C_p &= \text{Call Premium} \\
F &= \text{Futures Price} \\
S &= \text{Strike}
\end{aligned}
$$

With August futures trading at 727.50 cents per bushel and the 775 call premium priced at 17.5 cents per bushel, the 775 synthetic put premium is

$$
\begin{aligned}
P_p &= [17.5 + (-727.50) + 775] \\
P_p &= 65 \text{ Cents/Bushel}
\end{aligned}
$$

Again, one can prove that being short the cash commodity with futures at 727.50 cents per bushel and buying a 775 call at 17.5 cents is equivalent to buying futures at 727.50 and buying a 775 put. First, the break-even of the put is

$$
\begin{aligned}
\text{Synthetic Put Break-even} &= 775 - 65 \\
&= 710 \text{ Cents/Bushel}
\end{aligned}
$$

This is the EHP since the importer can only reduce the final price if the synthetic put moves beyond its break-even. Second, consider the outcome when the importer loses the entire put premium at 775:

Futures at:	775.00
Loss on long 775 Put:	+65.00
Gain on Long Futures:	−47.50
Basis:	+73.50
Final Cash Price:	866.00 Cents/Bushel

III. Managing the Hedge in Options Hedge II

The same follow-up strategies that are recommended for the standard minimum and maximum price hedges are valid here. The producer should sell the call on market rallies and roll-up the strike. As the market falls, the producer should sell the call and roll-down the strike. For the consumer, a strategy of selling the put and rolling-down when the market moves lower, and selling the put and rolling-up when the market moves higher is appropriate.

The equations for measuring the impact of rolling-up and rolling-down on the minimum and maximum price hedge are easily derived from the equations in Chapter 5:

$$\Delta\text{Min\_Price} = -\Delta\text{Call\_Premium} = -[\text{Call\_Premium2} - \text{Call\_Premium1}]$$

$$\Delta\text{Max\_Price} = \Delta\text{Put\_Premium} = [\text{Put\_Premium2} - \text{Put\_Premium1}]$$

The new EHP is the break-even of the new put or call; there is no need for an equation to calculate that.

A short example using the soybean importer's maximum price hedge will suffice. Assume August soybean futures fall to 662.50 cents per bushel by mid-June and the 725 put is now in-the-money and worth 66 cents per bushel. The importer decides to roll-down and buy the 650 put that is trading at 12.5 cents per bushel. The effect on the maximum price is as follows:

Put_Premium2:	12.50
Put_Premium1:	−66.00
ΔMax_Price:	−53.50
Old Maximum Price:	832.00
ΔMax_Price:	−53.50
New Maximum Price:	788.50 Cents/Bushel

The importer clearly buys high value (that is, the near-the-money 725 put) and receives a high return in the form of a lower maximum price by rolling-down when futures collapse. The EHP is now the break-even of the second put or 637.50. This is lower, but not too far away from the current futures price of 662.50 cents per bushel.

IV. Price Cap as a Synthetic

The price cap strategy can also be viewed as a synthetic short put with a strike price at 220 dollars per ton. From Chapter 4, Synthetic Futures and Options, a synthetic short put premium is

$$
\begin{aligned}
-P_p &= (-C_p) + F - S\text{, where} \\
-P_p &= \text{Short Put Premium} \\
-C_p &= \text{Short Call Premium} \\
F &= \text{Futures Price} \\
S &= \text{Strike Price}
\end{aligned}
$$

With December meal futures trading at 221.90 and the 220 call priced at 11.10 dollars, the 220 synthetic short put is priced at

$$
\begin{aligned}
-P_p &= [(-11.10) + 221.90 - 220] \\
P_p &= 9.20
\end{aligned}
$$

The break-even for the 220 synthetic put is 210.80 (220 − 9.20), which is equal to the EHP. The maximum possible gain for writing the synthetic put is the premium, or 9.20; hence, the price cap of 236.10 dollars per ton is equal to the futures price of 221.90 dollars per ton, plus the basis of 5 over, plus the synthetic put income of 9.20 dollars.

Notice that the processor sold an at-the-money call. A more aggressive strategy would be to write an out-of-the-money call, while the least aggressive approach is to write an in-the-money call. Graph 5-14 shows the effect on the synthetic put EHP's and the price cap as the strategy changes from writing an in-the-money to an out-of-the-money call. The more aggressive the strategy, the higher the price cap and the higher the EHP.

V. Price Floor as a Synthetic

As in previous examples, one can view the price floor as a synthetic strategy. Selling puts against a short in the physical commodity is equivalent to a synthetic short call. Again, this is useful in order to understand how the price floor of 22.40 cents per pound and the EHP of 24.20 are formulated; it also gives an indication of how aggressive the strategy is.

From Chapter 4, Synthetic Futures and Options, we know that the formula for a synthetic short call is

$$
\begin{aligned}
-C_p &= (-P_p) + (-F) + S, \text{ where} \\
-C_p &= \text{Short Call Premium} \\
-P_p &= \text{Short Put Premium} \\
F &= \text{Futures Price} \\
S &= \text{Strike Price}
\end{aligned}
$$

With July soyoil futures at 23.70 cents per pound and the 23 cent put at .50 cents, the synthetic call is worth

$$
\begin{aligned}
-C_p &= (-.50) + (-23.70) + 23 \\
C_p &= 1.20 \text{ Cents/Pound}
\end{aligned}
$$

The break-even for the synthetic short 23 call is 24.20, which is equivalent to the EHP calculation above. Since the maximum potential income from the short synthetic 23 call is 1.20 cents, the price floor is equal to the current futures price of 23.70, less the 1.20 call income, less the basis of .10, or 22.40 cents per pound.

VI. Managing the Price Cap and Floor

The management dynamics of the price cap and the price floor strategies follow the pattern already established in other strategies. In the case of the price cap, as prices move up the hedger buys back his or her short call and rolls-up to a higher strike; in the event of lower prices, the hedger takes profits on the short call and sells a lower strike. In the floor strategy, as prices move higher the hedger takes profits on his or her short put and rolls-up to a higher strike; on price breaks the hedger buys back the short put and rolls-down to a lower strike. But as before, the decision to roll the hedge is not made until the maneuvers can be quantified.

For the price cap:

$$\Delta\text{Price\_Cap} = \Delta\text{Call\_Strike} + \Delta\text{Call\_Premium}$$

$$\Delta\text{Price\_Cap\_EHP} = \Delta\text{Futures\_Price} - \Delta\text{Call\_Premium}$$

For the price floor:

$$\Delta\text{Price\_Floor} = \Delta\text{Put\_Strike} - \Delta\text{Put\_Premium}$$

$$\Delta\text{Price\_Floor\_EHP} = \Delta\text{Futures\_Price} + \Delta\text{Put\_Premium}$$

The equations for the change in the put and call premium (ΔCall_Premium, ΔPut_Premium) are the same as given in previous sections.

Here is an example using the price floor. The processor sold puts at the beginning of May, that is, at the start of weather season when crop prices are subject to volatile swings. Soybean oil—even though it is a derivative product of soybeans—will also be subject to wide price movements. This calls into doubt the appropriateness of selling volatility at that point in time (as outlined in Chapter 3); however, assuming that the decision is already made and the trade is executed, the processor must be prepared for active management of the strategy.

By mid-May, July soyoil futures have dropped 1.14 cents to 22.56 cents per pound. Although this is still above the original price floor of 22.40 cents per pound, it is beyond the processor's predicted ranges of 23.20 and 24.20. Hence, the processor wants to gauge the impact of buying back the 23 put (now worth .90 cents) and rolling-down to the 22 put worth .40 cents. Using the above equation, the new price floor is

Put Premium2:	00.40	
Put Premium1:	−00.90	
ΔPut_Premium:	−00.50	
ΔPut_Strike:	−1.00	
ΔPut_Premium:	−(−00.50)	
ΔPrice_Floor:	−00.50	
Old Price Floor:	22.40	
ΔPrice_Floor:	−00.50	
New Price Floor:	21.90	Cents/Pound

Similarly, the new EHP is

Old Futures Price:	22.56	
New Futures Price:	23.70	
ΔFutures_Price:	−1.14	
ΔFutures_Price:	−1.14	
ΔPut_Premium:	+(−00.50)	
ΔPrice_Floor_EHP:	−1.64	
Old EHP:	24.20	
ΔPrice_Floor_EHP:	−1.64	
New EHP:	22.56	Cents/Pound

Although the processor has succeeded in lowering the price floor, the equivalent hedge price is right at the current futures price of 22.56.

Therefore, the processor must be bearish in order to roll-down to the 22 put since he or she gives up the upside buffer. The problem here is that the July options are close to expiration and premiums fetch very low values. The 22 put is hardly worth selling. If the processor is indeed bearish, he or she should be unhedged and thus liquidate the short 23 put and not roll-down. Otherwise, the processor should stay with the original hedge to earn back some or all of the loss on the short put if the market rallies.

In short, the roll-down decision depends entirely on how the new price floor and EHP fit into the processor's market outlook at that moment. Objectively, the new floor and EHP are too constricting. In the volatile market at hand, perhaps a maximum price hedge is more appropriate.

VII. Managing the Option Fence and Window

The management of the option fence or window is complex as there are two option legs involved: The hedger has to make a decision to roll-up or- down both legs or just one depending on how the maneuver will affect the minimum/maximum price, the cap/floor, and the EHP. All the changes must be congruent with the hedger's market outlook. However, the overall maneuver is the same as in other strategies, that is, take profits and roll-up or roll-down, or cut losses and roll-up or roll-down.

To introduce formulas now to quantify the decision outcome would only confuse more than enlighten; therefore, an example will be given in order for the reader to gain an appreciation of the impact of the roll-up or roll-down maneuvers. Assume that the soybean producer has implemented an option fence by buying a 700 put at 35 cents and by selling an 800 call at 36 cents for a one cent credit. The minimum price and price cap are 671 and 771, respectively. Futures are at 743.25 and the basis is 30 under.

Assume that two months after implementing the fence, futures prices collapse to 685 cents per bushel. The 700 put is now worth 55 cents and the 800 call is worth 15 cents. Three manuevers are possible at this point: The producer can take profits on the long 700 put and short 800 call and roll both legs down, or he or she can roll-down one or the other separately. To simplify the example, each maneuver rolls-down to the next strike (700 to 675, 800 to 775, and so on). Each case is considered below:

Scenario 1: Roll-Down Both 700 Put and 800 Call

The Producer can roll-down and buy a 675 put for 36 cents and sell a 775 call for 18.5 cents. The net result is,

Profit on Long 700 Put = [55 − 35] = 20 cents
Profit on Short 800 Call = [36 − 18] = 18 cents

New Minimum Price:

a. New Put Strike Price:	675.00
b. Profit on Long 700 Put:	+20.00
c. Profit on Short 800 Call:	+18.00
d. Cost of 675 Put:	−36.00
e. Income From Short 775 Call:	+18.50
f. Basis:	−30.00
g. New Minimum Price:	665.50 Cents/Bushel

New Price Cap:

a. New Call Strike Price:	775.00
b. Profit on Long 700 Put:	+20.00
c. Profit on Short 800 Call:	+18.00
d. Cost of 675 Put:	−36.00
e. Income From Short 775 Call:	+18.50
f. Basis:	−30.00
g. New Price Cap:	765.50 Cents/Bushel

New EHP = 664.50 Cents/Bushel

In sum, the income flows from lines *b* to *e* are the new credit or debit. In this case the new credit is +20.5 cents per bushel. The result here is to lower the minimum price and lower the price cap. The new EHP is the current futures price less the new credit.

Scenario 2: Roll-Down the 700 Put Only

Profit on Long 700 Put = [55 − 35] = 20 cents

New Minimum Price:

a. New Put Strike Price:	675.00
b. Profit on Long 700 Put:	+20.00
c. Income From 800 Call:	+36.00
d. Cost of 675 Put:	−36.00
e. Basis:	−30.00
f. New Minimum Price:	665.00 Cents/Bushel

New Price Cap:

a. Call Strike Price:	800.00

b. Profit on long 700 Put:	+20.00	
c. Income From 800 Call:	+36.00	
d. Cost of 675 Put:	−36.00	
e. Basis:	−30.00	
f. New Price Cap:	790.00	Cents/Bushel

New EHP = 665.00 Cents/Bushel

Scenario 3: Roll-Down the 800 Call Only

Profit on Short 800 Call = [36 − 18] = 18 cents

New Minimum Price:

a. Put Strike Price:	700.00	
b. Profit on Short 800 Call:	+18.00	
c. Cost of 700 Put:	−35.00	
d. Income From Short 775 Call:	+18.50	
e. Basis:	−30.00	
f. New Minimum Price:	671.50	Cents/Bushel

New Price Cap:

a. New Call Strike Price:	775.00	
b. Profit on Short 800 Call:	+18.00	
c. Cost of 700 Put:	−35.00	
d. Income From Short 775 Call:	+18.50	
e. Basis:	−30.00	
f. New Price Cap:	746.50	Cents/Bushel

New EHP = 683.50 Cents/Bushel

Table B-1 presents a summary of the relevant numbers from the above calculations:

TABLE B-1

Hedge Maneuver	Minimum Price	Price Cap	New Range Min Price to	EHP
Do Nothing	671.00	771.00	100	742.25
Scenario 1 (Roll-down Put and Call)	665.00	765.50	100	664.50
Scenario 2 (Roll-down Put only)	665.00	790.00	125	665.00
Scenario 3 (Roll-down Call only)	671.50	746.50	75	683.50

Now that some solid, quantifiable statistics are generated, it is easy to conclude that the second scenario of rolling-down only the 700 put is the optimal decision. The benefits of a higher price cap, lower EHP, and a wide range for pricing the soybeans, far outweigh a small 6-cent reduction in the minimum price.

VII. Fence and Window Hedge Management Formulas

For the mathematically inclined, and for the sake of completeness, the formulas for sidestepping the lengthy arithmetic presented previously are as follows:

For The Option Fence:

ΔMin_Price	= ΔPut_Strike + ΔCredit/Debit
ΔPrice_Cap	= ΔCall_Strike + ΔCredit/Debit, where
ΔCredit/Debit	= ΔCall_Premium − ΔPut_Premium, and
ΔCall_Premium	= [Call_Premium2 − Call_Premium1]
ΔPut_Premium	= [Put_Premium2 − Put_Premium1]
Premium1	= Current value of the original option.
Premium2	= Current value of the new strike under consideration.
ΔEHP	= ΔFutures_Price − ΔCredit/Debit

For The Option Window:

ΔMax_Price	= ΔCall_Strike − ΔCredit/Debit
ΔPrice_Floor	= ΔPut_Strike − ΔCredit/Debit, where
ΔCredit/Debit	= ΔPut_Premium − ΔCall_Premium, and
ΔEHP	= ΔFutures_Price + Credit/Debit

The reader can use these formulas for the option fence in order to check the results in the soybean importer example. Again, these formulas are not meant to intimidate; they are meant to speed calculations and are quite useful when used with a spreadsheet application.

Bibliography

There are a few good books on options that I have read cover-to-cover and which I highly recommend to others. I li3t them here in order of difficulty:

1. Labuszewski, John W. and Nyhoff, John E. *Trading Options on Futures* New York, NY: John Wiley & Sons 1988; 264 pp.
2. Chance, Don M. *An Introduction to Options and Futures* Chicago, IL: The Dryden Press 1989; 560 pp.
3. Natenberg, Sheldon *Option Volatility and Pricing Strategies* Chicago, IL: Probus Publishing 1988; 392 pp.
4. Cox, John C. and Rubinstein, Mark *Options Markets* Englewood Cliffs, NJ: Prentice Hall 1985; 498 pp.
5. Jarrow, Robert A. and Rudd, Andrew *Option Pricing* Homewood, IL: Richard D. Irwin, Inc. 1983; 239 pp.

Here are general books on futures trading:

1. Hieronymus, Thomas A. *Economics of Futures Trading* New York, NY: Commodity Research Bureau, Inc. 1977 (2nd Edition); 368 pp.
2. Marshall, John F., *Futures and Option Contracting* Cincinnati, OH: Southwestern Publishing Co. 1989; 636 pp.
3. Chance, Don M. *An Introduction to Options and Futures* Chicago, IL: The Dryden Press 1989; 560 pp.

The reader may also find some of the following articles of interest:

Black F., and Scholes, M. (1973): "The Pricing of Options and Corporate Liabilities," Journal of Political Economy, 81:637–659.

Black, F., (1976): "The Pricing of Commodity Contracts," Journal of Financial Economics, 3:167–179.

Black, F. (1975): "Fact and Fantasy in the Use of Options," Financial Analysts Journal, 31:36–41, 61–72.

Choi, J.W., and Longstaff, F.A. (1985): "Pricing Options on Agricultural Futures: An Application of the Constant Elasticity of Variance Option Pricing Model," The Journal of Futures Markets, 5(2):247–258.

Hauser, R.J., and Neff, D. (1985): "Pricing Options on Agricultural Futures: Departures from Traditional Theory," The Journal of Futures Markets, 5(4):539–577.

Jordan, J.V., Seale, W.E., McCabe, N.C., and Kenyon, D.E. (1987): "Transactions Data Tests of the Black Model for Soybean Futures Options," The Journal of Futures Markets, 7(5):535–554.

Merton, R.C. (1973): "Theory of Rational Option Pricing," The Bell Journal of Economics and Management Science, 4:141–183.

Webb, R.I. (1987): "A Note on Volatility and Pricing of Futures Options During Choppy Markets," The Journal of Futures Markets, 7(3):333–337.

Wilson, W.W., Fung, H.G., and Ricks, M. (1988): "Option Price Behavior in Grain Futures Markets," The Journal of Futures Markets, 8(1):47–65.

If the readers have access to any college bookstore, they will find numerous texts on statistics that they can select to fit their expertise level and taste; however, I have been using the following as a general primer:

Wonnacott, Ronald J. and Wonnacott, Thomas H. *Introductory Statistics* New York, NY: John Wiley & Sons 1985; 649 pp.

Glossary

American options Option contracts that permit the buyer to exercise the option at any time prior to the expiration date.

Arbitrage In options trading, any situation where a risk-free profit can be earned by buying (selling) an undervalued (overvalued) future or option and simultaneously selling (buying) synthetic the actual future or option.

Assignment Occurs to an option writer when the option buyer exercises the right to buy or sell the underlying futures. The writer is then assigned the other side of the buyer's futures position at the strike price of the option.

At-the-money When an option's strike price is equal to the futures price, it is at-the-money.

Basis The difference between the local cash price of a commodity and the futures price. The basis reflects local supply and demand factors, transportation, and storage costs.

Bearish strategy Any option strategy that profits with a fall in the underlying futures price.

Bid/ask spread The spread between the price a buyer is willing to pay and the price a seller is willing to offer. The more illiquid a market is, the wider the bid/ask spread. In illiquid markets, buyers must often buy at the offer and sellers must sell at the bid, which results in added transactions costs.

Black formula A theoretical formula for calculating the fair price of an option on a future contract that was elaborated in an academic paper by Fischer Black in 1976 (see Bibliography).

Breakeven (the) The futures price at which the option strategy results in no net gain or loss.

Bullish strategy Any option strategy that profits with a rise in the underlying futures price.

Bushel A unit of dry measure used in the United States. A standard bushel of soybeans or wheat weighs 60 pounds. Since one metric ton equals 2,204.59 pounds, there are 36.7431 bushels of soybeans or wheat in one metric ton. A standard bushel of corn weights 56 pounds; thus there are 39.3676 bushels of corn in one metric ton.

Calendar spreads The purchase or sale of a put or call in one contract month and the simultaneous sale or purchase of a put or call in another contract month (see **Diagonal spreads; Horizontal spreads**).

Call option A call option grants the owner the right, but not the obligation, to buy an underlying instrument such as a futures contract at the call's strike price.

Class of options All call and put options on the same underlying contract month and which expire on the same day are in the same class of options. For example, May '89 soybean calls and puts.

Contract month Futures contracts are traded by months; for example, November soybeans, March corn, July wheat, etc. For every futures contract month there are corresponding options contracts.

Contrarian An investor who buys and sells contrary to the prevailing market sentiment. The idea is that as more people become bullish or bearish the more the underlying bullish or bearish inputs are already discounted in the market; the market then corrects as there is no longer any reason for it to go up or down.

Convexity The phenomenon caused by gamma where a call (put) option's delta equivalent expands at an increasing rate given increases (decreases) in the underlying futures. Given a favorable move in the underlying futures, profit (loss) thus grows at an increasing rate for the trader long (short) options.

CRB Index The Commodity Research Bureau Index. An index of a basket of 21 commodities: corn, oats, soybeans, soybean meal, soybean oil, wheat, cattle, hogs, pork bellies, lumber, cotton, orange juice, cocoa, coffee, sugar, copper, gold, silver, platinum, crude oil, and heating oil. Often used as an indicator of commodity inflation or deflation. Futures and options are traded on the CRB index.

Credit All option sales are credits since there is a cash inflow. A net credit occurs when an option strategy's cash inflow is greater than its cash outflow from option purchases (see **Debit**).

Debit All option purchases are debits since there is a cash outflow. A net debit occurs when an option strategy's cash outflow is greater than its cash inflow from selling options (see **Credit**).

Deferred (the) Used in reference to the deferred futures or options contract month. For example, if November is the first option or futures contract month traded in soybeans, then January is the first deferred month, March is the second deferred month, etc.

Delta A derivative of the Black formula that gives the precise change in an option's premium given a change in the underlying futures (for small changes in the underlying futures).

Delta equivalent An option position's delta defined in the same units as the underlying futures. Bushels are the delta equivalents of soybean, corn, and wheat options; short tons are the delta equivalents of soymeal options; pounds are the delta equivalents of soyoil options (see also **Position Delta**).

Delta neutral Any position consisting of options and futures or options in combination with other options where the net delta of the position is zero.

Diagonal spreads An options strategy that involves buying and selling options with different strike prices and in different contract months. For example, a trader sells a nearby May soybean put option and buys a deferred July soybean put option at a higher strike price.

Direct relationship A direct relationship means that two variables move in tandem: when one variable increases (decreases), the other variable increases (decreases).

Equivalent hedge price The futures price at which an options hedge has returned the same cash price as an initial futures or flat-price cash hedge.

European options Option contracts that permit the buyer to exercise only on the expiration date.

Exercise When an option buyer carries-out the right to buy or sell the underlying instrument, he or she exercises the option and receives a long or short position in the underlying instrument at the strike price of the option.

Expected volatility The volatility that market participants expect in the future. In this book, expected volatility is used as an equivalent term for implied volatility.

Expiration date The day on which the right granted to the option buyer terminates. The option buyer must exercise the right by or on the expiration date if the option has intrinsic value or abandon it if it does not.

Extrinsic value For both calls and puts, the extrinsic value is the option premium less the intrinsic value (see **Intrinsic Value**).

Fence An options hedging strategy available to people long the underlying cash commodity or futures whereby a put is bought and a call is simultaneously sold at a higher strike to defray the cost of the put. The strategy maintains a minimum price via the put, but limits the upside pricing potential at the call's strike price.

Flat price As used in this book, refers to the futures price of a commodity, but can also refer to the cash price in hedging applications.

Futures contract A contract that calls for the buyer to deliver a commodity at a future date or for the seller to take delivery of the commodity at a future date. Contracts are bought and sold on organized exchanges via the open outcry system. Futures contracts have uniform specifications regarding the grade and type of commodity that can be delivered.

Futures price The per unit price (bushel, pound, etc.) of a futures contract.

Gamma A derivative of the Black formula that gives the precise change in an option's delta for a given change in the underlying futures.

Gamma equivalent An option position's gamma expressed in the same units as the underlying futures for a predefined change in the underlying futures price (see also **Position gamma**).

Hedge ratio The inverse of an option's delta. An option's hedge ratio gives the number of contracts that equate to one futures contract, and which thus mimic the change in value of one futures contract for small changes in the futures price.

Hedging The strategy by which a position is offset with an equal but opposite position such that any adverse price movements in one position are compensated by the other position.

Historical volatility The volatility reflected by the standard deviation of the underlying futures. Usually, the standard deviation is calculated from the last twenty days of futures prices, and then adjusted to represent an annual figure.

Horizontal spreads An options strategy that involves buying and selling options with the same strike price but in different contract months. For example, a trader sells a nearby December corn call and purchases a deferred March corn call at the same strike price.

Implied volatility The volatility (annual standard deviation of futures prices) that equates an option's market premium to an option pricing formula, given all other known parameters such as the option's strike price, the underlying futures price, time to expiration, and the interest rate.

Interest rate In options trading, interest rate refers to the return on a treasury bill that matures around the expiration date of the option.

In-the-money When a call (put) option's strike price is below (above) the futures price, it has intrinsic value and is thus in-the-money.

Intrinsic value For calls, the difference between the futures price and the strike price; if the difference is negative, the intrinsic value is zero. For puts the difference between the strike price and the futures price; if the difference is negative, the intrinsic value is zero.

Inverse relationship An inverse relationship means that two variables move opposite to each other: when one variable increases (decreases), the other variable decreases (increases).

Legging into a spread A risky method for implementing a spread position where one strike (leg) is initially bought or sold and the other strike (leg) is bought or sold at a later time. For example, a trader can leg into a short straddle by first selling a put and then selling the call at a later date.

Leverage As used in this book, leverage refers to the fact that a small investment in long calls (puts) can result in a substantial long (short) position in the underlying futures when prices increase (decrease) dramatically.

Limit move The maximum allowable daily future or option price move up or down from the previous day's settlement as defined by a futures exchange. An exchange may increase the limit as markets grow more volatile, and then reduce the limit to its normal level as market volatility decreases.

Locked limit A situation where a limit move occurs and trading stagnates (is locked) at one price caused by an imbalance of buyers and sellers (see **Limit move**). For example, if soybeans are locked limit-up at 850 cents per bushel, then there are either no sellers or more buyers than sellers at that price. If there are some sellers, buyers are served on a first come first serve basis.

Long In options trading, long refers to the purchase of either a call, a put, or both. If a trader buys a call, a put, or both, the trader is long options. In futures trading, or as used to describe the position delta of an option position (see **Position delta**), any position where a trader profits with a rise in the futures price.

Margin The amount of money that a trader must deposit and maintain with his broker. During an adverse price move, money is taken from the trader's margin fund; money is added to the trader's account when price moves favorably. All futures and short options positions require margin funds. The amount of margin required depends on the size of the trader's positions and on the commodity traded.

Margin call Additional monies that must be deposited when an adverse price move occurs or when margin requirements are increased. Holders of futures positions or short option positions are subject to margin calls, while buyers of options are not.

Maximum price An options hedge whereby a person short the cash commodity can create a maximum price for his future purchases, while maintaining the ability to buy at a lower cash price should prices weaken. The most common method of creating a maximum price is to purchase a call.

Minimum price An options hedge whereby a person long the cash commodity can create a minimum cash price for future sales, while maintaining the ability to sell at a higher cash price should prices strengthen. The most common method of creating a minimum price is to purchase a put.

Near-the-money Option strikes that are closest to the futures price but still out-of-the-money are termed near-the-money.

Neutral strategy As defined in this book, a neutral option strategy can be one of two types: (1) option strategies that profit when futures prices trade within a sideways range, or (2) option strategies that profit when futures prices rally or collapse out of a sideways range.

Option book A risk summary of all option positions/strategies in a given commodity. The summary indicates the trader's aggregate delta, gamma, theta, and vega risk, and helps to point to contradictions among strategies or to areas where the trader needs to reduce risk or take on more according to individual preferences.

Option buyer A trader who buys a call, a put, or both. It is important to remember that a trader can be long options but net long, short, or even in the underlying futures (position delta) depending on if the option long is placed in a call, put, or in a combination of calls and puts respectively (see **Long; Position delta**).

Option markets A market where buyers and sellers come together to trade options (calls and puts) on an underlying instrument such as a futures contract. Options markets exist for a number of reasons; but in general, the ability of options to give hedgers and speculators a wider range of profit/loss outcomes is what stimulates such interest in these instruments.

Options on futures Options are a conduit for obtaining an underlying asset such as a stock, a currency, or a futures contract. Options on futures are a conduit for obtaining a long or short position in a futures contract.

Option seller A trader who sells a call, a put, or both. It is important to remember that a trader can be short options but long, short, or even in the underlying futures (position delta) depending on if the option short is placed in a put, call, or in a combination of puts and calls respectively (see **Short; Position delta**).

Out-of-the-money Any put or call option whose premium consists solely of extrinsic value.

Overbought/oversold Extreme market conditions that are reflected by various technical indicators (relative strength, oscillators, stochastics, put/call ratios, contrary opinion, etc.). When such conditions exist, technicians take them as a sign to sell if the market is overbought and to buy if the market is oversold.

Perfect hedge A hedge that perfectly compensates losses in one position with gains in another. Perfect hedges are rare since markets often diverge for different reasons. For instance, futures and cash markets diverge caused by changes in the basis, while futures and options diverge caused by discontinuous jumps in the futures price and/or changes in an option's implied volatility.

Position delta The sum of all the deltas of an options position taking into account the correct sign for each option (put or call, long or short) and the number of contracts at each strike price. Effectively equates the options position to an equivalent position in futures, which can then be defined in delta equivalents (see **Delta equivalent**).

Position gamma The sum of all the gammas of an options position taking into account the correct sign for each option (put or call, long or short) and the number of contracts at each strike price. The position gamma can then be defined in units of the underlying futures (see **Gamma equivalents**) given a predefined change in the futures price.

Position taking Speculative trading that involves taking a long or short position in futures, options, or in the physical commodity with the idea that prices will move up or down depending on the position.

Premium The per unit (bushel, ton, pound, etc.) price of an option.

Price cap A more speculative form of options hedge where a person long the cash commodity or long futures sells calls and thereby caps any upside pricing potential at the call's strike price. Downside protection is limited to the premium income received from the short calls. This type of hedge is implemented with the expectation that the futures price will trade in a sideways range.

Price floor A more speculative form of options hedge where a person short the cash commodity or short futures sells puts and thereby creates a floor to any downside pricing potential at the put's strike price. Upside protection is limited to the premium income received from the short puts. This type of hedge is implemented with the expectation that the futures price will trade in a sideways range.

Put/call parity The relationship among the price of the underlying futures and the premiums of a put and call with the same strike that must hold in order for there to be no risk-free arbitrage profit opportunities available. Specifically, the difference between a call and put premium of the same strike must equal the difference in the underlying futures price and the common strike price.

Put/call ratio The ratio of daily put volume traded to daily call volume traded. The ratio is then graphed over time to determine extreme movements away from put purchases and towards call purchases and vice versa. In the narrowest sense, often taken to be a contrarian overbought/oversold indicator.

Put Option A put option grants the owner the right, but not the obligation, to sell an underlying instrument such as a futures contract at the put's strike price.

Quantity risk In hedging, the risk associated with the inability to perfectly forecast future production or consumption. For example, a farmer may sell forward all his crop under the assumption of normal yields; however, a drought or bumper crop will alter yield and thus cause losses on the hedge.

Risk/reward In simplest terms, the ratio of the amount of money that can be potentially lost to the amount of money that can be potentially gained. Trades with low risk to reward are obviously more favorable. When risk and/or reward cannot be quantified, a surrogate is found (such as gamma, vega, or theta) that effectively represents sources of loss or gain depending on the position.

Rolling-up/rolling-down A tactic by which a hedger or speculator takes profits or cuts losses on an options position and then rolls up or down the strike price to either improve the hedge parameters or increase the likelihood of profit on a speculative position.

Seasonality The phenomenon where the price and the volatility of the underlying futures predictably rises, falls, or stabilizes during the same time period each year. In agricultural futures and options, the seasonal pattern is directly linked to the production, harvest, and marketing cycle of agricultural commodities.

Series All options in the same option class that have the same strike price. For example, May '89 soybean 750 calls and 750 puts.

Short In options trading, short refers to the sale of either a call, a put, or both. If a trader sells a call, a put, or both, the trader is short options. In futures trading, or as used to describe the position delta of an options position (see **Position delta**), any position where a trader profits with a fall in the futures price.

Short straddle An options strategy that involves selling both a put and a call at the same strike price. In order to be profitable, the underlying futures must trade in a sideways range and volatility must stabilize or decrease.

Slippage As used in this book, slippage refers to the cost of an imperfect hedge or covered write strategy. Since trading takes place in discrete time intervals (it is discontinuous from one trading session to the next), traders cannot continually adjust their hedges and are thus vulnerable to sudden shifts in the underlying futures price or in implied volatility.

Speculating Whenever there is no offsetting cash or futures position, a futures, options, or cash position is defined as speculative because the trader is speculating that prices will rise, fall, or trade in a range depending on the strategy used (see **Position taking**).

Spreading In options trading, spreading involves one-to-one or ratio combinations of long options, short options, or both long and short options. The combinations can involve only calls, only puts, or both calls and puts with the same or different strikes and in the same or in different contract months. In futures trading, spreading refers to the purchase of one contract month and the sale of another contract month on a one-to-one basis.

Standard deviation A statistic that measures the extent of fluctuations of a random variable around its mean.

Strike price The predefined price that is stipulated in an option contract at which the call (put) option buyer can buy (sell) the underlying instrument.

Synthetic futures Combinations of call and put options with the same strike price that effectively replicate a futures contract. For example, a long future is equivalent to a long call and a short put; a short future is equivalent to a long put and a short call. The price of the synthetic future should be equal to the price of the actual future; otherwise an arbitrage profit can be earned (see **Arbitrage; Put/call parity**).

Synthetic options Combinations of options and the underlying futures that effectively replicate the behavior of an actual option. For example, a long futures contract and a short call are the synthetic equivalent of a short put. The price of a synthetic option should equal the price of the actual option; otherwise an arbitrage profit can be earned (see **Arbitrage; Put/call parity**).

T-Bill Short for treasury bill. A short term debt instrument issued by the United States government with a maturity of three months and a face value of $10,000. The interest rate on this instrument is considered the risk-free rate.

Theta A derivative of the Black formula that gives the precise change in an option's premium given a certain fixed passage of time (a day, a week, a month, etc.).

Time decay The gradual decrease in the extrinsic value of an option premium over time due to the fact that, at expiration, an option can only be worth either its intrinsic value or zero.

Time value A term used interchangeably with extrinsic value; that is, an option's premium less its intrinsic value (see **Intrinsic value**).

Transactions cost A broker's commission for a round-turn trade of futures or options. Transactions costs vary according to the broker used (full service versus discount). In options trading, transactions costs are often determined on a sliding scale according to the number of contracts traded and premium costs.

Type of option Refers to either puts or calls.

Uncovered option Any option that has no offsetting position in the underlying futures or physical commodity. An uncovered option is often referred to as a naked option because the buyer or seller is fully exposed to the risk inherent in a long or short option position.

Underlying (the) Refers to the underlying instrument on which an option is bought or sold. For example, the underlying instrument of a soybean call option contract is a soybean futures contract.

Vega A derivative of the Black formula that gives the precise change in an option's premium given a fixed change in the implied volatility of an option. (For example, the change in an option's premium given a one percent increase or decrease in implied volatility.)

Vertical bull call spread An options strategy that involves buying a call at one strike and selling a call at a higher strike. The strategy reduces the cost of the lower strike option but caps profits if the market moves higher. It also decreases volatility and time decay risk.

Volatility In general, the extent of the fluctuations in futures price (increases or decreases) over the course of one year. Usually measured by the statistical measure of standard deviation (see **Standard deviation**).

Window An options hedging strategy available to people short the underlying cash commodity or futures whereby a call is bought and a put is simultaneously sold at a lower strike price to defray the cost of the call. The strategy maintains a maximum price via the call, but limits the downside pricing potential to the strike price of the put.

Writer The option writer sells the right to buy (sell) the underlying instrument at the call's (put's) strike price. Option writers are sometimes referred to as option sellers or option grantors.

Index